GENTLE BRIDGES

Gentle Bridges

Conversations with the Dalai Lama on the Sciences of Mind

Edited by

Jeremy W. Hayward

and

Francisco J. Varela

Shambhala *Boston & London* 1992

Shambhala Publications, Inc.
Horticultural Hall
300 Massachusetts Avenue
Boston, Massachusetts 02115

Shambhala Publications, Inc.
Random Century House
20 Vauxhall Bridge Road
London SW1V 2SA

© 1992 by Jeremy W. Hayward and Francisco J. Varela

9 8 7 6 5 4 3 2 1

First Edition

Printed in the United States of America on acid-free paper ⊗

Distributed in the United States by Random House, Inc., in Canada by Random House of Canada Ltd, and in the United Kingdom by Random House UK Ltd

Library of Congress Cataloging-in-Publication Data

Bstan-'dzin-rgya-mtsho, Dalai Lama XIV, 1935–
    Gentle bridges: conversations with the Dalai Lama on the sciences of mind/edited by Jeremy Hayward and Francisco J. Varela.
       p.   cm.
    ISBN 0-87773-613-8 (alk. paper)
    1. Buddhism—Psychology. 2. Buddhism and science. 3. Buddhism—Doctrines. 4. Cognitive science. I. Hayward, Jeremy W.
  II. Varela, Francisco J., 1945– . III. Title.
BQ4570.P76B77   1992   91-52525
294.3'42—dc20   CIP

CONTENTS

SHAMBHALA PUBLICATIONS, INC.

Mailing List
P.O. Box 308, Back Bay Annex
Boston, Massachusetts 02117

*If you wish to receive a copy
of the latest Shambhala Publications catalogue of books
and to be placed on our mailing list
please send us this card.*

PLEASE PRINT

Book in which this card was found

NAME

ADDRESS

CITY & STATE

ZIP OR POSTAL CODE   COUNTRY
                            (IF OUTSIDE U.S.A.)

Preface

In October of 1987 a small group of scientists traveled to northern India to meet with His Holiness the Dalai Lama, the spiritual and temporal leader of the Tibetan people. All the scientists were professionally involved in some aspect of research or thought concerning modern scientific approaches to mind and life. In addition, most of them also had an interest in Buddhism. For six days, morning and afternoon, the scientists met with His Holiness in the living room of his residence. With them were two Tibetan scholars, two translators, and a few observers. This was an unprecedentedly thorough, rich, and friendly exchange between eminent representatives of two great world traditions: science in the West and Buddhism in the East. It later turned out to be only the first of a series of conferences between His Holiness and Western scientists on the theme of "Mind and Life." This book, then, is an edited record of that first series of meetings.

His Holiness the Dalai Lama was accompanied at the meetings by Geshe Yeshi Thabkhe, professor of Buddhist studies, Central Institute of Higher Tibetan Studies, Sarnath, India; and Geshe Palden Drakpa, Tibet House, New Delhi, India. The Tibetan title *geshe* is roughly equivalent to the Western doctorate. The participating scientists were Newcomb Greenleaf, Ph.D., professor of computer science, Columbia University; Jeremy W. Hayward, Ph.D., professor, Naropa Institute, Boulder, Colorado; Robert B. Livingston, M.D., professor of neurosciences, University of California, San Diego; Luigi Luisi, Ph.D., professor of chemistry, Federal Polytechnical Institute, Zurich; Eleanor Rosch, Ph.D., professor of cognitive psychology, University of California, Berkeley; Francisco J. Varela, Ph.D., professor of cognitive science and epistemology, Ecole Polytechnique and Institute of Neuroscience, Paris.

At the time of the Chinese takeover of Tibet in 1959, His Holiness led thousands of Tibetans to safety in India and now serves as head of the Tibetan government in exile in Dharmsala. The Dalai Lama has visited Europe and North America on numerous occasions and is known the world over as a great spiritual teacher and a tireless worker for peace. In 1989 he received the Nobel Peace Prize. All his life His Holiness has shown an interest in science; he has said that if he had not been a monk, he would have liked to be an engineer. Going beyond this personal interest, he has taken a leading role in encouraging Buddhists to enter into a true dialogue with scientists.

How did this meeting come about? Dr. Varela had encountered His Holiness a number of times in public meetings in Europe and had been frustrated by the feeling that a fruitful dialogue was not possible because of shortness of time and too much exposure to the public. When visiting Paris in 1986, the Dalai Lama again invited Dr. Varela to meet for discussion. Their conversation went on for over an hour, during which Dr. Varela was intensely questioned about neuroscience. At the end of the hour, His Holiness' attendants insisted that it was time to go to a reception at the French House of Representatives (Assemblée Nationale). As he left, he said to Dr. Varela, "We must talk more, but I cannot give much time to it when I am visiting the West. I will make a week of my time available if you can come to Dharmsala. And bring anyone else you want." At about the same time, a student of His Holiness, businessman Adam Engle, was aware of the Dalai Lama's lively interest in science and was looking into the possibility of organizing a gathering with scientists. Engle and Varela met, and thus the first of the *Mind and Life* conferences was born. Financial support came from a grant-in-aid from Mr. Branco Weiss of Zurich, Switzerland, and donations from Adam Engle Associates. The conference was coordinated by Engle and Varela as well as Michael Sautman, M.A., of Berkeley, California.

The Dalai Lama's residence is several miles from Dharmsala,

up a steep mountainside, near a small town known as Mcleod Ganj, which is inhabited by Tibetan refugees. The visiting group stayed in a guest house about half a mile down the mountain from the residence. Each morning we ate breakfast while sitting on our veranda overlooking the valley below and then were driven up to the residence in jeeps. At the entrance to the residence we always had to go through a polite security check. Then we would go on to the living room. His Holiness would enter promptly at nine, and we would immediately plunge into intense discussion. After the morning session, we would ride or walk back down the mountain for a quick lunch, then return for the afternoon session. The mornings were crisp and cool, but the bright autumn sun warmed us through the day. From His Holiness' residence we could see the brilliant snowcapped front range of the Himalayas. In the evenings, we sat on our own veranda and watched the sun go down and the busy town of Dharmsala light up, far below.

The atmosphere of the meetings was intentionally very informal. The meetings were recorded in both audio and video, and there was a general intention to make the proceedings public in some fashion, yet we had all agreed that our primary purpose was genuine discussion with the Dalai Lama on matters of mutual interest. Sometimes gatherings of scientists and religious leaders are like a stage show in which set speeches are made to impress the public and little real dialogue happens. We all wanted to avoid this. The key ingredients were plenty of time, a group of scientists who also cared for respectful transcultural exchange, and shelter from the immediate presence of the public. Another key element was the help of two excellent translators, one Tibetan and one Westerner. These were Thubten Jinpa of Ganden Shartse College, Mundgod, India; and B. Alan Wallace, spiritual director of the Dharma Friendship Foundation, Seattle, Washington. Often during the discussions, there would be long pauses as the translators conferred, searching for English and Tibetan equivalents. This was a process that was essential if numerous misunderstandings were to be avoided. Nonetheless, translation remained mostly an auxiliary function, since the Dalai Lama usually spoke to us directly in English and only occasionally required our English to be translated for him.

Each morning one of the scientists gave a general talk on his or her field. These talks were to be informative for nonscientists, such as His Holiness and his Tibetan colleagues. They were to present essential elements of the discipline in a simple fashion and provide inspiration for dialogue. The afternoons were set aside for discussion or for the Dalai Lama to present related topics in Buddhism. The scientists had been chosen to cover the spectrum of what are presently called the cognitive sciences, which represent a convergence of neuroscience, experimental psychology, artificial intelligence, and philosophy of mind. The sequence of presentations each day was designed to aid exploration of this multidisciplinary area.

As the days progressed and we all began to relax and understand each other better, large parts of the mornings, as well as the afternoons, began to be taken up with dialogue and debate. The atmosphere in the room was always one of warmth, friendliness, and informality. Laughter and humor were rarely absent. Yet within this there was also a feeling of sharpness, of everyone being very much present and on the spot. It was the ideal environment for intellectual exploration and deepening understanding.

On the last morning there were expressions of gratitude from both sides for this genuine and meaningful exchange. The scientists, especially, were deeply grateful to the Dalai Lama for giving so much time out of his extraordinarily busy schedule. We were also profoundly impressed at his grasp of the issues and his attitude of fearless inquiry.

In this book, we have tried to convey the flavor of the meetings as much as possible within the structure required by a written presentation. The conversations themselves sometimes moved back and forth from topic to topic and often returned to a topic some days after it had first been raised. Our presentation of the conversations here represents a weaving together of the themes that ran throughout the six days. Readers well versed in either of the two traditions will see that the dialogues were not necessarily always profound and ground-breaking, although they consistently contained golden seeds. We feel that their main interest is the nature of the questions posed, the coming to grips with the difficulties of vocabulary and framework, and the identification of some sensitive areas. They provide, for the first time, a sort of cartography of the terrain of encounter between the two traditions.

This was not the first dialogue between science and Buddhism, and others have taken place since. It is hoped that these conversations will continue to provide a model for other such occasions in various formats and localities around the globe. The meetings reported here were followed in 1989 by a shorter two-day meeting, *Mind and Life II*, in Los Angeles. That event, coordinated by Dr. Robert B. Livingston, brought four North American neuroscientists together with the Dalai Lama. *Mind and Life III* took place in November 1990, again for a week in Dharmsala. On this occasion the emphasis of the meetings was emotions and healing. It was coordinated by Dr. Daniel Goleman and had six participants from Europe and North America. The fourth meeting is now being planned for 1992; the topic will be sleep, dreaming, and dying. So we are delighted to report that the dialogue continues.

GENTLE BRIDGES

Opening Remarks

DALAI LAMA: I welcome you. I deeply appreciate the efforts of the organizers of this meeting as well as of the participants. For quite some time I have had a great interest in the close relationship between Eastern philosophy, particularly Buddhism, and Western science. My basic aim as a human being is to speak always for the importance of compassion and kindness in order to help build a better, happier human society, and a brighter future.

I believe such deep human feeling is the key factor for positive developments. With respect to this positive human feeling, there is some potential for Buddhist teachings to contribute to further development. Naturally this can happen only through mental training, not by surgery or injections. The results of such training are mental qualities like compassion or kindness and awareness. But in order to develop these it is very important to know more about the nature of mind or consciousness.

Western civilization's science and technology bring society tremendous benefit. Yet, due to highly developed technology, we also have more anxiety and more fear. I always feel that mental development and material development must be well-balanced, so that together they may make a more human world. If we lose human values and human beings become part of a machine, there is no freedom from pain and pleasure. Without freedom from pain and pleasure, it is very difficult to demarcate between right and wrong. The subjects of pain and pleasure naturally involve feeling, mind, and consciousness.

So it is most important for Western science and material development and Eastern mental development to work together.

Sometimes people have the impression that these two things are very different, even incompatible. However, in recent years this has changed. Some Western scientists have reached highly sensitive and deep issues in their research work, such as: What is the mind, what is "I," what is a human being? A more philosophical inclination, a new trend is developing. In order to contribute something for the future of humanity, dialogue between people who are professional in these fields is extremely important. I hope this meeting will be a start, that we will raise new interest, that others from different places and different fields will take more interest, and that there will be further research.

Our first aim is to benefit humanity in the future. Then, the second level is the study itself. As a Buddhist I think it is very important to know the latest scientific findings about mind, the relation between mind and brain, and so on. For example, I would like to know from the scientific viewpoint whether or not there is a separate entity such as mind or consciousness. On certain levels there is a very close link between body and mind, yet basically when you reach the deepest nature of mind, you find it is an independent and distinct factor. Through this meeting I want to introduce Buddhists in general, particularly Tibetan Buddhists at various learning centers, to the Western explanations of mind, of the relation between mind and body, and so on.

In Buddhism in general, particularly Mahayana Buddhism, including Tantrayana, there are many explanations and methods regarding mind and the mind-body relation.* The highest Tantrayanic teachings are very much involved with a special kind of energy. There are techniques to control bodily functions such as temperature, and in fact there are still people today who have ex-

---

*Tibetan Buddhists, among others, consider Buddhism to be divided into two major traditions, the Hinayana (Skt., lit. "small vehicle"), represented primarily today by the Theravadin schools of Southeast Asia and Sri Lanka; and the Mahayana (Skt., lit. "large vehicle"), represented by Tibetan, Chinese, and Japanese Buddhists. According to the latter, the Mahayana subsumes the Hinayana. In addition, according to the Tibetans, there is a higher level of the Mahayana, called variously Tantra (Tantrayana), Mantrayana, or Vajrayana. This highest level is thought to subsume the lower Mahayana and the Hinayana.

traordinary experiences through practice. There are Western scientists who are looking into this, and already they have found help in Eastern explanations of mind and the relationship between the mind and the nervous system. A joint effort may be useful for researchers in these fields. For all these reasons, I think this meeting may be helpful.

To those old friends who organized and made preparations for this gathering, I want to express my deep thanks. It is completely informal here, and I always prefer it this way. One's own individual nature can be fully expressed, and that is important, isn't it? Here you may find it uncomfortable because of poor facilities, but the weather is very nice. In spite of the lack of facilities, the snow mountains are beautiful and provide the facility of beautiful scenery. Just a few days ago it snowed, but now we have brilliant sunshine, and I hope these weather conditions may remain.

FRANCISCO J. VARELA: Thank you, Your Holiness. For all of us who are participating here, as you pointed out, this possibility of a real dialogue between the Buddhist meditative tradition and science is of the utmost interest, both for the benefit of the world and for our own individual interests as scientists. The fact that some of us have already been involved in Buddhist practices inevitably has led us to ask certain questions, some of which I hope can be explored during the following days. I do not think that this dialogue will settle anything in particular, but I do hope that we can establish for both traditions a standard of how to do things respectfully and carefully, of how to build gentle bridges.

I would like to briefly go through the program so that we have an overall sense of where we're going.

Your Holiness, we are aware that most of your exposure to science has been to the physical sciences. Now, I happen to be convinced that the natural bridge between the Buddhist tradition and the sciences is not through the physical sciences but through the sciences concerned with mind and life itself, roughly what we call today the cognitive sciences, and the life sciences, certainly. That's why we have entitled the program "Mind and Life," rather than "Science and Buddhism."

It seems that in previous dialogues you have had with scientists, it has not been clear what science is as an activity. What is it that scientists do? It seems really important to have a basic understanding of the scientific process. This is why we included as part of the program a discussion of science as a human activity. What is it to do science, and what is science in terms of its theories and their validation? How does it validate its own theories?

Then, to move into the more substantive areas, to start we will have a presentation of neuroscience (neurobiology and the brain sciences). And because neuroscience is a huge field and we couldn't possibly cover everything, we have decided to focus first on the basic principles of the nervous system and how it organizes behavior. The next area will be cognitive psychology, which is a direct examination of behavior and hence plays a role in the cognitive sciences that makes it very close in some sense to Buddhist theories of mind.

A very interesting part of the Western view of how to approach mind is in the modern theories linked with artificial intelligence. This is the notion that if you know how mind works, then you should be able to build one. It is a very important part of today's Western understanding of how to go about explaining mind.

Next, we felt it important to understand the development of the brain from fertilization to birth. This offers much insight into how the complex human brain develops from the basic structure common to all nervous systems. And, finally, we will have a presentation on evolution. Classically, evolution is not part of the cognitive sciences, which center more on neuroscience, cognitive psychology, artificial intelligence, and linguistics. However, we thought it was important to include evolution here because without understanding the Western view of how living things come into being, it is very difficult to understand the view of how they function.

In the morning presentations, each of us has agreed to speak, as it were, as a classical scientist; that is, we agreed to present our fields in their most standard form. Now, speaking for myself (but I know it's also the case for the others), I am rather a heretical neuroscientist. In many cases I do not hold the same views as my colleagues. But in the mornings, out of fairness to you, Your Holiness, we will try to be as average scientists as we can. It will be slightly odd for every one of us, but I think it is important to give you a representative view. In the afternoon conversations, we will speak our own minds. I am delighted that you have invited us to work with you in this informal setting.

Scientific Method and Validation

JEREMY W. HAYWARD

The Search for Objective Reality

I believe that those few people who have been trained as scientists and also have studied some Buddhism view Buddhism and science as having a great deal in common in their view and methods of inquiry. In both the Buddhist and scientific traditions, one doesn't come to something through blind faith, but looks at things with the intention of overcoming personal bias. Thus, this dialogue between science, or the sciences, and Buddhism seems to be a tremendous opportunity to bring together the views of modern civilization and the great tradition of Buddhism. Dr. Varela has asked me to open the meeting by outlining the scientific view and method, and by describing our changing understanding of what it is to do science.

What is this activity that we call science? One of the things that I would like to suggest is that there has been evolution in the interpretation of that activity. Often, when we talk about science we have at the back of our minds the assumption that there is a unified view, *one* science; that all scientists subscribe to this view; that the various fields of science—physics, chemistry, biology, psychology, astronomy, anthropology, sociology, and so on—are based on the same assumptions and that their results are compatible and even often interchangeable or reducible one to another.

In this presentation, I will show that this assumption—which attained its greatest strength, almost universal support, at the end of the nineteenth century—has been the object of extensive and almost irrefutable criticism, especially over the past quarter of a century.

One of the principal characteristics of the activity of "natural philosophers," or scientists, over the past three centuries has been the search for objective knowledge. Objective knowledge is true knowledge that is not in any way dependent on the subject, the mind of the knower, or the society of knowers. In order for there to be objective knowledge, there must be something for this knowledge to be true *of.* That is, there has to be an objective reality: a reality or world that is not dependent on the minds of the knowers of that world. This objective world is supposed to be independent of the minds of its knowers, both in its inherent existence and in its various characteristics. We shall see how the firm belief in such an objective world as a foundation for certainty in science has begun to break down.

If there is one objective world that is independent of human thought, then we would expect that there would be a unified system of knowledge about this world. This system of knowledge would in the end be able to include all separately acquired individual observations in a description that uses a single set of assumptions, terms, and methods: this would be a unified science. The ideal of a unified science was set forth some fifty years ago, and now it is very widely thought that this too has failed, not just because of the difficulty of its execution, but in principle.

The theory of scientific theories is a topic for very intense debate and is by no means resolved by a single view. We can no longer look for a unified science with a single set of assumptions and terms to explain all observations. Instead we find there are many different activities going on under the name of science, with different basic assumptions and terms. The domains that these various sciences cover may not be the same or even overlapping. Where the domains of two sciences are overlapping, they might well provide different and even incompatible explanations of a single observation.

Generally, there is some agreement among those who assent to the failure of a unified science that theories are intimately bound up with human activity and communication within particular communities of scientists. Thus the search for an objective reality is replaced by recognition of intersubjective validation of theories; how these theories relate to a world independent of them is an open question.

Beginnings in the Middle Ages

Let us begin with a very short historical view of how modern science began. Between the fourth and the tenth centuries, the view of the world around us was a very negative one. This period is sometimes called the Dark Ages in the Western tradition, although I don't think this is quite fair. What we believe to have been the great civilizations of Greece and Rome had collapsed. The continuity of knowledge was kept alive primarily in Christian monasteries. The Christian view of the period was that this world is terrible and that there is a parallel or different world that we wish to reach—the heavenly realm.

The beginning of opening up after these Dark Ages, the great flourishing during the early Middle Ages, was in large part due to the discovery of Greek texts, particularly the writings of Aristotle. One result of reading Aristotle was that people began to conceive of nature as a realm that has its own reality, its own modes of functioning, and its own regularities, which people could come to know through careful use of their senses and reason. So a duality was postulated between the heavenly realm, knowable through faith, revelation, and deductive rational thought, and the earthly realm, knowable through the senses and inductive rational thought.

For some centuries, there was debate about whether the doctrines of medieval Christianity could be combined with this extraordinary new view of the world that was being discovered through the Greek texts. In the thirteenth century, Thomas Aquinas managed to put together the view of the Greeks, especially Aristotle, with the view of Christian contemplation. A conception of the universe was created in which the earth was at the center and surrounding it were nine spheres on which the planets moved. The outermost, tenth sphere was the dwelling place of God and did not move. The eight spheres beyond the moon were considered to be relatively perfect. This was shown in the fact that the stars moved in perfect circles and the planets almost in perfect circles. Below the sphere of the moon, in the earthly realm, all was unstable and restless, not so perfect. Matter here is composed of the four elements in various combinations. The natural place of the earth is at the center of the universe, since earth is the heaviest element. Next comes water, then air, and then fire. However, in the imperfect earthly situation, the elements are out of their natural places, and they are constantly striving to return to them. This is the source of unrest, noncircular motion. This is why a stone falls to earth when it is dropped, and why fire rises.

The beauty of this system—which of course was very well thought out—was that everything known to human beings was included in it. The physical universe was the same as the spiritual universe. These nine spheres on which the planets moved were the spheres through which the human soul moved toward God.

The writings of Aristotle had now been harmonized with Church doctrine. However, although the Greeks had themselves been great observers of nature, Europeans of this period relied on the written word as the source of knowledge. So much so that even the drawings of herbs in medicinal texts were copied from ancient texts rather than observed in nature.

Breakdown of the Medieval View

Even at the time Aquinas was proposing his synthesis, other scholars were finding contradictions in Aristotle's writings, contradictions that became the seeds for the dismantling of the entire medieval belief system about three centuries later. In the sixteenth century, Galileo argued that one should actually look at how things are to decide whether Aristotle was right, not just rely on the authority of texts. For example, in Aristotle's view, objects should fall at different rates depending on which is heavier. And Galileo decided to experiment to find out whether this was so. He created artificial situations, for example, balls of different weights rolling down a plank. If a piece of lead falls faster than a piece of wood, then it should also roll down the plank faster, and he tested this and found that the wood and lead rolled down in the same time. This went against Aristotle's view that heavier things fall faster because they are trying to reach the place of earth at the center of the universe.

Galileo also heard that someone had just made lenses for the first time and realized that he could now look at the heavens and see if they really *are* perfect. So he made a telescope and looked at the moon and saw bumps. He also looked at Jupiter and saw moons that changed position around it, which represented a further irregularity in the pattern of celestial movements. Some people said they wouldn't look through his machine because they *knew* the moon was perfect and therefore didn't need to look. Others looked through the machine and saw the bumps on the moon but concluded that although the moon appeared to be imperfect, it must be covered by a perfect sphere you can't see. But Galileo trusted his own observations, and for Aristotle's view (and therefore Aquinas's and the Church's view as well) this was terrible, because the moon and Jupiter, being part of the heavenly realm, should be perfect.

Now what was Galileo actually doing? Number one, he looked and saw, rather than just believing the texts. Secondly, he created a situation that made things simple so that they could actually be tested. This is experimentation. Thirdly, he created a language, in this case mathematics, in which he could precisely say what he saw.

The Success of the Newtonian Program

In 1642, the year Galileo died, Isaac Newton was born. Newton showed without any doubt the exact way in which the planets moved around the sun. Moreover, he showed that earthly motion followed the same laws as heavenly motion, and that the language of mathematics was the language in which the laws of motion were to be written. Whereas in Aristotle's world there was a necessary role for God and the soul, in Newton's world all these were swept away. The planets moved automatically, mechanically, without any intervention from a creator.

The program of Newton and his followers was to explain all phenomena on the same principles as he had explained the motion of the planets: a few basic laws of motion with mathematical language for their description. Furthermore, initially the program also tried to explain all phenomena by the motion of small material particles, which obeyed the same laws of motion that Newton had found to apply to planets and stones. The action of a creator was no longer a part of these laws.

By the end of the nineteenth century, two centuries after Newton, there was a widespread certainty that the general program originating with Galileo and Newton had been successful. In the realm of physics, a tremendous amount had been explained by Newton's approach. In addition, work in chemistry—which at that time was the study of the way in which various natural elements interact with each other—had suggested that the theory of atomic activity as the basis of everything was valid. There was tremendous confidence in the scientific approach because so much of its program had been carried out, at least in the realm of physics and chemistry, that is, in connection with objects believed not to have life. The belief that living things are made out of cells, developed in the eighteenth century, was an effort to establish even biology on the basis of a kind of atomic theory—even biological function is based on the activity of an organism's smallest units. Charles Darwin's theory of evolution appeared in the nineteenth century, saying that, over a long period of time, the more complicated kinds of living things developed mechanically from some very simple kinds of living things. Darwin's theory suggested a mechanical, automatic process by which this happened. According to Newton's followers, all natural processes are simply mechanical. They all occur without intelligence or consciousness guiding or driving them.

Scientific Certainty

By the beginning of the twentieth century, this sense of certainty about scientific knowledge had made science the dominant belief system in Western countries. During the two hundred years from Newton's time to the turn of the century, this belief system was unfolding amid great debate between the Christian viewpoint in which God was creator and the so-called scientific viewpoint, which was gradually diminishing any role for God. Once Newton had shown that the planets just move around by themselves, there was no more need for God. When Darwin suggested that different kinds of organisms just evolved mechanically, that meant that even in the creation of humankind there was no need for God. Thus began a fierce debate between people who hold the Christian viewpoint and those who hold the evolutionary viewpoint; the debate has continued into the present. However, by the end of the nineteenth century, the view that science was the one and only true belief system began to prevail and continues to do so, at least in the popular mind. This rather simplistic belief is also held by most working scientists, who do not reflect much on what they do.

Let me try to characterize this sense of certainty, that science is really able to find out the truth about the real world. An aspect of this view is what is called reductionism. Reductionism builds on the idea that the objective world is fundamentally space, time, and material particles, and nothing else. The study of how these material particles behave is physics, and how they combine to make bigger particles is, very simply speaking, chemistry. The study of how those bigger particles combine to become living particles is biology, and how the living particles become more complex so that they appear to feel is the study of physiology and neurophysiology. The study of the way those even more complex particles behave in such a way that they seem to have what we call intelligence is psychology. My description has moved upward from physics, from small particles to bigger particles, and ultimately to intelligent, living things. Reductionism is the belief that the description can run the other way as well. Phenomena that seem to be intelligent should be explainable by phenomena that seem to be living, and those in turn should be explainable by phenomena that seem to be chemically complex molecules, and those should be explainable by the laws of basic atoms. So in the end, everything is explainable by physics.

Another tenet of the turn-of-the-century scientific viewpoint is objectivity, which is the notion that the results of the scientific process are independent of any individual human perceiver or group of perceivers. The presumption is that, independent of the whole society of human perceivers, there is a world that exists

and has its own structure. This structure can be known by observing it, but it exists independently of the observer. The reason
it can be known by the human observer is that the structure of
this objective world follows certain laws. Therefore it is testable
by experiment. By the experimental method, the observer can
know the objective structure of that world. This was the view at
the end of the nineteenth century of what science does, and it
remains the view of most people, certainly of 99 percent of the
ordinary, nonscientific, public. It is also the view of perhaps 80
or 90 percent of practicing scientists. This is very important in
that it provides for the Western world a sense of guarantee of a
real world beyond personal bias and beliefs. Science provides, so
the scientist believes, a way to get around wishful thinking, to see
how things really are, independently of what I, or anyone else,
wants.

Another aspect of the established scientific viewpoint was determinism. Because everything we experience, including our
own lives, comes down to the movement of particles, and these
particles obey fixed, unchanging laws, then if we could know the
state of all the particles in the universe right now, we would know
the state of the universe at any time in the future. Similarly if all
phenomena could be accounted for on the same basis, then all
phenomena would be predetermined. Human thought and aspiration has no more place in these laws than does the action of a
creator.

By the 1920s, the classical Newtonian outlook began to break
down. The relativity theory and the development of quantum
mechanics undermined its principles and also called into question
the possibility of pure objective perception. Doubt arose that the
scientific method could in fact produce certainty about an objective world. However, in the Western tradition, when you doubt
the existence of a real objective world, the only alternative you
have is subjectivity. Everything is thrown back on the individual
subject. We simply perceive whatever we invent. The world becomes whatever we make up in our minds. So, subjectivity again
brings us back to wishful thinking. Why are we stuck with only
these two alternative extremes of subjectivity and objectivity?

Because deeply rooted in Western thinking is a belief in the duality of mind and matter, subject and object.

Science, according to the classical view of the nineteenth century, was the great method for overcoming wishful thinking and finding out how the world really is. Many could not let go of the classical belief in an objective world. Therefore, when doubt about it began to arise in the 1920s, scientists had to find a way to make the foundations of science firm again. In the 1930s, a whole new approach was worked out and has now become the mainstream view of science. This current outlook of science is called logical empiricism.

Logical Empiricism

The method by which we supposedly discover the nature of the objective world is the scientific method. This is taught at the beginning of every science schoolbook regardless of whether it is physics, biology, chemistry, or even psychology. There are four steps to this method. First, we look and see—we gather data, information. Second, we form a theory that explains the data. The theory puts the data into some simple, singular formula or description. Third, with that theory, we predict further observations that we should be able to make. Number four, we look for those predicted observations. These are the four stages of scientific method. It was through this method that the Newtonian program is supposed to have been accomplished, according to the school textbooks. This method incorporates the basic ideas of logical empiricism.

Logical empiricism has two parts: logic and empiricism. The logic of propositions deals with the way in which several true statements can be combined to produce another true statement. It is a system that consists of axioms and rules. Axioms are statements one knows from somewhere else, outside of the logic, to be valid. In addition, there are the mechanical rules, the laws of logical operations, which show how one can produce new statements by combining different axioms. These are the basic elements of the logic of propositions. This kind of system is very familiar in the Buddhist tradition, which also has a highly developed logic of propositions.

Now we can use this system in science. The axioms are drawn from observations, from experiments. So, in our scientific method, the axioms come from the first step: we look, we derive facts, data. This is the empirical aspect of logical empiricism. Next we have to rewrite our initial observations in a language that the logic machine (mathematics) can work on. We really have two layers of initial statements, or axioms: there are observation-statements speaking directly about our observations; and these are turned into theory-statements that combine the conceptually formulated observational elements of our theory with the laws of the theory. Let me give an example. We look a the night sky and see little lights, and as time passes we observe that some of the lights change position. The description of the paths of these lights across the sky is a pure observation-statement. When we say each of those lights is an object (a planet) with a particular mass and distance from the earth, that is the theory-statement. And that they move around the sun according to Newton's laws is the theory itself. You can see already that there is here a circularity between theory and observation—a point we will take up soon when we discuss the objections to logical empiricism.

Next we have to process those theory-statements according to mechanical rules of logic, in combinations (the equations of the theory) suggested by our theory, to produce new theory-statements. This produces the third step of the scientific method: a new theory-statement that can be turned into a prediction about new observations. These predictions can then be tested, and this is step four of the scientific method. For example, some observations (step one of the scientific method) of the planets showed that they did not exactly move as Newton's laws required (step two), and this gave rise to the prediction (step three) that if a telescope was pointed in a particular direction in the sky at a particular time, another planet would be found. The planet was found in 1846 (step four), and it was called Neptune.

This is how, in a simple way, the logic of propositions becomes the core of science, with the observations being the input. You put in an observation statement and turn the logic crank in the direction suggested by your theory. Out comes a new statement, and you make a new observation to check this new statement. If it checks, then your theory is correct.

That is a brief sketch of the theory of logical empiricism. This is how people convinced themselves in the 1930s, and continue to do so today, that there is a good foundation for science. Many people still suppose that logical empiricism is the basis for scientific activity. And because it works, because there is a step four where we can check our prediction and find "yes," we can work back and verify that our theories are correct, that is, that they correspond in some way to an objective reality.

I wanted to be sure that we understood the principles of logical empiricism and the importance of it, because the next stage of the presentation is how this has been challenged in the past thirty to thirty-five years. Although these challenges are very important, among philosophers of science there is nevertheless great debate about their significance. There is no longer a feeling that the foundations of science are clear, definite, solved, no problem. As we saw, there was this certainty up until 1900. And again, following roughly a quarter of a century of shaking foundations, from 1930 to 1960, a new feeling of certainty arose, based on logical empiricism. And that false sense of certainty still goes on in some quarters. Many practicing scientists get very angry if asked, "But aren't there problems at the very foundations of science?" Nevertheless, there is now a great debate among people who think about science as an activity. In the early 1970s there was a major conference on the structure of scientific theories. In the proceedings* of that conference, one of its organizers, Frederick Suppe, said: "The situation today, then, in philosophy of science is this: the positivistic analysis of scientific knowledge erected upon the Received View [logical empiricism] has been rejected, or at least is highly suspect, but none of the alternative analyses of scientific knowledge that have been suggested enjoy widespread acceptance. For more than fifty years philosophy of

---

*See Frederick Suppe, *The Structure of Scientific Theories* (Champaign, Ill.: University of Illinois Press, 1974).

science has been engaged in a search for philosophic understanding of scientific theories: today it is still searching."

Problems with Logical Empiricism

Now I would like to talk about the refutation of logical empiricism. There are two ways to look at the refutation. One is from within and one is from without. Even in the 1930s, the people working very hard to make logical empiricism completely certain and clear came up with problems. These problems are still unresolved. After fifty years, even the logical empiricists themselves say we still haven't solved these problems.

The first question to ask concerns whether logical empiricism works as a theory about scientific method. In considering this, we can apply the experimental method to logical empiricism itself. Here we have a theory about the scientific method, and we would like to test this theory by making observations of various sciences to see if this is really how they are done. When we look at, say, atomic physics or evolutionary biology or cognitive psychology and ask whether they have the form that logical empiricism says they should, the answer almost universally is no. Logical empiricism as a philosophical basis for science may be very nice, but that's not how these sciences are done in reality. So, as a theory of scientific method, logical empiricism fails its own test.

Another major internal problem for logical empiricism is related to the idea of confirmation, step four in the scientific method. At step three, we have a prediction, and we want to confirm that. If we can prove by observation that the prediction is correct, then we can say our theory is a good one. But how do we confirm? We cannot absolutely confirm an observation. In a way this is very obvious, but it is difficult for anyone, including scientists, to accept. Suppose I want to find out whether all swans are white. I see a swan, and it is white. Good. I see another swan. It is white. Good. I see a million swans. They are white. Good. Does this prove that all swans are white? No, of course not. It just so happens that the million-and-first swan is green! In principle, the theory of confirmation by observation just does not work.

This requires the creation of a theory of falsification—the first step in the breakdown of logical empiricism. I can certainly falsify the statement that all swans are white. If I find a green swan, that theory is falsified. We have to agree that we cannot develop a view of confirmation of theories by observation, but we can perhaps develop a view of falsification. Now what do we have? We have this so-called objective world. How does it speak to us? It only tells us when we are wrong; it does not tell us when we are right! Thus it becomes clear (and in a way this is still within logical empiricism as it has now been rethought) that we must think of theories as more or less *probable*. We cannot say that observation or theory *certainly* describes the way the world is. We can only say that so-and-so is *probably* how the world is. Then we must develop a theory about what would make a theory most probable. This is as far as we can push logical empiricism. I think that most scientists are familiar with the idea of falsification and feel that science gets closer and closer to a description of objective reality, but this description can never be a sure one. This is the challenge from within.

Now turning to the challenge from without. Studies by cognitive psychologists challenged the idea of pure observation, that is, objective observation. In the 1950s, experimental psychologists began to suggest that perception is in some way an active process, that the eye and brain do not purely take photographs of what is out there but in some way influence what seems to be out there. This challenges step one and step four, the observation stages. Can we actually get pure data that is free from our wishes or our theories? The many external challenges to logical empiricism focus on that question. There are several aspects to this challenge. One is that all of our observations are in some way filled with previous theory. The catch phrase here is "Observation is theory laden." A second aspect is that the terms in which we describe our observations add a further theoretical and subjective layer to what were supposed to be objective observations. Of course the meanings of theory terms are theory laden, but even the observation terms are theory laden. A third aspect of this involvement of subjective factors is that what is allowed to count as a fact also depends on one's theory.

Let us look at these three aspects a little more closely. One of the classical examples of how theory influences what we see is the old woman–young woman drawing [see figure 1]. You could regard this drawing as a young woman or as an old woman; it depends on your view. This kind of perceptual ambiguity is taken as a key indicator that something else happens in perception other than just simply seeing. How do we decide which interpretation is correct? In this case we might say: "Oh well, this is actually a patch of black ink on a piece of white paper." A more basic reality than old woman or young woman is the line on the paper. But what about when Galileo's colleagues looked through his telescope and insisted on seeing Jupiter's moons as imperfections in the instrument? Or, in a more recent example, people simply refused to accept the observations of an experiment measuring the speed of light in different directions (the Michelson-Morley experiment) because these observations did not conform to their theory about the ether—the subtle medium that light was then supposed to travel through. It took the genius of Albert Einstein to ask what would be the consequences of accepting these results. One of the consequences was that people had to stop believing in the ether!

The second aspect of the challenge concerns the meaning of the terms that we use in our theories. What do we mean by electron? At the end of the nineteenth century, when electrons were first "discovered," people thought that they were little particles. "Electron" meant a tiny particle of a certain kind with a certain electrical charge. Then quantum mechanics came along and said that an electron cannot be thought of simply as a tiny particle. It is much more complicated. It is also a wave. Now the meaning of the term *electron* has completely changed; that is, the meaning depends on our theories. Each time a scientific theory changes or new observations are made, the meanings of the terms change to include the new understandings about them. But if that is the case, we have no scientific method, because the terms in which we have formulated our hypothesis keep changing in meaning through the course of our work. Anything observed becomes included in our new term *electron*. In order for logical empiricism to work we have to agree on a definite meaning of electron. We

FIGURE I

have to say, This is our theory about electrons, now we will do experiments. But instead, the meaning of *electron* keeps changing, as the experiments themselves bring changes in the theories that give meaning to the term. It is a circular situation. For this reason it is said that the meanings of terms are *theory-dependent*, and do not correspond to an independent reality.

Finally, as to the third aspect of the challenge, it was pointed out that any fact suggested by observation that goes against prevailing theories tends to be screened out, just as other "facts" are created to corroborate prevailing theories.

FRANCISCO J. VARELA: I will give one example of how what counts as a fact depends on theory that is very recent. In 1984 the Nobel Prize was given to an American geneticist by the name of Barbara McClintock. She received the prize because her theory was finally accepted: that genes jump from one place to another within a cell. This idea of jumping genes was unacceptable, was abhorred in biology and genetics for thirty years. During this time, Dr. McClintock had been publishing her results, but people in genetics would not accept them as factual. They would say that they were not possible, although her finding was fact, a pure observation in the classical view. It took thirty years for biologists to say, "This is a fact."

JEREMY W. HAYWARD: The theory-dependency of facts is

very difficult for practicing scientists to accept, because the fundamental belief today is that we, the scientists, are the ones who are open. We simply look and survey the world and make our theories that way. But if you look at history, you find that, as Francisco's example and many other examples have shown, facts are not that simple. Here is another example: In accordance with his little-particle idea, Newton said that light is made up of little particles; he developed a whole theory about light with the idea that it is made up of little particles. Although there were people who were doing experiments that could be explained more easily on the basis of light being waves, these experiments were discounted for more than a hundred years. People said that a mistake must have been made, that light cannot be waves. This was just like when people looked through Galileo's telescope and refused to acknowledge what they saw. So, facts are selected rather than all being accepted.

This selectivity about facts is explained by the kind of training a scientist receives. In order to become a physicist or a biologist or a doctor, one receives a certain kind of training. In receiving this training, one learns to see certain things. They become part of one's system in a sense, and only people who have received that training can see those things. This gives us further understanding about what scientists do. One must consider what scientists do in the context of the entire system of beliefs that they grew up in and were trained in. This is what is known as the worldview criticism of logical empiricism, which places science as a human activity within a group of humans and takes into account the kinds of training that group receives. The new view that came in was that science is a human activity, and observations are theory-dependent within a society of scientists. The scientists are like a lineage that passes on the principles of how to see and what to see.

So far, we have dealt mainly with how the belief systems of individuals affect observation, what they see. They do not just see the world as it is but see it as affected by their belief systems. Now I would like to go a little more into the role of presuppositions. I want to mention particularly the work of Thomas S. Kuhn, a scientist and historian who wrote an important book called *The Structure of Scientific Revolutions* [University of Chicago Press, 1962]. One of his basic ideas is that the classical view, including the logical empiricists' view, regards science as a progression, moving gradually closer and closer to the truth. Each discipline—physics, biology, chemistry, astronomy, neuroscience—in its own way gets closer to the way things are. Each time there was a change in the mainstream scientific view, for example, from Newtonianism to relativity, this was progress. The idea is that relativity includes Newtonianism and goes beyond it. Kuhn proposed that this is not at all the way things happen. For example, through his work Newton established a worldview, and for a long time after that people were working out Newton's ideas in more and more detail but always within the same worldview. As they continued to elaborate the Newtonian view and see that it worked, occasionally there were observations that did not fit in with it. At first, observations that do not accord with a prevailing worldview are put aside. They are called anomalous, or unacceptable observations, like the jumping genes of Barbara McClintock. Newtonianism also remained impervious to various conflicting observations for a long period of time. But such observations put pressure on this prevailing worldview, this system of beliefs, and tensions begin to arise in the community of scientists. Still they hold fast to their worldview, until at a certain point the pressure from the unacceptable observations is too great and the whole system breaks down, as has happened to a great extent with Newtonianism. An entirely new worldview comes to replace it. In Kuhn's view, then, science cannot be seen as a progression, but should be seen as a continual series of shifts from one view to another. And we are not really able to say that the current view is better than any that have gone before.

There are many worldviews. Perhaps we could say that each scientific discipline—physics, biology, neuroscience—has its own worldview. A word that expresses the idea of a particular model of the world is *paradigm*. Each of those sciences has its own paradigm, on the basis of which it forms a view of what it observes. Thus biologists may be forming a notion of ultimate reality on the basis of a hidden paradigm that is not the same as that of the physicists. The idea of paradigms was part of Kuhn's theory of scientific revolutions, and it is also part of the criticism of logical empiricism. This view of how science changes is not by any means completely accepted. Moreover, Kuhn's early statement of it was a rather extreme one. Nonetheless some form of Kuhn's view is fairly widely accepted now among those who think about the foundations of science.

Kuhn also introduced, as a development of the notion of a prevailing paradigm, the idea of the *disciplinary matrix*, which is the shared commitment of a particular scientific community, say, of physicists or psychologists, to particular models and shared values. These shared commitments provide a basis for professional communication and a relative unanimity of professional judgment within that community.

Let us say that a group of students decide, perhaps in their second year of college, that they want to be physicists. They take courses in physics and gradually become acquainted with the language of physics. The experience of learning in this way is familiar to many of us. First you hear new terms that you do not understand; but you leave your mind open and work with them. You perform the activities, do the examples, that exemplify the views and methods of a discipline. You do lots of problems and still have the uncomfortable feeling that "I don't understand what this is, but I'm doing it anyway." One day suddenly you feel: "Ah! Now I understand what it is all about." At that point you can say, "I have become a physicist now, because the language is part of my system." The way you became a physicist was by doing hundreds of examples until suddenly you understood. A biologist or a medical student, an astronomer or a psychologist goes through this same process. Maybe it takes up to ten years to go through this process. Then finally one *is* a biologist or a psychologist.

There is an extreme view that says that, in view of the part played by all these subjective elements, there are no grounds for speaking of an objective reality that science produces knowledge about. The opposite extreme, of course, is the classical view that science is capable of pure objective observation of an objectively existing reality. Kuhn and others espoused a kind of middle view, according to which we cannot speak of a single objective reality, and therefore it is acceptable to have several incompatible theories about the same phenomenon. One group of scientists is satisfied to explain a phenomenon within its own disciplinary matrix. Another group of scientists with a different disciplinary matrix might explain that same phenomenon with a different theory. And really there is no reason that the theories have to be compatible. Some people argue that it is good to have many incompatible theories, because in any case facts are theory laden. If we have more theories, we might let in more facts. Two theories might be quite incompatible, yet both equally good. In the extreme point of view this approach leads to saying that there is no objective reality or that it is meaningless to speak of an objective reality.

The idea of disciplinary matrix points to the role, perhaps deeply hidden, of conceptual presuppositions in scientific discovery, but it also goes beyond these to take into account the background of outlooks by which any society interprets what it is to be human. This background cannot be made explicit or fully conceptualized because as a background it is all-pervasive. To make it an object of analysis would be to separate parts out of it and thus lose touch with its quality of being a background. Several writers have pointed to the vital role of this background of communication and outlooks and practices within which science arises. For example, David Bohm, a physicist working within the scientific tradition, argues that science is communicative action within an unbroken wholeness that is infinite in its qualitative and quantitative depth and complexity. The communicative actions of a group of scientists bring into consciousness an abstract picture of a particular limited domain and thereby separate out this domain from the unbroken wholeness. Any laws and theories formulated in relation to this domain are necessarily relative, valid only within that domain, and possibly false beyond it. The activity of scientists is to extend the domain of a particular theory to its limits. When it reaches those limits, it is falsified and an entirely new theory must be found to relate to a new domain. No theory can ever be regarded as absolute because of the infinite depth of the unbroken background.

Questions of Method

A Conversation

Buddhist Epistemology and Logical Empiricism

FRANCISCO J. VARELA: One of the interesting things about logical empiricism is that it is a way of satisfying a distrust of common sense. In other words, when the Newtonian world began to break down, it was a breakdown of common sense. It was a discovery that space is not what it seems to be; time is not what it seems to be. The idea was that science went beyond common sense. Answers were no longer just simple; they were complex. So began a notion in science that common sense cannot be trusted. What you can trust is the logical apparatus of mathematics and logic, which is very complex. The distrust of common sense brought about the entire reformulation of science so that it would have a very precise machinery that would not depend on common sense. This is why the results of science oftentimes are contrary to common sense. But scientists are very proud of this. They say because we have a clean method, we can actually get to results that correspond with reality.

JEREMY W. HAYWARD: I agree, Francisco, but what you call common sense is the belief system that has been brought to us as the result of two hundred years of science itself. In the tenth century, empty space was not common sense; absolute time was not common sense. So what you mean by common sense is nineteenth-century science.

VARELA: Absolutely right, but I was just being a scientist! [laughing] The phrase that one reads a lot in logical empiricist texts is "cleansing the foundations," making things work. This means cleaning out what seems to be just the noise of ordinary ideas that don't match the standard of what should be a scientific theory. Hence the whole search for foundations in mathematics, foundations in physics, foundations in biology.

ELEANOR ROSCH: Whatever the criticisms of it are, the classical view Jeremy outlined is described at the beginning of virtually every science textbook. This is what students are taught from the time they take their first science course, whether it is physics, psychology, mind, biology, whatever. This is the view.

HAYWARD: Yes, the experimental method, logical empiricism, is at the front of every textbook. That is the only philosophy that students receive, and then they are taken into the science, into the "facts."

DALAI LAMA: In relation to the disciplinary matrix, or the way a scientist is trained to be part of a community of scientists, is this whole process a conditioning of the mind that eventually leads you to have a certain view due to a particular opinion or theory? In Buddhist training, for example, when studying Madhyamika,* first you hear that things have no inherent existence or intrinsic existence. You hear it and it doesn't mean much, but then you hear it again—there is no true existence, no inherent existence, no intrinsic existence—and after a while an understanding of this comes vividly to mind. Then you say, "Ah! Now I know what this means." So the mind has been conditioned, and a kind of new vision or understanding arises.

There are two cases, one is as just explained, when you first hear the phrase *noninherent existence*, or *nonintrinsic existence*, you don't know what it means, but later you learn. You hear it many times and after a while you get to know it, and you may eventually understand it. The moment you hear the phrase, you know

---

*Madhyamika is a school of Buddhist philosophy that emphasizes that no individual entity or thing exists in virtue of an essence or nature of its own. Thus it is "empty," or devoid of inherent existence. This emphasis, *shunyata* in Sanskrit, is a central tenet of Mahayana Buddhism. The Madhyamika school has a number of branches or subschools. The main ones are the *rang tong* (Tib., lit. "self-empty," which is further subdivided into the Prasangika and Svatantrika schools) and the *shen tong* (Tib., lit. "other-empty"). The Prasangika position is the one advocated by the Gelugpa Order, of which His Holiness the Dalai Lama is the head.

what it means; it is actually more convincing, it comes closer to reality. In the other case, the phrase becomes something very alive, something very meaningful, but not in a way that corresponds to reality. Due to your own too-close feeling for that phrase, you see it in a way that does not correspond to reality.

So the conditioning can go both ways. It can lead you deeper into reality or it can lead you right away from reality and actually distort your mode of experience. With the "disciplinary matrix," which of these two cases are you referring to generally?

HAYWARD: In one extreme view there is no external objective reality. It is simply that what we learn molds our way of seeing, and our beliefs follow along with that. For Kuhn, there is still some objective reality, and the disciplinary matrix makes a difference only in the color of our spectacles. We can never see reality as it is; we always see it colored through biological or physical spectacles. There actually still is some reality there, but it depends on the viewer to some extent. Then there are still the scientists with the classical view who say that there is a reality there and we do see it. You have that side, and you have the side that says, we can't say now that there is a reality, and you have the people in the middle who say, yes, there is a reality but we never really know it.

VARELA: But in general the belief is that there is some kind of a progress toward a reality, so in the disciplinary matrix it is neither of the two cases that His Holiness was talking about. There is not an immediate apprehension of what seems to be totally true as in the Madhyamika, for example. Nor is it a case of pure opinion, as when people have an ideology that they have picked up in society. This middle Kuhnian or loosely Kuhnian scientist would say that in this disciplinary matrix you learn a worldview that is not completely true, but it's better than anything else because it leads you little by little, closer and closer to the truth. There is a sense of getting better and better, which is why a scientist would prefer to be a scientist than something else.

ROSCH: Kuhn himself would challenge the idea that there is progress from one paradigm to the other. It's more like different-colored spectacles.

HAYWARD: Even among those who agree with Kuhn, a large number still think there is progress. So, there is a whole range. But I think that the ordinary scientists would have to ask His Holiness, How do you know the Madhyamika view of emptiness is reality any more than I know that the matter view is reality or the biologists know that the brain really is equivalent to the mind? From the point of view that I'm presenting now, very sadly, when we lost logical empiricism, we lost forever the possibility of actually knowing a complete objective reality. Now, this is the scientists speaking—we have to go with some level of Kuhnian view.

DALAI LAMA: Another question is, Within one field, whether physics or another discipline, do you find different views arising in different countries, in Germany, the United States, and so forth? Perhaps there are certain differences with a scientist from Russia, from a Communist country. The Chinese have a long tradition of some kind. So, is there any sort of nationalistic factor from one country to another, or not?

HAYWARD: Yes, there are influences at every level, and Kuhn points to the social structure of any particular group of scientists as the source of such influences. Whatever way they hold themselves together and define themselves as a group—through articles written in professional magazines and journals, through conferences, through memberships in professional societies—all this forms a group interaction that is self-confirming. This society is the group that determines whether a fact is acceptable or not. In each discipline, say, in the discipline of quantum physics or the discipline of evolutionary biology, this group has an international aspect. Journals are published internationally and there are international conferences. The discipline goes beyond national boundaries. But at the same time, the influences of local cultural ideology does affect particularly which facts are regarded as acceptable. There was a famous situation with a Russian biologist, Lysenko, who later became the head of agriculture in Russia. Lysenko, for ideological Marxist reasons, argued that Darwin's theory of modification by descent was not correct. He argued for the possibility of the inheritance of acquired characteristics, which had become heresy in Western science. Because he was able to argue it in ideological terms, all biological evolutionary science in Russia followed the Lysenko view, all through the time until he became the head of agriculture in Russia in the 1950s.

VARELA: I want to warn against the impression that this could only happen in a Stalinist society. In fact, it is something that happens all the time. One beautiful example that happened in the United States was the following study: Using scientific articles that had been published in good journals (which therefore contained facts accepted by the scientific community), people changed the names of the authors and the name of the place where the paper was written. Instead of saying the research was done at Stanford or Harvard, or some place like that, they said it was done in Chile, or in Tibet—someplace that people wouldn't trust too much for scientific reliability. They sent these articles back to the same journals. The result was that out of a hundred papers resubmitted, 80 percent were rejected with comments saying they were not good science, their method was bad, the interpretation was bad! Yet these were the same papers that had previously been published by the very same journals! This means that a fact, just because it comes from a place that is not considered reliable, isn't reliable. This was not Lysenko and Stalin, who represent an extreme. This phenomenon is a lot more subtle and pervasive than one might think. It is part of this entire social context that Jeremy was talking about. This sociological matrix that science sits in the midst of is not separable from why a theory is accepted and why one fact is considered good and another fact is not. This is extremely important and very unsettling for most scientists, who would not like that to be the case.

ROBERT B. LIVINGSTON: I could give an example of long-term differences in approach between Russian neurophysiologists and European-American neurophysiologists. The Russians have a much deeper concern for the social implications of scientific work. For example, the Nobel Prize was received by David H. Hubel and Torsten N. Wiesel for the discovery of specific neurons that receive a message through the retina and the cortex as to a location and a field size of what activates them. In the [former] Soviet Union the same experiments were repeated, but this time the conditions were altered from those used in the Hubel and Wiesel experiment at Harvard. They did the same experiment with the same animals, cats and monkeys, but now with dim light instead of bright light, or with a conditioning in respect to the signal as compared with an unconditioned signal. They found that the map of the units they were investigating changed as a consequence of darkness, or it changed because of conditioning. They went through six or seven different variables that made the whole physiology much more dynamic and plastic than it would have been if everything had been accepted on the basis of the Hubel and Wiesel paradigm. It has been very difficult to get these findings published in the West. So the channels of science get affected by the sociocultural conditions.

DALAI LAMA: But in the field of research work, was what the Russians did in their experiment helpful?

LIVINGSTON: Yes, exactly.

VARELA: But it wasn't listened to. It was a good experiment, good data, but it wasn't listened to.

ROSCH: Everything everyone has said is true, and I could give more examples from my field, but when you are at a conference with Russian or Chinese scientists, there can be a great deal of communication. The way analysis is done and discussion is conducted, the fact that logic is respected to a certain extent, that empirical experiments are appreciated—all these show that scientists everywhere have much in common. It is not as though you are talking to a Martian or a rock. There is a kind of international community among scientists despite very real cultural problems.

LIVINGSTON: You might say that communication is better among the scientists than the general public.

VARELA: That point is important, because for people like myself, who come from a place that is not a dominant center like the United States or Europe (although I have worked most of my life in the U.S. and Europe), it is very clear that what is called international science is a particular style of science. This is not to say that the system prevents different voices from coming in, but today what ordinary citizens all over the place would consider real science is fundamentally European-American science.

NEWCOMB GREENLEAF: Of course, a good example of that is the Chinese science of acupuncture. Westerners are still very puzzled that acupuncture seems to work. How does this work? They don't like it. Most Western scientists would like to ignore the whole thing and feel that in non-Western cultures there really was never any significant understanding. They would like to regard the Third World as always somehow scientifically primitive.

LIVINGSTON: Here's a case with acupuncture; we have two different theories that account for the same phenomena but are based on a very different argument. For instance, if you apply the meridians of the acupuncturists to the Western practice of using procaine injections to relieve spasms and tensions, you will find that there is a great deal of overlap between the acupuncture points and the injection points. But the interpretation of what happens in the process of massage, heat application, or acupuncture, on one hand, and injection of procaine on the other is radically different. Both interpretations account for the phenomena.

DALAI LAMA: That is my point. National origin is not an especially fundamental problem; differences arise unconsciously due to a variety of environmental factors. You are very sincerely trying to explain the truth, but due to other factors you are unconsciously conditioned; as a result, you have a different explanation. That was my question, and I got a good answer from you [laughing]!

It is my view that generally Buddhism, and particularly Mahayana Buddhism, is very close to a scientific approach. Consider, for example, that Lord Buddha himself gave different kinds of teachings, depending on whether they were given publicly or not. According to the general Mahayana point of view, there were three major turnings of the wheel, as the three main cycles of Buddha's teachings are traditionally called. The teachings that were given during these three major turnings of the wheel are literally contradictory—some elements are really incompatible. Since all these teachings were genuine words of the Buddha himself and they contradict each other, how do we determine which are true and which are not? If we were to make the distinction on the basis of some scriptural citation, then that again has to depend on something else to validate its authenticity. Therefore, eventually the final validation has to be done on the authority of reasoning, logic. One example of this is that in some sutras Buddha says that things do inherently exist and in another one he says they do not inherently exist. Then where do you go? The only way is to establish a conclusion by reasoning and not simply further scriptural authority. Therefore Mahayana Buddhists divided the words of the Buddha into two categories: those that are definitive, and those that require further interpretation; those that are literal and those that are not literal.

The explanation I have given just now is from the point of view that regards all the teachings of Buddha—the Mahayana and Hinayana teachings—as genuine words of the Buddha that were actually taught by the Buddha himself during his lifetime.* But then there is another viewpoint that maintains that the genuine words of the Buddha, the original teachings of the Buddha, were only the Hinayana sutras, which are very practical, clear and simple. Then later on, according to this view, Buddhist doctrine, no longer ascribed to the Buddha himself, became more complicated and more confusing, but I am not sure this is true. Now this second point of view is mainly based on historical facts, because historically speaking, it was the Hinayana teachings that Buddha taught publicly. In the Hinayana view, then, we take for granted that the Buddha taught only the Tripitaka, or the three collections of scriptures that are included in the Hinayana tradition. As one analyzes these, there may appear to be certain contradictions and points of lack of clarity, things that are open to refutation. To respond to those, further additions were made. In this way the teaching grew through history—by finding the shortcomings or soft spots that appeared through analysis.

From either of these two perspectives, the Hinayana or the Mahayana, we find that analysis and examination through reasoning, the basic Buddhist attitude, is very important. Once you find a fact through investigation, then you accept it. Even if that fact

---

*See note, page 2.

appears contradictory to Buddha's own words, it doesn't matter. Because of this, I feel the basic Buddhist attitude is quite similar to the scientists' attitude. Be open and investigate, find something, confirm it, then accept it. Whichever way you go, whether you think that all the teachings of Mahayana and Hinayana were taught by the Buddha, or whether you think that they were progressively created by later people, either way there is a strong emphasis upon your own analysis and investigation and not simply a dogmatic adherence out of faith in the Buddha.

Now, on another topic: Buddhists divide phenomena into three categories, depending on how ordinary beings relate to objects and perceive them. It's very important to recognize that the Buddhist usage of the term *phenomenon* includes everything that exists. In the first category of phenomena are those that are obvious, that can be directly perceived through the sense faculties, that are immediately apparent to the senses. In the second category are hidden types of phenomena that cannot be perceived directly by ordinary living beings but depend on some kind of logical process in order to be perceived. You can perceive them only through inference. Relying on certain logical processes, you can infer their existence. The first type requires no reasoning and the second one necessarily does.*

Now, with respect to the second category of phenomena, the slightly concealed phenomena, although at that moment you can only understand them through inference, that experience of inference also has to trace back to a certain direct experience you had. The initial access may be only through reasoning, but eventually it must lead to a direct experience, and also the inference itself must depend upon a certain direct experience. In the case of understanding something that is not obvious, you require examples so your perception of the examples can be direct. For example, you perceive this pen as impermanent; then you need reasoning and you need an example. The inference that perceived the impermanence of this pen is just an inference, therefore it is

---

*The third category, extremely hidden phenomena, is discussed below on pages 48–49.

conceptual, but it depends eventually upon the experience of directly seeing this pen.

GESHE PALDEN DRAKPA: The reason that inference should eventually lead to a direct experience is that if it doesn't, then it is questionable whether the inference has really touched, perceived, the object or not. For example, by seeing smoke on the mountain you could infer that there is a fire, but if you are not able to perceive the fire directly when you go there, then the earlier thought was just a presumption. It did not lead you to that direct experience.

With respect to your explanation of the tradition of logical empiricism, I would like to discuss your point that you can only falsify the logical empiricist statement "All swans are white"; that you can never prove it. According to Buddhist logic, there is a way of proving positive statements too. For example, when you say, "Wherever there is smoke, there is fire," just as you can prove that wherever there isn't fire, there cannot be smoke in a negative way, in the same manner you can also positively prove that wherever there is smoke, there is fire. In order to prove that, there is no need for you to see each and every instance of fire and smoke. It is not necessary to see each and every instance of fire.

The Logic of Existence

DALAI LAMA: To understand that, it is important first of all to be familiar with the basic theories of Buddhist logic. For example, we talk of *pervasion*. This is a difficult term. The condition that wherever there is smoke, there is fire is called pervasion. That relationship is pervasive, all-inclusive. In order to prove pervasion, you need three elements. The first is that the presence of smoke should follow and pervade only instances of the presence of fire. Smoke should never be present where there is no fire. That yields a conditional negation of smoke: where there is no fire, there cannot be any smoke. The existence of fire and the nonexistence of fire are mutually exclusive, a dichotomy. Now, there are different types of these mutually exclusive phenomena. For example, this pen and this book are mutually exclusive, meaning that there cannot be something that is a pen and a book. The absence of fire as opposed to the presence of fire is not like that. It is more than that. It is directly contradictory, a dichotomy. Either there is a fire or there isn't a fire. It is a deeper incompatibility, and the presence or absence of smoke pervades it.

VARELA: That seems all to be very reasonable and within the range of what logical empiricists would argue; but it doesn't seem to me to escape precisely the counterargument that, in fact, if you have seen a hundred fires and have never seen a fire without smoke and smoke without a fire, that doesn't positively prove that the next day such a thing will not happen. Scientists have been painfully aware of this. Let me give you an example of an actual scientific situation. For about thirty years in biology, it was asserted that the presence of DNA* permits the specification of a protein. It was thought to go in one direction only. It could never be the case that a protein could affect the DNA. This one-directional flow of information was called the central dogma of molecular biology. It was asserted on the basis of what? On the basis of examining thousands and thousands of examples, with every single example turning out like that. On this basis they made this positive assertion that it is always the case that DNA precedes protein. Until one day someone found that this was not true. In some cases it goes in the other direction. This is a perfect example of something that seemed to have been proven. But scientists have learned since the decay of logical empiricism not to say that something is proven but only that so far it seems to be true. There is nothing that can be established on the basis of "It has always been the case." It doesn't seem to me that the Buddhist logic escapes this argument, does it?

DALAI LAMA: I think the basic Buddhist attitude is we have to discriminate between things that are existent and things that are not. We determine that something exists by whether or not it is established by a valid cognition or not. If something is established by a valid cognition, it is existent; if it is not, then it is

---

*DNA (desoxyribonucleic acid) and RNA (ribonucleic acid) are the two chemical substances involved in the genetic transmission of characteristics from parent to offspring and in the manufacture of proteins.

nonexistent. What is meant by valid cognition is consciousness. I am defining consciousness here as a perception that perceives the object and is not mistaken with respect to the object; that is, the object can indeed perform its function in accordance with the way consciousness perceives it. By discriminating between existence and nonexistence in such a manner, we escape the danger of accepting something that might just be conjured up by a conception. Therefore, as a Buddhist I find that discoveries made by scientists through the scientific method, that have been proven as facts by scientists, really help the Buddhist way of thinking rather than harming it.

Buddha divided all phenomena into four: suffering, origin of suffering, cessation, and method. These divisions are especially pertinent to sentient beings. Within those divisions you will find two sets of causes and effects: those that are desirable and those that are undesirable.* Also, the way that he taught is based on the cause-and-effect relationship between phenomena. The manner and content of his teaching was not just something created by himself but was a natural outgrowth of the way things are and interact. In order to change results you must deal with causes. This also shows that the Buddhist emphasis is not confined to mere mind; it is also something that has to tally with reality. It is not simply subjective, but really there is something objective there as well. One may have a great aspiration to be free of suffering—"Oh, I wish I could be free of suffering"—but simply having that yearning doesn't free you from suffering. You have to discover for yourself the actual causes for the suffering you are experiencing and eradicate those. Wishful thinking alone does not produce the result. This is the basic Buddhist attitude.

Within Buddhism, then, when you speak of the truth of suffering, this includes the external world that sentient beings ex-

---

*This classification corresponds to the Buddha's fundamental doctrine of the four noble truths: (1) existence is characterized by suffering; (2) the cause of suffering is desire or grasping; (3) the cessation of suffering is possible; (4) the path of meditation and intellectual understanding taught by the Buddha leads to the cessation of suffering. The two sets of causes and effects are: (1) suffering and its cause; (2) the cessation of suffering and its cause (the Buddhist methodology or path).

perience as well as the inhabitants of that environment, so both of these are included in the truth of suffering. If we look at the very orthodox presentation of this world found in the Abhidharma,* you have a flat earth with Mount Meru in the middle, something that is in some ways comparable to the medieval notion of the various spheres described by Dr. Hayward. But you do not find a unified front in the Buddhist teachings on the nature of the universe or the nature of the world. In fact you find different presentations. Some of them say that the world, traditionally called Jambudvipa, is triangular and some say it is circular. Some say there is an up side and a down side. So even within Buddhism you don't have just one dogmatic front, but you have a little more looseness or flexibility for interpretation because of the different presentations.

Nowadays if you go up in a spaceship, you look back on planet Earth and see something very pretty, a blue ball, which is almost perfect! It is very beautiful, more beautiful than the moon. On one hand, you have the experience of being able to go up in a rocketship and look down on the earth and have a perception, a direct experience, of what the world looks like; and on the other hand, you have the orthodox literal interpretation of the Abhidharma that says the world is flat. Now, a general basic stance in Buddhism is that it is inappropriate to hold a view that is logically inconsistent. This is taboo. But even more taboo than holding a view that is logically inconsistent is holding a view that goes against direct experience. Here there is direct experience of what this world looks like, that it is round, not flat. I feel that it is totally compatible with the basic attitude of Buddhism to refute the literal interpretation of Abhidharma that says the earth is flat, because it is incompatible with the direct experience of the world as being round.

---

*The Abhidharma is the third part of the three collections of Buddhist scriptures known collectively as the Tripitaka, or "three baskets." This third collection is a compendium of Buddhist psychology and philosophy. A rich commentarial literature based on it has accumulated over many centuries, and this commentarial activity has given rise to many of the Buddhist philosophical schools.

In terms of the four noble truths that I was referring to before, the whole presentation of Mount Meru and the flat earth is simply one rather peripheral element that is part of the truth of suffering. It is really quite peripheral. Among these four topics, what is really of crucial importance are the final two truths, the truth of cessation and the truth of the path to cessation. These are really what deserve the greatest emphasis. On these topics that deserve our chief attention, we find there are many, many teachings of the Buddha. Some of them are interpretive—meaning you don't take them literally—and others are definitive; they are simply right on as they are. If you look at the many teachings of the Buddha, from the Abhidharma system on to the Sautrantika and so on, right up to Madhyamika,* you get many presentations of what is meant by the truth of cessation. Then you come to the finer points of the nature of *shunyata*, "emptiness." What is meant by this? What is the nature of the path? These are the crucial elements; the whole business of Mount Meru and the flat earth I find really very peripheral, very secondary. That part can be changed, can't it? Actually I am thinking that in the near future I would like to gather together some Buddhist scholars who are very conservative and orthodox, as though they were from a few centuries back, and express my own view on what type of attitude contemporary Buddhist scholars should have toward these points that are incompatible with experience.

Perceptual Illusion

HAYWARD: Your Holiness, that explanation seems to be very close to the logical empiricists in that one assumes in that presentation that one can trust one's observation.

DALAI LAMA: Yes. Now here one should also take into account the question of illusion. Can your basic experience be trusted? There are certain causes of illusion, and Buddhist texts speak of temporary and more essential causes of illusion. There are two forms of deception: one is adventitious or simply tem-

---

*The Buddhist philosophical schools developed differing interpretations of the four noble truths.

porary; one is more fundamental. For example, different colors of glass affect your vision, and certain diseases affect your sight—these are temporary. The causes of temporary deceptions are within the object, in your own sense organs, and in the consciousness that immediately perceives the cognition. For example, if someone is very angry and loses his temper, at that moment he will see the whole earth as sort of reddish. He is having an illusion. The causes of his illusion are in the immediately preceding consciousness, which was under the influence of this anger. When you are physically exhausted, at that moment your sight might be affected. You see people differently from the way you normally do. This is also a sort of deception that comes from the immediately perceiving moment of cognition or awareness.

Then there are other, more essential, deeper levels of deception of the type we discussed earlier in connection with the kind of conditioning one goes through in society, one's background. Buddhists place a great deal of emphasis on the search for the truth or reality. But at the same time, Buddhists maintain that our perception of reality cannot be heavily relied upon. There is a disparity between the way things appear to us and the way things exist. Since the actual reality appears to us in a different manner, it cannot be cognized directly because there is this disparity. What ultimately remains to us as a means of approach is a logical process. Since reality does not appear to us as it exists, you cannot simply rely upon appearances, you have to use logical means. Therefore we make divisions of different categories of phenomena. When speaking of dispelling the faults of our perceptions, I do not mean having poor hearing and getting ear surgery done, or anything like that. Rather, I mean dispelling faults of the mind, of the consciousness itself that is misperceiving reality.

A very major issue, which is discussed at great length in Buddhist epistemology, concerns the progression of one continuum of cognition focusing on a particular entity. Let us say that you are focusing on a state of affairs that is not evident but is concealed. You must resort to logic. The one continuum may start out with a false view. You are miscognizing the object in question. You have misconstrued it. From that, in the same continuum of awareness, you may then shift over to nonrealistic doubt. "Nonrealistic" means, to take the electron as an example, you are cognizing this thing and saying it may be an electron, but it is probably not. (We are assuming for the sake of argument that in fact what you are concerned with *is* an electron.) So you then have a nonrealistic doubt. You are wavering, but away from reality rather than toward it. Then, as you investigate further, you may come to a state of doubt that is in equilibrium. This thing may be an electron and it may not; you are not quite sure. You don't lean one way or another; it's really fifty-fifty for you. As investigation continues, the same continuum of one person's awareness may eventually arrive at a realistic doubt: "I'm not really sure, but it seems likely that it is an electron." You investigate yet further and then you may reach a conviction that this is an electron. But still you don't have any confirming or verifying evidence. You do have conviction; you are sure of it; and in fact your conviction is realistic. But you still do not have what is called a valid cognition or a verifying cognition, because you don't have sufficient evidence. With the same continuum of awareness, you investigate further and you find conclusive evidence on the subject in question. You still have the conviction, but now you also have had what we would call a valid or verifying cognition of an inferential nature. You have found evidence that leads conclusively to the presence of an electron. You have a completed inference, which is better than just a conviction, although it may feel the same. Having arrived at this inferential conclusion, you now investigate even further, and finally you arrive at perception. By "perception" we mean here a nonconceptual valid awareness. This whole process takes time. It is a gradual process.

In the context of this kind of process, which proceeds from a wrong view and winds up with a valid perception, we speak of the various sources of deception, discriminating those that are of an adventitious nature from those that are of an essential nature. In probing toward the inferential conclusion, we use different logical tools, such as inferring a consequence, then syllogism, and finally, conclusive reasoning. These are the three major tools in a logical investigation or analysis. So that is a kind of standard modus operandi of starting from a false view and winding up with a valid perception.

Applying Logic to the Question of Existence

These logical tools are applied by the philosophical schools within Mahayana. Within Mahayana there are two main approaches or avenues of philosophical investigation, with their corresponding schools. One of these, the Yogachara school, arrives at the conclusion that there is indeed no objective world out there. The other one, the Prasangika Madhyamika, asserts that there is an objective world, although not in the old Cartesian sense of being totally independent of consciousness.

B. ALAN WALLACE [interpreter]: For the Prasangika Madhyamika there are objective entities but in a very special fashion that is non-Cartesian, non-Newtonian. For the Prasangika, if you investigate an object that seems to be out there, really seeking out its essential nature, asking what is the nature of this phenomenon from its own side exclusively, you don't find something out there as an objective entity. It winds up to be something unfindable under analysis. Then the Prasangika says that although it is not findable under analysis, nevertheless it exists in a conventional fashion by the force of verbal and/or conceptual designation or imputation.

DALAI LAMA: There is a distinction between something *existing* and existing *by its own nature*. If you ask, Does the pen have a nature? you have to say yes. It has characteristics, defining characteristics; these are its nature. But then, it is a different meaning when you ask, Does it exist by its own nature? Saying it exists by its own nature suggests that it exists independent of contributing circumstances or factors.

There may be some relationship here with what Jeremy Hayward was speaking about. When one really investigates very deeply the objects that we posit, be they electrons or what have you, it becomes really questionable whether they have this thoroughly objective existence, independent of consciousness. But then what do you do? Upon very deep investigation, if you find that they don't stand up to that analysis, then what is your conclusion? Do you conclude that there is no objective world? Now, there may be an appropriate area of dialogue here with the Prasangika, since it also engages in an analysis of apparently objective phenomena and finds that under analysis they simply cannot be found. The Prasangika then does not conclude there is therefore no objective world but says there is an objective world—that verbal or conceptual designation is sufficient for an objective phenomenon to exist, but that this conventional nature is the only kind of existence it has as an object. So here is a school of Buddhism, the Prasangika, that says yes, there is an objective world, yes, there is a subjective world, a subjective mind. And in fact it says these are both equally weighty. It is not a view that says it is all purely a world of mind, nor is it a materialistic view. Both mind and matter exist; they both have a conventional, conceptually designated existence.

In contrast to the Prasangika view, which asserts the conventional existence of an external world or objective entities, there is another view among the Mahayana views, the Yogachara, which in its own fashion really investigates, really analyzes: Do these phenomena that appear to be objectively existent in fact have objective existence? The Yogacharins also say that objective existence is not findable under analysis, but they come to a different conclusion beyond that. That is, they come to the conclusion that although these things appear to have objective existence out there, in fact this does not stand up to analysis, and therefore they are purely of the nature of mind. But then there is another problem. As soon as you say that these phenomena that appear to be objective out there are of the nature of mind, then the question is: Is it possible for the mind that cognizes these phenomena to be in error? Is there realistic cognition as opposed to unrealistic cognition? The Yogacharins must say, Yes, there is. But how do they establish that one thing is realistic and another is unrealistic when everything is coming from the nature of mind anyway? This becomes problematic.

Thus far I have been speaking in the context of the Sutrayana, of the different philosophical schools within Sutrayana.* Now let

---

*From the point of view of Tibetan Buddhism, the Hinayana and the lower

us shift into the context of Tantra. In the context of Tantra there are four authentic agents of authority: scriptures, commentarial texts, an authentic teacher, and one's own experience. The original scriptures, the Tantras, themselves are authentic. Because of their authenticity, there may arise authentic commentarial literature based on the Tantras. On the basis of these scriptures and commentaries, teachers arise who are themselves authentic. By encountering an authentic teacher, one can arrive at authentic experience. This is the sequence of events that establishes authenticity. Now, how does this work in terms of your own process of ascertainment? You do have that progression, that established authenticity in the first place. But when it comes to verifying or confirming that authenticity, you do not first verify the authenticity of the scriptures and then of the commentary, and so on. Exactly the opposite sequence comes into play. Relying on an authentic teacher, you have your own experience, which you know for yourself to be authentic, so in a sense it is self-authenticating. On the basis of complete ascertainment of the authenticity of your own experience in your meditative practice, you then infer the authenticity of the teacher upon whose guidance you have been relying. On the basis of that ascertainment, again a very subjective conviction, you then infer the authenticity of the commentarial literature that your teacher has been relying upon. On the basis of that, you infer the authenticity of the scriptural basis of the commentaries, the Tantras themselves. This is where your own certainty comes from. It basically comes down to your own experience.

HAYWARD: Your Holiness, there are two particular points I see in what you have presented that relate to the question of scientific method. One is in your discussion of the Prasangika and Yogachara views. You said that, in the Prasangika view, if we analyze, we don't find inherent existence but say the objective world exists due to conceptual imputation. My question is, Doesn't this

---

part of the Mahayana together comprise the Sutrayana, or "sutra vehicle," because they are based on the basic Buddhist scriptures known as the sutras. The higher part of the Mahayana is variously called the Tantra, Tantrayana, Mantrayana, or Vajrayana. This highest part of the teaching is based on another class of scriptures known as the Tantras.

conceptual imputation itself come from mind? From where does this conceptual imputation come?

DALAI LAMA: When you say that phenomena are conceptually designated, this does not imply that just any old thing is true. For example, if you take this pen in my hand and you insist that this is a human being, simply calling it that or thinking that does not make it a human being. If that were the case, if any old thing you thought were true, then there would be no distinction between valid and invalid cognition. That is the predicament. When we speak of phenomena as being conceptually designated, what criteria are there for establishing something as being existent? If just any old thing you think of is true, then what are the criteria for establishing something as existent?

There are three criteria. One of these is that it must be in accord with conventional experience. This does not simply mean that if everybody believes something, then it is true, because many people may believe something that is not true. This has happened many times. The second criterion is that you cannot assert the existence of something that is controverted by a conventional valid cognition. If something is controverted by a conventional valid cognition, then it cannot be asserted as existent. The third criterion concerns deeper issues such as the existence of *prakriti*, a Sanskrit term designating a primordial substance that is posited, for example, by the Samkhya school* as something that has an ultimate intrinsic existence. Now this is not conventional parlance, so how do we refute it? Ordinary people do not ask, Have you seen a prakriti lately? and so it is neither confirmed nor denied by ordinary experience. So the third criterion is, the existence of something like prakriti cannot be posited if it is controverted by an ultimate analysis or an ultimate investigation. If one investigates prakriti with ultimate reasoning, ultimate analysis, and finds that it does not exist, then it would not fulfill the third criterion. Those are the three criteria that are used in the Prasangika system to establish the existence of something.

So we do not say that phenomena exist by the force of concep-

---

*The Samkhya school is one of the six orthodox philosophical schools of Hinduism.

tual designation just because we are enamored of conceptual designation, or simply like the whole idea. Rather, when we look at a phenomenon, a pen, for example, on one hand we investigate whether it exists from its own side, that is, independently of being cognized. Upon such analysis, we find that no such entity exists from its own side. If you investigate the pen, you investigate its shape, its color, its components, and you take each of these apart; you don't come across something that is the very pen itself. It doesn't satisfy that mode of analysis. But having come to the conclusion that there is no pen-in-itself to be found, then you can't simply say there is no pen. When you pick up the pen and write something, it performs functions that can harm you or benefit you. Any phenomenon that can harm or benefit you cannot simply be written off as nonexistent. But now you are in a quandary. You can't say it is nonexistent, yet at the same time you have investigated it and not found the thing-in-itself. So the question becomes, How does it exist? It exists by the force of conceptual designation. It is not that you like the idea so much, but rather that you have no alternative.

Verification of Meditative Experience

VARELA: If I were now to play a naive Western scientist, I would say, "Well, there is a way in which we can use logic to gain further and further conviction in several stages until we gain the final conviction." Then, as a slightly more sophisticated Western scientist, I would say, "No way, because in the West we have been trying to do that for two hundred years too." We have quite good evidence that calls into question just believing our convictions. Our convictions are just our convictions. There are all sorts of examples showing how even the clearest logic, the most impeccable reasoning, can lead you to something that can change tomorrow. What we call immediate experience, whatever that is that we always exemplify with pens and things, is all good and fine. But Newton was misled by that. Science now says that space is not three-dimensional, right? We know that the earth does not stay put; it is moving, although I don't see it moving. It is not my experience. Why do I believe that?

Now I want also to ask this question in relation to discoveries made in meditation practice. In my very limited understanding of Buddhism, meditation does give you access to a different mode of experience and that enables you to validate assertions made with Buddhism. What is interesting is precisely that the mode of validation doesn't really seem to be all that different from the mode of validation in science. Therefore it is subject to the same problems. When the Buddhists say, "We're absolutely certain that . . .," it raises the same kinds of problems as when the scientists say, "We're absolutely certain that. . . ." It is subject to the same kinds of criticisms of what is ultimately valid and so on.

What Buddhism has said so far in my experience has proven quite accurate, which is why I am interested in it and find it valid. However, the reasons I say it is valid seem to be the same reasons I use in science to say, "This is valid." I have the same kind of logic of observing, validating, listening to what other people say, convincing myself through my own experience, and so forth.

HAYWARD: In the scientific approach we always begin and end with an observation. Scientists would call this observation a direct perception in their understanding of direct perception. And in a way, in the end we validate our inferences through another direct perception. That is also very similar to the way Your Holiness has described the Buddhist approach—that it must begin and end, especially end, with what you call a direct perception, which is also a valid cognition. Now, in the last part of my presentation of the alternate view of science, scientists had begun to doubt that there could possibly be any observation that was not laden with concepts. So the question I would ask the Buddhists is, What is your method of validation of a direct perception and does it also validate that it is totally free from concept?

DALAI LAMA: One point of importance is that in Western science when you speak of direct experience, you seem invariably to mean *sensory* direct experience; whereas in Buddhism the sensory aspect of experience is really quite peripheral. When you go through this whole progression from false view to perception, the whole idea is not to wind up with some sensory perception. That's not the point at all. Rather, the aim is to wind up with a mental perception, or better yet, a contemplative perception, which is the yogic perception. So it is really a different order of perception than simply what you were talking about, namely, ordinary visual perception.

According to the Prasangika presentation, there are three types of direct perception. Yogacharins present four types of direct perception: sensory, mental, yogic, and apperception or self-cognizing. The reason for asserting the presence of this apperception is the fundamental Yogacharin belief in the inherent existence of mental phenomena, which Prasangikas refute.* Because the Prasangikas don't accept the existence of this apperception, they acknowledge only three types of direct perception: sensory, mental, and yogic.

It is quite easy to identify sensory perception. There are many different viewpoints about direct mental perception, even among the Tibetan scholars. According to the Madhyamika Prasangikas, anything that is subjective experience—like the biologists' sensation, awareness of some kind of perception—is regarded as direct mental perception. Then there are other types of consciousness; in Buddhism we have precognition or heightened awareness. All these kinds of experiences are also direct mental perceptions. Yogic direct perception is not easy to describe; suffice it to say that it is a separate category.

HAYWARD: How is yogic direct perception validated?

DALAI LAMA: [laughing] That is quite complicated! Mental perception refers to types of experience like feelings—mental feelings like happiness or anxiety.

There are two types of direct mental perception, yogic perception, that are not there initially, that you achieve as a result of your meditation. With either type, since what you have is a new realization, you need agents or factors that validate it. That agent of validation itself has to be a direct perception, so Buddhists maintain that until you perceive the ultimate nature of phenomena directly, until you reach the path of seeing, in other words,

---

*The Yogacharin idea of apperception, or self-cognizing awareness, is explained in "Perception and Consciousness," pp. 190–212.

you are not able to overcome the influence of your own doubts.* By the time you get to the path of seeing, you have the direct realization of ultimate truth, *shunyata*, emptiness. The nature of that direct realization is a yogic perception or a yogic realization. This provides your criterion, a kind of a standpoint or perspective from which to verify other experiences. This would be a major step. Until the majority of the population has achieved the path of seeing, all this doubt will be there.

HAYWARD: Suppose someone meditates for many years and says he has direct perception of ultimate truth. He feels this to be certain. Is he not deluded? How do I know he is not deluded? How does he know he is not deluded?

DALAI LAMA: Buddhist literature describes certain signs through which you can validate whether you have reached that level. There are two kinds of signs: external and internal. Through external signs, other people can verify your level of realization. The internal signs are more reliable. Here I think there are big differences from science. In Dharma [the Buddhist teaching], first of all, someone who already has this experience knows it. As a follower, you have every right to carry out an investigation, analyzing according to your own experience and reasoning. The difference is that in science, you don't accept any authority at all; you just pursue things based on your own investigation.

In this context we speak of three categories of phenomena: obvious phenomena, hidden phenomena, and extremely hidden phenomena. This last category of phenomena cannot be verified or established even through logical processes, through pure reasoning. To establish these phenomena and to verify them, you have to depend on certain authorities or reliable sources.

It seems that we actually employ these three modes of verification in our day-to-day life experience. We perceive things through direct experience, obvious things. We also understand things through inference by seeing certain signs and anticipating

---

*One of the ways that Buddhism delineates levels of spiritual development is by dividing the journey to enlightenment into five paths: the paths of (1) accumulation, (2) application, (3) seeing, (4) meditation, and (5) no more learning.

what normally follows. Extremely hidden phenomena are also represented in everyday life. For example, I know the earth to be a round bluish globe, although I have never seen it and have not done any conclusive reasoning about it. Nevertheless I know the earth is round by relying on the words of someone who has seen it and proven it with photographs. First you must prove that the person is reliable by various reasonings. There is no reason why he should tell lies and produce false photos. Through such considerations as this, you prove that the person is reliable. After this, you understand that the earth is round although you haven't seen it. This is called inference based upon belief, a different type of inference. All of the actual inference is based on belief in someone, but still that belief has been supported by certain reasoning, like proving that the person is reliable. It is an informed belief and not a blind belief. Some time you might be asked to describe something that is beyond thought, beyond reason. No matter how you attempt to analyze, to see, and to feel this thing, it is impossible. So you have to rely on a person who has already had this kind of experience and has no reason to tell lies. However, it is also important to verify that there are no logical inconsistencies within the statement or series of statements made by that person.

VARELA: You said there are also external signs of yogic perception. Perhaps some of those external signs could be explored?

DALAI LAMA: It would be quite difficult but there is a possibility. When you see a human being who doesn't lose his temper or doesn't have fluctuating moments of emotion in a situation that would ordinarily give rise either to attachment or anger, seeing that these do not arise you might infer some kind of realization in that person. But it would be very difficult to determine objectively whether this person has direct realization of *shunyata*, or emptiness.

Perception and the Brain

FRANCISCO J. VARELA

My job is to present some ideas on what a brain is. In thinking about how to do this, I decided that I would eliminate what I consider inessential details and focus on the most essential insights. To do this, I would like to begin by taking us away from the brain proper and then to come back to this subject armed with some insights.

The Nervous System and the Capacity for Motion

When we talk about the brain, we are always referring to something you might call *behavior*, something that an animal or any sentient being does. First I want to get across here that in the history of life there is something very interesting that happens when sentient beings acquire a capacity to *move*: the nervous system is fundamentally bound up with the capacity for motion. Consider, for example, a very tiny animal called an amoeba. We have some of them in our intestines, and these amoebas can move. They stretch their fingerlike protrusions. The amoeba in figure 2 is about to engulf and eat a smaller cell. Here you have motion, and people feel very comfortable in describing that motion as eating behavior or prey catching, in spite of the fact that this is just one cell and it is doing something very simple.

The point I'm trying to make is that the moment we have movement, we have a natural tendency to describe it as some form of behavior. I want to concentrate now on the question of movement or action. How does this prey catching happen? According to biologists, molecules in the cell surface are able to

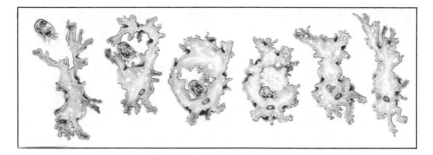

FIGURE 2.   An amoeba displaying eating behavior by chasing and ingesting another single-celled organism.

sense the presence of the prey. This sensing causes changes inside the cell, which then pushes out those fingerlike protrusions.

DALAI LAMA: Now, when the amoeba senses a prey, it sends out these fingerlike things and takes it. Have there been any cases to the contrary, where it senses danger and contracts?

FRANCISCO J. VARELA: Yes, that also happens. In either case we have two fundamental things. One is a *sensory* element or a surface that senses, and the other is a *motor* surface or an effector surface, which in this case is the same thing, because it is also the inside of the cell that pushes out its boundaries. By motor surface here, I mean anything that can cause a motion, such as the inside of a cell pushing out its boundaries. We may call that the motor surface or motor component. By motor we don't mean a mechanical thing, but anything that produces a visible effect. These two elements are very important: the moment we see a behavior (in this case catching a prey), we may assume that there is something that senses and something that causes a motion. These two things are related to each other, in this case because they are in the same cell.

Let me give you another example. Single cells with a moving tail or flagellum are very tiny; you need a microscope to see them. Each of these creatures has this hairlike thing sticking out, and it swims by moving it. Interestingly, when it encounters an edge, the hair bends, and when it does so, the cell is capable of shifting its direction and moving away from the obstacle. The sum of what you see is that this little organism is able to avoid bumping into edges. Again, here you have something that senses, because having its hair bent amounts to sensing something it encountered when the environment modified it. That produces a change inside the cell, and it swims in a different direction.

In these two single-celled cases we have the two fundamental phenomena you find throughout life that are related to the existence of movement. Every time you have behavior and movement, you have a sensory and a motor side, and this is the story of the nervous system, no more and no less.

DALAI LAMA: Take, for example, a plant with its root system. Where there is fertilizer, is it not true that the root system develops in that direction? Is that counted as movement? Is it the same kind of movement or not?

VARELA: Yes, it is the same kind of movement. The plants' strategy of life is to be settled always in the same place. They move their roots a little but that's about all. Therefore, they do not have a nervous system. Animals, on the other hand, have chosen a style of life that includes moving around all the time. Here there is a nervous system, because there is always this behavior of seeking food, and encountering each other, and so on. But you are absolutely right that the root movement of the plant is of the same nature as in the previous example, which is movement by membrane extension.

Neurons Allow Communication between Distant Cells

DALAI LAMA: The plant roots sense that there is something beneficial and so grow toward it.

B. ALAN WALLACE [interpreter]: I think perhaps an implicit question here would be, When the root system reaches out in the direction of the fertilizer, would you actually say that the root system senses the presence of its food?

VARELA: This is a question that is highly debated among biologists. I think that I could represent general opinion in the field by saying that maybe there are some sensory phenomena happening, some kind of a discriminating phenomena at the cellular level. This is why, in the case of the amoeba, biologists wouldn't feel uncomfortable describing that as a primitive form of behavior. They would say the same for the plant root. But when you move to animals, this very primitive behavior can become more interesting. This is where the nervous system really begins to show up.

To explain, let me use the example of a very simple animal. We are moving from a single cell to an animal that has several thousands of cells. A hydra is an animal that can be seen with the naked eye and can be found in ponds in the West. This is a so-called free-living hydra, because it floats free in the water and exhibits various kinds of behavior. For example, when little organisms flow by, it catches them with its tentacles and ingests them. Or if you touch one, it contracts and moves away. Let's take a look at how this animal is composed.

The arms of the hydra can be recognized in this cross section of its body [see figure 3]. You can see also that there is an opening like a mouth, and inside it there is a hole. What I want to call to your attention is that this animal is basically composed of two layers of cells. There is an external row of cells and an internal row of cells. That's the animal.

On the surface of the external and internal layers you find different *kinds* of cells which have various things that are capable of sensing, perceiving, and producing motion. For example, some cells have little needles. When you touch these, they sense they have been moved; they are sensory cells. In contrast, in the inside layer there are muscles, which can contract and relax. The animal can move its tentacles by acting on these contractile fibers or muscles.

So we have a sensory component and a motor component. It is interesting that biologists have found that these animals have, for the first time in the developmental history of life, something that grows *in between* these muscles and sensory cells. Growing in between (indicated in black in the figure) are very long cells that are called nerve cells, or *neurons*. *Neuron* is a term that will be very important for the entire discussion of the brain. It is the class of cells that compose any brain. This animal has a very simple brain, which is just a whole net of these neurons that connect muscles to sensory cells. They extend all over the animal. Neurons con-

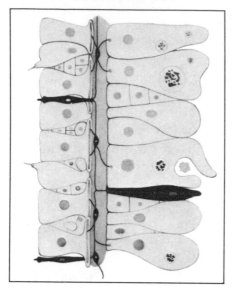

FIGURE 3. Sketch of cell diversity in tissues of the hydra, with neurons highlighted.

nect things that are distant from one another and put them in relationship. A neuron is a special cell: it can extend like an amoeba and put into contact things that are distant from each other in the animal.

DALAI LAMA: The amoeba does not have a brain?

VARELA: The amoeba has no brain because it has no neurons; it has sensory-motor correlations, behavior. But then in a hydra, since there are many, many cells, how does a sensory cell on one end know what another one is sensing on the other? If the muscles of this arm contract, how are the cells in the bottom going to know about that? This is precisely where the neurons come in.

The hydra contains the basic story of the nervous system: sensory cells, motor cells, and a network of cells that grow in between. The latter network of neurons allows things that were impossible before. There is sensing by the tentacles to which the base responds with movement so that the hydra is actually able to follow a prey, for example. When you observe this behavior you wonder: How is it possible? The explanation biologists would like to give is that it is possible because things that sense and move in different parts of the body are in contact.

I want to call your attention to the fact that even up to 1910 it was in dispute among scientists how the brain was constituted. The study of neuroscience proper, as we understand it today, only goes back to about 1900. We have been at it for only about seventy years—not a very long time.

What I want to do now in the second part of the presentation is move on to some essential points that have been accepted about neurons and brains. First, what are neurons? How do they work?

What Are Neurons?

Neurons like to get in touch with lots of other neurons, many neurons, normally several thousands for each. In figure 4 you can see that a neuron has many branches—through each one of these branches it makes connections, points of contact with other neurons. If I were a neuron, I would be touching some ten thousand other neurons. In turn I would be touched by some ten thousand other neurons. A neuron is really a very highly interactive, sociable cell. This is very important because it is through this interconnectedness that the nervous system correlates all the sensory and motor surfaces.

DALAI LAMA: If we go back to the plant root and the amoeba, we have something that seems to be a sensory process or a sensory phenomenon as well as some type of motor phenomenon at the same time. What then is the crucial role of neurons, when the plant and the amoeba apparently can do the same thing without neurons? What is the essential role there? What is the discriminating factor? In both cases the sensory element is there, so what is the difference between a sensory message that is due to a neuron and one that comes through without a neuron?

VARELA: The difference is that without neurons there is no way in which a sensor on one end of the plant can know what a sensor detects on the other end of the plant. This is the whole point: neurons can accomplish that because they are so long. For example, if somebody lives up here and somebody lives down there in Kashmir Cottage, where we are staying, we have no communication unless there is a phone. But the moment we have a phone, a new phenomenon occurs. We can now do things to-

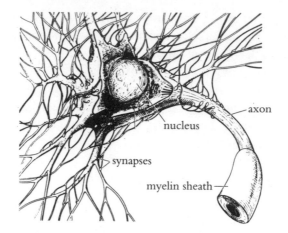

FIGURE 4. The neuron and its multiple synapse sites, the functional units of the nervous system.

gether. If you have muscles or effectors and you have sensors, and they don't know how to come together or act together, then there is very little that can happen. That's why plants don't move. They just sit there.

DALAI LAMA: Then for the root system of a plant, the movement can occur right there, but it will not be related to other aspects of the plant.

VARELA: Or only in a very diffuse way. If a plant had a nervous system, or a brain, there would be a neuron that would go from the tip of the root all the way up to the top of the tree and would sense how much sunlight is coming in. Thus, I can sense something itching on my head, and that can be correlated with what my foot does. This sensory-motor correlation allows us to generate the whole spectrum of behavior. This is really the central point; this is the basic logic of the nervous system.

In figure 4, the neuron has been sectioned to show its inside, and you see the fingerlike contacts that come from other neurons. These points of contact are called synapses. They are the way neurons can affect each other. One of the big advances in neurobiology during the last forty years has been to understand quite a bit how one neuron can affect other neurons. Before we go into this, let me point out that, in fact, neurons have many different shapes, so that neurons that come into contact with one another can be very different. But always they have the same logic: a receiving end, a long intermediary part and a terminal end.

Our little hydra had more sensors and motor cells than neurons. In humans, however, for every sensory neuron there are one hundred thousand interneurons, that is, neurons that lie along the path inside the body on the way between a sensory end and a motor end. This is an enormous increase, but the logic is still the same. As the brains of animals have evolved in history, they have grown a mass of interneurons. When you see a human brain, you say, my goodness, where do I start in order to understand this mess? The way to understand it is to try and trace this basic logic. We have eyes, for instance, which are a sensory surface. The eyes connect inside to different places in the brain. Whatever happens with the message the retina takes in results in some form of motion. I see something and I turn my head. The behavior of turning my head because I notice something is a sensory-motor correlation. A sensation, something that comes into my sensory surface, produces a motion by moving my muscles. Although human beings wouldn't like to admit it, we have a close bond with our little sister hydra. We seem to be built on the same logic.

Communication between Neurons

When one neuron touches another, they communicate in many different ways. The best known one is through an *electric impulse* that travels as though along a cable, and once it gets to the surface of a cell where the synaptic button* is sitting, the current becomes a chemical signal for the next neuron. But a neuron receives many synapses and senses all of them simultaneously. On the basis of all the signals it receives, the cell makes a decision: it either transmits an impulse or it doesn't. It's almost like a consensual decision.

---

*The synaptic button, or knob, is the place where the electric impulse constituting an electrochemical communication from another neuron can be received.

DALAI LAMA: So when we speak of a single cell or possibly a group of cells making a decision, the final decision is made how, by majority or . . . ?

VARELA: Your question is one of the most difficult questions in the whole of neuroscience. The decision is made down at the soma, or main body, of the neuron, so we can tell that the decision is not made simply on the basis of yes, yes, no, no—a mechanical compilation of the various impulses from the other neurons—because it depends on how far the impulse travels, how strong its influence is, how great the efficacy of its transport. It is based on a number of things. The final decision is far from being a simple one; a neuroscientist wouldn't be able to predict what would happen in a particular case. We can know the answer in some simple cases, but most of the time the neurons have to do very complex spatial and temporal comparisons of all of the synapses. It is an extremely delicate process.

When you talk to neuroscientists, it is important to know that much of what they do in their laboratories is to measure these electrical impulses. They use small probes to measure the current down one neuron or maybe a small group of them. For example, figure 5 shows a typical experiment: The monkey is trained to press a lever on a given signal. The scientists have put tiny little probes inside of its brain, and they can record electrical impulses from just a few neurons—just a few. In this case, a neuron in the motor cortex produces muscle contraction when stimulated. Each one of the little lines in figure 5 indicates that one of those impulses has gone down the nerve. When the monkey has relaxed its hand and when it has contracted, it is indicated in the upper and lower parts of the figure, respectively. You see that, interestingly enough, when it relaxes its hand, the neuron tends to become very active, but when it flexes it, the neuron stops firing. There is a relationship between the behavior of the monkey and the electrical behavior of the neuron. Of course, you can record the activity of many other related neurons. These are the kinds of things neuroscientists do to try to find patterns of activity that correlate with specific behaviors, in this case arm-and-hand motion.

motor cortex

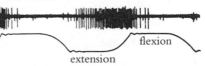

flexion

extension

FIGURE 5. The monkey's arm movement can be followed by the discharge rate (spikes) of a motor neuron recorded simultaneously from its brain (motor cortex).

Another example is from the other end of things—from sensation or perception. The way the word *perception* is used in neuroscience, it does not imply any form of consciousness or any form of internal observer. It only means that some discrimination has happened. Normally, we speak of perception in humans only. But, from the point of view of neuroscience, animals like the frog can perceive their visual world. One of the classical experiments for understanding sensory phenomena such as vision as opposed to motor phenomena (as with the monkey's hand) was done many years ago with the retina of a frog. Imagine that an electrode is now sitting inside a frog's brain, and we present the frog with different kinds of visual stimuli. A stimulus according to neuroscientists is anything that you can use to make a neuron react. If I am recording from a neuron and I present something, say a bar that moves, and the neuron doesn't do anything, we would say that the stimulus is not appropriate or adequate. It will not make the neuron fire. What these researchers found with the frog's retina was that, for example, a small dot, a large dot, an edge that moves are adequate stimuli. They found that particular neurons would not respond to everything but only to one simple item: small dark things that move. The neuroscientists concluded: this neuron is a "fly detector."

DALAI LAMA: Does this particular neuron only activate at a particular time? In response to that particular stimulus and not to others?

VARELA: Yes, and that made these scientists very happy. They could say: This is a frog, which likes to catch flies with its tongue, so this neuron must be a fly detector, because flies are small dark things that move.

DALAI LAMA: It is almost like, before the information is perceived through the brain, the eye itself makes some decision.

Circuits of Neurons

VARELA: That is correct, not the entire brain but a small segment, a subcircuit. A subcircuit of neurons can perform the function of detecting a fly. This is the kind of idea that entered into neuroscience very strongly: to explain a behavior like detecting a fly, you need to find the specific circuits within the brain that can do it. (By circuits I mean a network of some neurons that connect with each other in some specific way.) The great surprise in this experiment was that even within the retina you have these local small circuits that can do interesting things like detect flies. That of course is the case throughout the brain. Also, in the previous experiment with the monkey, we can say that the neuron is doing something similar. It "knows" how to activate that muscle to contract and to relax. It is making a decision as to which of those is appropriate behavior, much the way a neuron in the frog's retina is making a decision about when to fire and when not to fire when presented with stimuli.

These are the kinds of phenomena that neuroscientists claim to explain or at least potentially to be able to explain. They include, for instance, movement, perception, learning, memory, decisions. So in the actual understanding of neuroscience today, some simple behaviors have some sort of explanation in terms of neuron circuits. Other problems are much more vague and people dispute for hours about them. How does planning behavior happen? There are enormous debates and nobody agrees. On some other things people agree a lot more. For example, in regard to vision there is a fair degree of agreement on how color, movement, or edges are distinguished.

Just to finish up, let me comment on a way of presenting neuroscience that is very typical of what you find in textbooks and what you see in neuroscience meetings. The idea is to replace the brain, the actual brain, with boxes [see figure 10, page 99]. These boxes represent specific circuits, and now the brain has become little boxes that do specific things. One box could be the idea of a motor program, that is, a pattern of neuron activity that accomplishes a motor behavior like walking. Another would be a motor program that is carried out by a particular group of neurons. Program is a word that we'll come back to when we talk about artificial intelligence. It is actually borrowed from the world of computers. To make a computer work, you write a program. This set of instructions, when taken together, performs a function. A computer program will allow you to calculate numbers or compile indexes of data. Neuroscientists took this idea of program from computers and proposed that the brain does the same thing. Neural circuits behave as if they have a program. A neuron recognizes a fly because it is part of a program. The neurons know what to do with respect to each other. So a motor program is a set of neural activities that accomplishes a function, for example, walking. Another motor program would be climbing stairs or lying down. Each one of those motor behaviors requires a different program. The task of a neuroscientist is to ask how that program is actually embodied in neuron activity, so that it is not just some abstract thing.

DALAI LAMA: If you were to cut out and set aside the whole system of the brain, is there any primitive interaction at all between the sensory input and the motor output, even if it's not very refined?

VARELA: Very primitive. I think that it is rather fair to say that if you were to remove the entire brain, then motor cells, muscles, and sensors would stay isolated from each other.

DALAI LAMA: So that being the case, why do you have the arrows going in both directions in the brain-boxes you just mentioned.

VARELA: Oh, this is important. On the whole, without the brain the sensory and motor circuits would remain insolated from each other. But there are some interactions between them at a very low level. For example, consider the famous knee-jerk reflex. If I tap my knee, as you know, it jerks. A muscle stretches, and the jerk happens. The muscle inside has sensory receptors, so that when the muscle moves, it affects the receptors right away. In this way, what happens on the motor side has a direct effect on the sensory side. And vice versa. Whatever happens on the sensory side can have a very low-level direct effect on the motor path. What is interesting is that when we move in the world we don't use that reflex alone; we use it only very marginally. Most of the time, neuroscientists would say, there is a so-called top-down pattern, in which a higher-level motor program flows down and takes into account these sensory-motor correlations. As an analogy, think of a government. A government has public offices where the public goes. For example, someone who wants a passport goes to a government office and asks for it. This office is like the sensory end in that there is an employee there who receives the application. There is some bureaucratic machinery, analogous to the muscles, that functions and presents the passport. That is a low-level sensory-motor interaction. On top of that, there is a very complex governmental structure that gives guidelines. For example, this higher level dictates who can have a passport and who cannot.

Allow me to summarize the main points that I have tried to make here. The first point is that the entire history of the brain has to do with one simple fundamental thing, which is sensory-motor correlation linked to motion. No motion, no nervous system. No motion, no behavior. No sensory-motor correlation, no brain. No brain, no pain [laughter]. So, brain arises from sensory-motor correlation. It doesn't matter what kind of brain—hydra brain, cat brain, fly brain, human brain—basically they are the same thing. Secondly, the neuron is the functional unit out of which brains are made because sensory-motor correlation happens by neurons connecting to each other in this interneuron network that is the brain. The third point is that these interneural circuits are the basis of behavior, because they are capable of carrying out programs such as detecting flies and moving muscles.

The Two Main Assumptions of Neuroscience

I want to end with what I think are the two main assumptions or fundamental beliefs, I could say, of neuroscience. The first one is that the brain circuits and programs, the two of them together, are the seat or the source of all mental phenomena or cognitive phenomena. Memory, planning, desires, emotions, moving, or perceiving—all are ultimately based on circuits and programs. The more complex the behavior, the bigger the circuit is, even to the point of including the entire brain. The second belief is that these programs or circuits that perform these behaviors function well because they are good representatives of the world in which the animal lives. For example, the fact that the frog has in its retina one little circuit that identifies flies is very appropriate because frogs eat flies. So you don't expect to find a horse detector. But it does the frog a lot of good to eat a fly, so this circuit and program are providing a suitable representation of the world. They are adapted to it; they are picking up the right information from the world. It is very adaptive to have emotions, for instance, because if I don't have emotions, I won't be motivated to undertake actions like avoiding dangers or reproducing.

These two notions—information picked up from the world being represented inside the brain, and the brain's programs being adaptive—are the entire foundation of the current dominant view of neuroscience. This is really quite important, because these are dominant assumptions.

Neuroscientists might argue a lot with each other about which circuits and programs do what, but they do not argue about the fact that those circuits and programs are operating on the basis of information picked up from the world out there, and that it is in the world out there that the brain produces a behavior that is adaptive and adequate.

Sentient Beings

A Conversation

What Is Adaptation?

DALAI LAMA: Is it true that for the process of adaptation to occur there needs to be emotion or desire?

FRANCISCO J. VARELA: I'm glad you raised that point, because in the minds of Western biologists and Western scientists, the word *adaptation* is very ambiguous. On the one hand, it means something that I as an individual do while I'm alive. It is adaptive for me to eat when I'm hungry. But by and large, what we mean by adaptation in this context relates to the evolutionary process, which goes beyond the individual. Neuroscientists say that this brain we have has evolved over many many thousands of years and has become the way it is because of evolutionary logic. Neuroscientists are very keen on saying that the reason the circuits and programs appear and work is because they have been selected by evolution—that is why they are adaptive. Animals that didn't have the right program for getting food when they were hungry died, and those that did have it survived and therefore, here they are. So it is extremely important to see that for Western scientists the word *adaptation* is inextricably bound up with evolutionary history and with the idea that evolution is a progressive adaptation to information coming in from the world.

DALAI LAMA: Let's leave aside for the time being the word *adaptation* in the context of evolution and focus simply on one sentient being. Let's imagine that this sentient being is instinctively a plant eater, a vegetarian, but while its natural instinct is to eat vegetables, by a process of conditioning or training, it is taught or learns to eat meat. In this case, in which it is shifting its programming, is there a corresponding shift in the neurons, such that in the plant-eating phase only certain neurons responded to certain kinds of stimulus, to vegetable stimuli, but now there is a shift to neurons stimulated by meat?

VARELA: Yes, Your Holiness, you put your finger on a very key point that I didn't touch in my talk, which is the following: The only kinds of programs I described are those that are already those which biologists would call innate programs. An example is the program for the frog to catch the fly. There is no way to change programs such as these. The frog was born with that. It was the frog's karma,* it will not change. But almost every animal, even flies and worms, has a capacity to change behaviors, that is, they have a capacity we call "plasticity" that allows a certain range of behaviors to be modified.

Of course mammals or vertebrates, mammals especially, are capable of much learning. We mammals can learn, for example, to recognize objects that were formerly completely unrecognizable. In such cases, neuroscientists would not say learning is due to new circuits. It's not that new neurons appear and start connecting with others. What happens, according to the current theory, is that the synaptic contacts of existing neurons are modified. Learning occurs, and it modifies the brain in the fine tuning of its circuits. Synaptic change is comprised of slight modifications in the way the neurons interact. New circuits do not grow. In fact, in the brain, very, very few neurons are added after a certain point of development, essentially after birth. All that can happen from childhood on is that neurons can change their synaptic conversation. It is not the case that where before there were two neurons, now there are twenty.

But it is very clear from observation of animal behavior that animals have an innate predisposition to learn. Not to learn this

---

*In Buddhism, karma is the universal law of cause and effect. A cause produces its effect when the right circumstances are present. Thus the idea arises that an individual's situation is the result of previous causes and thus can be called his *karma*. This view does not constitute a determinism, since many choices are always open. Dr. Varela's remark about the frog's karma is a jocular one.

or that specifically, but to *learn*. And this is extremely important in mammals, especially in primates. Human beings can be described, from this point of view, as specialists in nonspecialized learning. We are generalists as opposed to specialists.

So the great question is, What are the differences in the brains of animals that learn and those that learn very little? For example, pigeons and chickens are very similar if you look at them, but the chicken doesn't learn very much at all, while the pigeon does. What is different in these two brains, one of which is capable of much more learning than the other? Neuroscience has very little to answer on that if anything at all. But it's a very interesting question for sure.

DALAI LAMA: It's not simply a matter of brain size then?

VARELA: Certainly not. From certain measurements we know that there are animals with large brains and very little capacity to learn, compared to pigeons, for example, which have a very small brain but a great capacity to learn. It's clear that the pigeon and the chicken have an enormous difference in learning capacity yet their brains are the same size. In fact, from the anatomist's point of view, it is almost an identical brain. I will not learn anything by looking at the shape and size of the brain. The idea that learning capacity has to do with brain size is far from being established and simply is not the whole story.

What Is a Sentient Being?

DALAI LAMA: Does a one-celled creature like an amoeba have the whole range of cognitive events, such as desire, sexual desire, feeling, and so on?

VARELA: This is a disputed point. Some amoebas can behave as male and female. Sometimes they get together and exchange, not as one male and one female, but nevertheless as sexual partners. They exchange genetic material.

Now, let's compare amoebas with bacteria. Bacteria are simpler cells. They also have sex. And they have the capacity to seek food and get away from things that are harmful, much like that little amoeba that I showed [see figure 2, p. 51]. Some people would say, with good reason, that in bacteria you'll find all of those behaviors, including cognitive behavior. Sensory-motor correlations happen inside the cell, all at the one-cell level. But of course a bacterium has no neurons. On this basis it can be said that the nervous system does not invent cognition. It only expands the range of sensory-motor capacity. This is very important.

DALAI LAMA: Therefore, would you consider a one-celled creature like an amoeba a sentient being?

VARELA: Yes. From *this* point of view, there is no question. There is no way for me to draw a line and distinguish my cognition from the cognition of frogs, hydras, amoebas, or bacteria.

DALAI LAMA: In your personal view, is a bacterium a sentient being? The question is important in the Buddhist context, because when you take the life of a sentient being, that constitutes a wrong deed. If that being has a desire for happiness and does not want suffering, then taking the life of that being constitutes a lot of suffering. So is it wrong to kill an amoeba? The Buddhist would say that if the amoeba feels pleasure and pain, wishes for happiness and to be free of suffering, then it is wrong to kill it, and otherwise it is not wrong.

VARELA: The behavior of the bacterium or amoeba is one of avoiding some things and seeking others, much like the behavior of clearly sentient beings like cats and humans. Hence I have no basis for saying that the behavior is not of the same kind, although I would say there is no *consciousness* of pain or pleasure. The amoeba intrinsically manifests a differentiation between what it likes and what it doesn't like. In that sense, there is sentience. Why do I say that a cat feels pleasure and pain and seeks satisfaction and is a sentient being? There is no way that I can know what the experience of a cat is.

DALAI LAMA: Yes, that's right.

VARELA: Exactly the same argument applies to the amoeba or bacterium. I cannot know what the experience of a bacterium is, but if I observe its behavior, it is of the same kind. This is why, as a scientist, I can say that the behavior of the bacterium is cognitive behavior in that it makes discriminations through this form of sensory-motor correlations I have described. The mechanism is the same as, say, in cats. I know psychologists shudder when I say this, but I'm talking as a neuroscientist. People who have studied bacterial behavior as a way to understand the simplest forms of behavior and they have no hesitation in referring to it by terms such as behavior, perception, and instinct. I must say, I find their approach convincing. Now, it is certainly true that from there to what we normally call cognition, which is some form of awareness, there's a large leap. But the question remains open as to whether this is not a continuum.

LUIGI LUISI: If you go back to a piece of calcium carbonate, which reacts with an acid and not with a base, would you call this a form of behavior?

VARELA: There is a transition between what I would call pre-life and life within the establishment of a cellular boundary. According to this approach, a cell has one new quality: a sense of self-determination or autonomy. That is, it can to some extent establish its own environment, or its own boundaries, which is not the case for calcium carbonate.

JEREMY W. HAYWARD: Well then, what would you say for the plant and its root?

VARELA: I would say that it is sentient.

B. ALAN WALLACE [interpreter]: The word *life* as it is used here in biology really doesn't translate easily into Tibetan. There are two words: *sok* [*scrog*] and *tse* [*tshe*]. You cannot say in Buddhism that a tree has *sok*, which is translated as "life," because *sok* implies awareness, cognition, desire, happiness, and so forth. The other word, *tse*, also means "life" but focuses more on duration, lifetime, and life span. *Tse* can be properly used to describe a tree. Then, does how long the tree lives mean how long before it ceases to be green? This is a very tricky point because the whole orientation of the two systems is different. It's a matter of semantics, and a very interesting one.

ROBERT B. LIVINGSTON: Actually this is a very crucial point for Western science and Buddhism, and we need to take the time necessary to understand each other.

GESHE PALDEN DRAKPA: Consider moss or fungus that

grows in the water. The Vinaya* says that moss has life, and that its life depends on water. Here we use *sok*, which means life or vital principle. If you take moss out of water, that life is cut. This does not mean that you are taking the life of a sentient being, however. Therefore, to do so is not evil, but the terminology used here is very interesting. The moss does have life, *sok*, in dependence on the water, its habitat. You take it out of that, and its life is cut. So the terminology used here suggests that maybe we do have a word in Buddhism that is very close to the biologists' term for life, applying both to the animal realm and the plant realm.

VARELA: Yes, and also in the Buddhist tradition, the definition of a sentient being is usually associated precisely with movement as an expression of volition.

I think an important fact here is that these behaviors of bacteria and amoeba cannot be seen with the naked eye. You need instruments. Once you have seen them though, they are very much "sentient-like." I think the reason we say only animals are sentient beings is basically that we have the bias of experience limited by the capacity of the naked eye. If one extends one's observation into the micro world, which comprises by far the largest chunk of life according to the biologists' definition of life as anything composed of cells, then that sentiency certainly seems to extend to single-celled life—amoebas and bacteria. Plants seem to remain outside the realm of sentience because they don't move; but they don't move only because their style of life is precisely not to move. The fact that they don't have a nervous system and all the rest of it doesn't make them less living in the sense of having the same quality expressed in cellular composition. So, in that sense, I think the biologists' definition is the most precise. Biologists have very specific criteria for deciding whether something is alive or not and whether something has a nervous system or not. The behavior of receptivity toward things that are good and avoidance

---

*The Vinaya is the first part of the Tripitaka, the part dealing with matters of monastic discipline. The Vinaya discusses this question in relation to the issue of what constitutes taking life.

of things that are bad extends all the way down. I don't see a way to escape that observation.

DALAI LAMA: It seems that you maintain that bacteria also have the faculty of feeling, as in feeling pain and pleasure? If that is the case, then even plants also have this kind of faculty?

VARELA: I observe the behavior of bacteria as movement toward certain things and avoidance of others; I cannot say that this is not the same kind of behavior as that of a cat. Just as I cannot project myself inside the cat and say the cat feels, I cannot project myself inside a bacterium and say the bacterium does not feel. However, I'm not forced to impute the kinds of feelings to the bacterium that I have when I avoid or when I see. What is proper to my experience is proper only to my experience. I don't have to impute feelings of the same kind to plants. I do have to impute to the bacterium the quality of sentience of seeking happiness. Who knows what happiness is for a bacterium, but it seems to manifest a discrimination that is akin to ours. That's why scientists would feel comfortable in describing the behavior of bacteria as cognitive. Still, they wouldn't dream of using the words *conscious* or *mental*. There is an escalation from cognition or perceiving, which is sort of neutral, to mentality, consciousness, which are far more loaded words.

LIVINGSTON: Would you also acknowledge that there are differences in quantity and quality of sentience and that one might have some kind of demarcations based on that?

VARELA: Yes. But the quality is the same and the defining line is the beginning of life, cells on up. Where I would stop with mental phenomena or conscious phenomena, I honestly don't have the slightest idea. Do I impute it to dolphins or to monkeys? My observations and reading suggest that monkeys have awareness. So I don't know, but I wouldn't like to impute the same type of consciousness to bacteria.

DALAI LAMA: The whole science of neurobiology is undertaken on the basis of some physical matter like the brain. But is the whole question of consciousness as Buddhists speak of it— which is formless and of the nature of clarity, and so forth—just ruled out?

VARELA: It is ruled out, yes. It is left out.

Living Matter

DALAI LAMA: On the level of the tiniest particles, atoms and subatomic particles, is there really any fundamental distinction between totally inert or inanimate things like rocks as opposed to that which goes into flesh?

VARELA: None whatsoever. What makes a cell alive is not the molecules it's made of but the *pattern* in which these molecules come together. In the same way, what makes a whole bunch of neurons perform a particular behavior is not the neurons themselves but the pattern in which they come together. This is a fundamental point for scientists—that it is not the components but rather the pattern of connections that gives a new property. So life is an *emergent* property of a pattern of molecules.* Behavior is an emergent property of a pattern of neurons. Language is an emergent property of society. So if I look at the cell and I see its molecules, they're just like the molecules of things that don't make up cells. For scientists there is no question about that. There is no such thing as a "living" molecule.

DALAI LAMA: Since all these cells, living organisms, when they are reduced to their smallest components, come down to the subatomic particle, there is some kind of continuity or continuum of matter. Would you say there was also some kind of continuum of this nature at the beginning of the universe, before the Big Bang?

VARELA: Your Holiness, here you touch on something that is very unusual in a Western biological context, because biologists deal with living systems. Elementary particles don't enter into biology. They are totally irrelevant as far as a biologist is concerned. A biologist's interest runs from molecules up. Elementary particles might as well not exist. So in fact the question you're asking is a question that you need to ask a physicist with a specialization in cosmology. Quite honestly, I don't know. I don't know anything about cosmology beyond the layman's

---

*An emergent property is one that comes about as a result of the interaction of local processes or agents, which does not exist before those local processes come together. The new property is said to emerge from their interaction.

reading. It's important to see that you switched us all of a sudden from biology to physics and that the question you asked doesn't arise from a Western biological standpoint. What biologists do know nevertheless is that all of our molecules get replaced every few days. If I paint an atom of a molecule in part of my body in order to identify it, and I keep track of its location, I find that within a very short time it either will have gone to another part of the universe or will have been transformed into something else, or become part of another bigger molecule. That includes the nervous system. There is a fantastic turnover.

So you don't need to go to the Big Bang to see that your sub-stantial basis is shifting. What stays and continues to constitute what we know as a body is not a molecule or a set of molecules but a pattern of molecules that keep being replaced constantly. A cell has a rate of change that is so fast that within hours or minutes the whole thing has changed, yet the overall pattern of the cells remains.

I would like to ask Your Holiness what prompted your question?

DALAI LAMA: The question arises because, according to Bud-dhist theories, there are two types of cause: substantial cause and cooperative cause. When you try to trace the beginning of the substantial cause, you can't posit any beginning at all. You can have fluctuations, but there isn't any absolute beginning to the continuum. If you posit a beginning, then all sorts of inconsis-tencies arise in relation to the question of why it came about in the first place. There is no creator; there is a cycle of cause and effect. Here we are not talking about karma, but cause and effect in the sense that this paper comes from wood, the wood from a tree, and so on. The wood is the previous seed of the paper; and the tree of the wood. In that sense, we can try to trace the begin-ning of the substantial cause. Suppose at the beginning there is empty space, nothingness, then all of a sudden something hap-pened. If that's the case, then there are a lot of unanswered ques-tions. I am interested to know what the answers are from a sci-entific point of view. In the Kalachakra Tantra,* there is mention

---

*The Kalachakra (Skt., lit. "Wheel of Time") Tantra, which dates from the tenth century, is the last and most complex Buddhist tantra. It is said to have been written down by a king of the mythical kingdom of Shambhala.

of what can be translated as "space particles" that are believed to be the source out of which the world evolves and what it dissolves back into during a cycle of destruction.

VARELA: That is interesting and fascinating and a puzzle for Western scientists today, but in some sense I find it somewhat irrelevant to the understanding of life. Life needs to be explained without primary reference to its substantial basis, which is fleeting. When it comes to the relevant direct analysis of human beings and sentient beings, you don't have to go back to the beginning. It is much more immediate—we can relate directly to what is there. One should certainly learn what physicists say about the Big Bang, but for life and mind, it's really only marginally relevant.

The Causes of Momentary Change

DALAI LAMA: I believe that the presentation of subtle impermanence, that all things are changing moment by moment, is more or less the same for both science and Buddhism. In physics, when we get down to the subatomic level, the small particles are all changing. We're speaking of very rapid rise and decay. That is like the subtle impermanence of Buddhism. So the Buddhist explanation and the scientific finding are basically exactly the same.

Now, within Buddhist schools, the position of the Vaibhashikas is different from that of other schools. The Vaibhashikas and others say that phenomena are dependent upon causes and conditions: they are produced, they abide, then they decay and disintegrate. And they go through this process sequentially. But then the Vaibhashikas say that the cause for the production and the cause for the disintegration are totally different. Disintegration requires another force, a secondary cause, some outside force. On the other hand, the Sautrantikas and all the other schools maintain that the very cause that produced a phenomenon is the cause for its disintegration. The moment it is produced, because it is changing from moment to moment, it has

Cosmology, time reckoning, and astronomy play a major role in the text, where they function as a basis for meditative practice.

the nature of being disintegrative from the beginning. By the very fact that something comes into existence, the cause is already there for its destruction. My question is from the point of view of subatomic physics: Which of those two Buddhist presentations is more valid: that the causes of a particle's destruction are already present in its arising, or that after it arises, a subsequent cause comes in, causing it to change or decay?

HAYWARD: Well, from the point of view of physics there are some particles that, so far as we know, are not destroyed from within. For example, the proton has never been shown to decay spontaneously.

DALAI LAMA: We are not speaking of destruction. "Destroy" means just to end. But momentary change is not ending; there is still continuity. I'm not speaking of duration but referring to momentary fluctuation or momentary change. So a proton may last for seventeen billion years, but on a momentary basis, is it not subject to change?

HAYWARD: Yes, but only through its interactions with other particles.

DALAI LAMA: Bearing that in mind then, and also the wave-particle aspect which makes it not static,* which of the two, the Vaibhashika or the Sautrantika view, is correct?

HAYWARD: It depends on whether you take the view that the interactions of the proton with other particles is part of the actual internal definition of the proton, or just its external relations. There are different schools on this.

VARELA: I would like to say something, Your Holiness, if I may be so bold. The answer that physics gives is completely irrelevant. Suppose that physicists say that it is the Sautrantikas who are right. That would be true for a very abstract thing called an elementary particle that nobody ever sees. Their existence depends on a long chain of inference that has nothing to do with the way your question applies to my body or to this table. At the level of mind and life, it is completely irrelevant what elementary par-

---

*According to quantum mechanics, electrons exhibit both particlelike and wavelike characteristics. Thus no one fixed nature can be ascribed to them.

ticles do or don't do. So if your question is about whether a body, when it is born, contains within itself the seed of decay, it is something that you have to ask at the level of the body's organization. You won't find the answer in the reductionist idea. There is nothing at the elementary-particle level that will give you an answer for what happens at the microscopic level of life. This is why I say that, while what physicists say applies to the realm of matter, it carries no implication for life or mind.

DALAI LAMA: There are two kinds of decay. It is very important to discriminate between subtle levels and gross levels of impermanence. When you talk of decay on the microscopic level, it is rather gross; it's obvious that it depends upon secondary causes.

VARELA: And who says that elementary particles are more basic? [laughter] This is precisely the Western myth that matter is more basic. But what is the basis of that? Why do we take elementary particles to be basic? I say they're not basic! They're a description of a human construction we call matter, but what is basic is my direct experience.

DALAI LAMA: Then let us talk on the microscopic level. Take the example of the human body. This body may last, say, fifty, sixty, or seventy years but it is changing momentarily. I am not referring to the gross changes that we can see but rather the momentary changes. What is the cause of this momentary change?

VARELA: Well, there are two causes, I would say. One is what I describe as the components of my body and the other is my perceiving those components. The two things together are the causes of momentary change.

DALAI LAMA: Now the question is: Is the fact that a body is produced the cause of its changing or are there other subsequent causes for its change? As a biologist focusing on the subtle impermanence of the components of the body, is subtle impermanence due to the Vaibhashika sense that arising, maintaining, decay, and destruction each requires a subsequent cause to keep on happening, happening, happening? Or is it by the very force of the production that the cause for destruction has already happened?

VARELA: As a biologist, I would say the second one.

DALAI LAMA: Interesting. That is a sort of confirmation. And would the physicist say a proton is a part-less particle, something indivisible? Are protons subject to aggregation, that is, do they enter into compounds?

VARELA: I would submit with all due respect that this is not the question you really want to ask! [laughter] You seem to fall into the reductionist impulse of wanting to seek the answers at the supposedly "fundamental" level.

DALAI LAMA: My question was quite broad, not just confined to something that is living alone. It concerns all things that depend upon causes and conditions for their arising and includes the entire range of phenomena that is subject to destruction or disintegration. This includes both organisms and things that are not organisms. For example, consider the very exalted state of mind of Buddha's omniscience, which realizes emptiness directly. Even that is subject to momentary change. There is no real end to it, and it is always there; yet it is momentarily changing. The scientists also realize that things are momentarily changing, not on a superficial, grosser level but on a deeper level. So particles are involved.

VARELA: Could you replace *deeper* with *smaller*?

DALAI LAMA: Sure! It is just my poor English vocabulary!

VARELA: No, no. It's part of the clearing up of the ground. In the Western context, Your Holiness, it is really important, because if you say deeper, it means that it's more fundamental. If you say smaller, it's just a different observation.

HAYWARD: Could we come back to this notion of momentary changing? I would like to ask His Holiness: How, in the Prasangika view, does a cognition momentarily change, or how does one cognition change into another cognition?

DALAI LAMA: Actually, the momentary changing of the consciousness is not something you need only in the Prasangika view; it is central to all the Buddhist schools. Each of the four noble truths itself has four qualities, and the first quality of suffering (which is the first truth) is impermanence.

The important point here is that when we explain impermanence, it is almost like presenting a view of emptiness in that we have to free ourselves from the two extremes of nihilism and eternalism.* Momentary change doesn't mean that a phenomenon disappears even in terms of continuity. We should be able to speak of a phenomenon momentarily changing while retaining its nature, its quality. In retaining the continuity of its nature, it is there—this frees us from nihilism. The fact that it is momentarily changing also frees us from the extreme of eternalism, or belief in absolute permanence. Since consciousness also has this nature of momentary change, an earlier moment of consciousness that is a wrong cognition or misconception could later turn into a valid cognition. For example, a person might be very wicked or naughty at the beginning and could later change into a better person. It is the same person—there is the continuity— but one whose nature involves momentary change.

The Kalachakra, Modern Cosmology, and Neurology

DALAI LAMA: It might be quite interesting, and also important, to point out in what kind of fields Buddhism has parallels with cosmology, neurology, psychology, and so forth.

Let us consider the question of space and time first. The Kalachakra Tantra† speaks of the space particle as the connecting link between the destruction of one universe and the evolution of the next. In between universes, it retains all of matter, so it is just like the fundamental source of all matter. That phase of cosmology between universes is said to be the "time of space." But in that empty space, very much as in modern cosmology [before the Big Bang], there is a potentiality for matter. Here it is called the space particle. How is this space particle, which is like the fundamental source, activated to give rise to the creation of the next universe? It is activated by the force of the karma‡ of sentient beings, which

---

*Eternalism in Buddhism is the view that phenomena have a real, eternal essence, and nihilism is the view that they have no reality at all. The view of emptiness is considered to defeat these two conceptual extremes, indeed to transcend any conceptual outlook whatsoever.

†See note on page 72.

‡See note on page 65.

acts as a cooperative cause for it. The next universe to arise has a substantial cause, which is these space particles. That is what is transformed into the new universe, but what allows it to happen? It also requires a cooperative cause, which consists of the karma of sentient beings.

This karma is based on the actions of the sentient beings who will take rebirth in this particular future universe. So, sentient beings have accumulated karma that will ripen into the universe now being created. As the substance of space particles is stimulated by the cooperative cause of the karma of sentient beings who are going to be born in the new universe, a motion of pure energy arises from the space particles. From that motion of pure energy arises heat, or fire. From that arises the water element (you speak of hydrogen), and then from that arise the solid elements of the universe.

After the formation of the universe, we have gross types of matter, and Buddhist texts speak of these types of matter as being composed of eight types of particles, an eightfold configuration of particles. Although this may be quite gross compared to the modern scientific theory of particles, still it is quite similar. I feel this is related to modern physics, and these issues within modern physics are something Buddhists should be aware of.

Leaving aside the question of how life originated in this universe, in terms of this body that we're now endowed with, we come to the topic of the *thigle* (drops) and subtler minds. So, looking at our present circumstances in which we have a body and mind, we're concerned with the relationship of the body and mind and the nature of consciousness or cognition. And in this connection we introduce the topics of the channels, energies, and drops.* I feel that channels, energies or winds, and drops may have a special relationship with neuroscience. On the one hand,

---

*According to Buddhist tantra, human beings possess a subtle body, which is composed primarily of *prana* (Skt., lit. "energy" or "wind"), *nadi* (Skt., lit. "channels"), and *bindu* (Skt., lit. "drops"; Tib., *thigle*). The points of confluence of these three elements are the chakras, of which the most common system enumerates six. This subtle body is associated with a subtler level of mind.

we're not assuming that there are these centers, these chakras, as they are described in books, because if you look for them in mundane research, you don't find them. Nevertheless we should mention the location of these centers: at the crown of the head, between the eyes or just above the point between the eyes, the throat, the heart, the navel, and the genital area. And if you actually direct your mind, your awareness, to these points, you find there really is a special kind of response, suggesting that there's something there, that this is not simply fiction. I feel that since there certainly is some reality here that has been discovered empirically through meditation, this could be an area for very interesting dialogue with neuroscience.

Now, in regard to the drops, or bindu, first there is the drop related to, or associated with, awakening from sleep. That one is related to the chakra just above the eyes, or the third eye. Then there is the drop associated with the event of dreaming, at the throat. The drop associated with deep sleep is located at the heart, and the drop at the navel is associated with bliss, ecstasy. I feel it is quite possible that there is a relationship of these drops with something to be found in neuroscience. There certainly should be some relationship between this presentation of consciousness and psychology, that's pretty obvious.

Dream Research

VARELA: Does His Holiness have some suggestion about how we in Western science, at least in neuroscience, could go about asking some of those questions you mentioned? You mentioned maybe there could be some experiments done?

DALAI LAMA: One important point is to experiment on the activity of the brain during the dream state. Some people, due to their previous karma or previous training, have extraordinary experiences in this life; their dream body actually separates from them. In the previous generation in Tibet, this kind of thing happened among Tibetans having this ability. I have not recently paid a whole lot of attention to the subject, but it has happened. So it's very important to engage in research on that.

VARELA: Well, I am aware of experiments recently done precisely on this, on people who have lucid dreams while they have electrodes on their head. The person goes to sleep in a laboratory, has a dream, wakes up in the dream and says to himself "I'm dreaming." He becomes an observer in the dream but remembers that he agreed with the experimenter that should this happen, that is, should he become an observer in the dream, he would then give a signal that somebody outside could see. The signal agreed on before the experiment is to move the eyes from side to side. This signifies that the observer in the dream is aware of himself dreaming. The person outside with the electrodes can record the movement. Then we know the person is an observer in his dream, and we have the electrical recordings for that moment. When we look at these recordings, what is interesting is the fact that, compared with the usual measurements for brain functions, there is no difference between the person in that lucid dream and in an ordinary dream.* From the external signs, there is no difference whatsoever. It doesn't seem that that lucidity, becoming an observer, shows up in the brain activity, at least with that method. So the machines we use today need to be refined for those kinds of experiment to be properly done.

These experiments represent the first time some kind of signal has been sent from the dream world out into this world by an agreed convention that can be measured and recorded. So this suggests that at least at that gross level—and they are gross measurements, it's just what we call an electroencephalogram—it doesn't show.

ELEANOR ROSCH: But in other kinds of measurements on the body, not on the brain, differences have been measured. Experimenters have instructed dreaming persons to have sexual intercourse in their dreams and have then measured the physiological responses. Although subjects report that the dream intercourse is like waking intercourse, and males may ejaculate,

---

*In both cases the brain is in the so-called REM (rapid eye movement), or paradoxical, sleep state. The signal sent by the lucid dreamer is the direction and frequency of his eye movements. See, for example, Stephen LaBerge, *Lucid Dreaming* (New York: Ballantine, 1986).

the physiological responses are quite different from those of the waking experience.

DALAI LAMA: Research on dreams where ejaculation takes place could be important. In terms of the arising of the clear light,* there is only one occasion when this happens fully, with full authenticity if you like, and that is the moment of death. However, there are four other occasions when a very gross form of the clear light arises: yawning, sneezing, the very moment of falling asleep, or fainting, and the moment of orgasm.

HAYWARD: And as a result of meditation?

DALAI LAMA: Yes, certainly, it also occurs as a result of meditation, but I was simply speaking of ordinary life, day-to-day life. In the course of ordinary living, the appearance of the very gross clear light is very, very brief in duration, whereas when it arises as a result of meditation, it is far more stable. When it's not a deliberate experience but rather a natural process, it is very momentary.

VARELA: But then would Your Holiness expect that in these moments like lucid dreaming or yawning or clear light one should see some kind of difference in the way that the brain works or the body works?

DALAI LAMA: Among these four, fainting is very strong, but the one that you experience at the time of orgasm is the strongest. That is one of the reasons why the practice of bliss comes into the highest yoga tantra. There is a lot of misunderstanding of the sexual and other imagery associated with the Anuttara yoga tantra.† The actual reason for this sexual imagery is precisely because among these four ordinary occasions in which the clear light appears, orgasm is the strongest. Thus this imagery is used in meditation to extend the experience of the arising of clear light and also to clarify it or make it more vivid. This is the point. During the event of orgasm, because the experience of clear light

---

*The subject of the clear light (*ösel*) is of interest, because the experience of it is tantamount to spiritual illumination, according to Tibetan Buddhism.

†In Tibetan Buddhism, the various levels of tantric meditative practice can be called the yoga tantra. In some systems, the highest of these is called the Anuttara yoga tantra. *Anuttara* is a Sanskrit term meaning "none beyond."

is longer in duration, already you have a greater opportunity to utilize it. There is also something to be researched here in the moment of fainting and its relationship to the clear light. One training method speaks of the technique of experiencing clear light by pressing some arteries.

ROSCH: The people doing sleep research at Stanford—without knowing any of this, just trying things—have arrived at the technique of training people to have lucid dreams by pressing the artery on the right side, that is, holding the cheek and pressing that when they go to sleep.

DALAI LAMA: This makes a lot of sense, because the drop associated with sleep is right near the heart at the throat center, so there is a very good connection. Moreover, it is true that if during the dreaming state, you direct your awareness, your concentration, to the throat, this will make your dreams clearer. Whereas by contrast, if you direct your awareness to the heart, then it will make your sleep deeper. So here is a subjective sleeping pill [laughter].

VARELA: I'm still not clear whether His Holiness would expect brain indications in any of these states.

DALAI LAMA: I think this subject is rather delicate, so if you are able to perform a successful experiment, you can derive a lot of benefit from it; but at the same time, since all these techniques are related to a very practical side of the tantra, it is important to have initiations. Without initiations these matters should not be pursued.*

ROSCH: Well, what is the point of doing the experiments? Suppose that you find some brain difference or other physical difference, is the point to prove to the world that believes in such things as little wiggles on graphs that there is something to this meditative dream practice, or is the point to find out something more that you don't already know about the relationship between mind and body?

---

*The Buddhist tantra requires training and initiation from an authentic guru before embarking on any of the practices connected with *prana, nadi,* and *bindu.*

DALAI LAMA: I think both. Even as a Buddhist there is great interest.

ROSCH: What do you want to find out that you don't already know?

DALAI LAMA: There are practitioners among Tibetan Buddhists who have gained some experience, but if this could be confirmed through scientific experiments, it would be reinforcing.

Cognitive Psychology

ELEANOR ROSCH

My field, cognitive psychology, is at the heart of the modern field of study that attempts to deal scientifically with the mind. Therefore, since Buddhism is about the mind, cognitive psychology may offer a special opportunity for dialogue with Buddhism. This is true not only because of what cognitive psychology might have to offer, but also because of its weaknesses. In biology, for example, in the presentation that we heard yesterday, where there is an agreed-upon body of data and explanation, experiments build on each other. That is the way science, as opposed to a field like art, is supposed to work. Nothing like that, however, exists in the Western study of mind. In cognitive psychology, there are instead many different ways of thinking, many approaches, theories, questions, experiments, and much disagreement. Cognitive psychology needs help as a scientific discipline. Because of this openness in the field, there may be the potential for actual two-way communication with Buddhism.

This is especially true because as His Holiness said the first day, in both Buddhism and science there is a common ideal of using observation, experience (empiricism, as it is commonly called by psychologists) as the basis. If you want to know how many teeth a horse has, the method for finding out is to look and see, to count the teeth. And if what you see when you look contradicts your previous theories or habits of thought, then you should go with the observation against what you previously thought. But because this ideal has manifested very differently in the Buddhist and Western scientific approaches, they may have interesting things to contribute to each other.

I should also say that just as biology doesn't consider itself reducible to physics, likewise, psychology doesn't consider itself just a branch of biology. Cognitive psychologists often frame this as an issue of method; they say that it is the job of the psychologist to describe accurately and powerfully what the mind does, how it functions, irrespective of physical mechanisms. Then, the idea goes, when biologists know enough, they can explain how the organism can do the things the psychologists have described.

Historical Roots of Cognitive Psychology

It will be helpful to start with an account of how the modern scientific study of mind evolved to its present state. The field is only a little over a hundred years old, because it was about a hundred years ago that people got the idea that you could treat the mind with methods of science. Right at the beginning there were two quite different schools of thought or methods relating to how to do psychology that were competing with each other. One was called introspectionism and the other behaviorism. Within about thirty years, the introspectionists had lost completely and disappeared, and behaviorism had taken over.

Introspectionism

It's very interesting to look at how that happened from the point of view of dialogue with Buddhism. It may be that when anyone first thinks to inquire about what mind is and how it works, there are a limited number of possibilities of what to look at and how to proceed. Since one has a mind, one obvious possibility is to look at and analyze one's own mind. And what one normally means by *analyze* is to break something into its elements, to try to find the smallest elements, the primitive elements that make up the thing and to analyze how they are related to each other. And that is what both the early Abhidharma schools of Buddhism and introspectionism in psychology tried to do.

A major difference between them, however, was the method. From the Buddhist point of view, the introspectionists did not know how to look at their minds. They had no method of meditation. What they did was decide in advance, on the basis of their theories, what the mental elements of mind should be and then trained themselves and others to analyze their experience into those elements. This took place primarily in the sociocultural context of nineteenth-century German academia. Each powerful professor had his own theory and would train his students and the subjects in his laboratory to introspect according to that theory. For example, in one laboratory it was believed that visual perception was ultimately composed of tiny patches of color, and so everyone was trained to describe their perceptions as tiny patches of color. In another laboratory it was considered that perception was a combination of sets of pre-intentions, and that is how subjects in that laboratory described their perceptions. In one laboratory it was believed that all thoughts were composed of mental images; another laboratory maintained the doctrine of imageless thought. The chaos that resulted was the very opposite of what is desired in science, namely, no laboratory could replicate what any other laboratory did. This was a much more fundamental problem than that of experiments not building on each other. The problem was that there was no way to establish agreement on any experiment at all. Each laboratory would work with its own trained subjects and would publish its results and would argue with the results of other laboratories. But there was no method for resolving any of the disputes. That was the undoing of the introspectionist method in Western psychology. It would seem that in the Buddhist sense, the introspectionists were not looking at mind at all. They were just thinking about their thoughts; they were tangled in their preconceptions about the mind.

To this day introspection is used as the model of how not to do scientific psychology. Textbooks in psychology normally begin with a chapter on scientific method, by which they usually mean logical positivism—that the terms of the theory must be reducible to observations, and so on, as described by Dr. Hayward. Often added to this description is the dictum that introspection is not the way to know anything about mind. So, modern psychology is in the situation that the one thing you cannot use as evidence for any claim you make about mind is what you know or observe about your own mind—such a self-observation is considered not objective. It is not considered to lead to agreement, and, according to the definition of a fact in logical positivism, it is not even a fact.

DALAI LAMA: I don't see the logic in the refutation of introspectionism. On the one hand, it's quite true that if you have laboratory directors impressing their views upon other people such that they're almost compelled to confirm the directors' theories, it is evident that that is a very wobbly approach. And if one speaks of (simply looking at the terminology) awareness being aware of awareness, then superficially one might ask, "Well, how can this be?" But in practice, although one cognition cannot observe its very self, nevertheless it is possible, and very practical, to observe cognition, because you'll have different mental events, different cognitions, and one cognition will be observing another. This seems very reasonable and a very authentic approach to investigating the mind. Are the grounds you mentioned the only grounds for refuting introspectionism, so that now you can't bring in your own inward awareness as evidence? Or are there other reasons for saying this is not factual, not scientific?

ELEANOR ROSCH: Yes, I think there are other reasons, at least four of them. First, there was the whole spirit of the times, the whole zeitgeist, of which Dr. Hayward spoke at length, regarding what science was and what it meant to be objective. Physics was the prototype of nineteenth-century science, the model of how to observe external, objectively observable phenomena and how to build theories that would predict and control those phenomena. Psychology was in awe of, and wanted to imitate, physics. The second reason is that the introspectionists did not actually have any way to observe their own minds. Because there was nothing like shamatha or vipashyana* or any other

---

Shamatha and *vipashyana* are two types of meditative training found throughout the Buddhist tradition. *Shamatha* (Skt., lit. "dwelling on peace") could be characterized as training in mindfulness, or bare attention. The discipline of bare attention to the breath or other present objects leads to tranquility and composure. *Vipashyana* (Skt., lit. "insight") is the discipline

such training of the mind, I assume that when the introspectionists tried to introspect, their minds were very wild like everyone
else's. Thus they couldn't have one cognition observing or ascertaining another, because by the time they might notice, they
were already ten cognitions down the line. So introspectionism,
in this sense, was never actually given a try. Third, the introspectionists served as an example to the whole scientific community,
of people who had tried something called introspectionism that
had not worked. It had turned out to be the very antithesis of the
ideal of science represented by physics. And fourth, there was
already a contemporaneous school that could provide an alternative to introspectionism. This other contemporaneous
school—behaviorism—took over and became dominant. Behaviorism had exactly the positivist ideology of logical empiricism
that Dr. Hayward spoke about. And it really was an ideology.
They were passionate about it. The behaviorists' idea was that
psychology could be done like physics, and the way to do that
was to eliminate mind entirely from psychology.

Behaviorism

In inquiring about mind, one obvious alternative to trying to
look inward directly at mind is to look outward at behavior. In
everyday life, for example, when you want to know what people
think, it is natural to look at what they do—like the old folk saying, "Actions speak louder than words." Behaviorism took this
approach to its extreme. The motto of behaviorism was "stimulus-response." Figure 6 is a diagram of the behaviorist worldview. The first arrow, the stimulus, is something that the experimenter does to the organism (human or other animal); it is in the
external world, observable by everyone. The second arrow is
what the organism does after the stimulus, also something observable by everyone. The square between the two arrows is the
mind, considered as a black box, a box that is not publicly ob-

---

of developing clarity in relation to a broader field of awareness. The two are
sometimes referred to in English as mindfulness and awareness practice,
respectively.

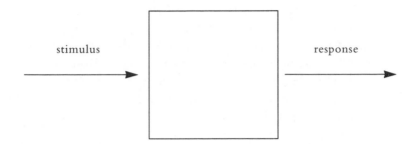

FIGURE 6

servable and hence not subject to scientific investigation, hence unnecessary to talk about. For the strict behaviorists, the biological organism was also in the black box. So psychologists could be completely objective; they need only chart the relationships between stimuli and responses.

The meaning of the behaviorists' claims lies very much in the kinds of experiments that they were led to perform. There are three major areas of experimentation (according to their current names): classical conditioning, operant conditioning, and certain aspects of memory. All have to do with lawful relationships over time, relationships between what happens to an organism at one time and how it behaves at a later time. So a third obvious direction that inquiry may take when someone first thinks to inquire about mind relates to the question of what effect the past has on the future. The relationship between past and future certainly does not seem random to people—what I do now seems to have results in the future. In Buddhism this is discussed in terms of karma; experimental psychology speaks of learning and memory.

The first kind of learning experiment, on classical conditioning, was devised by the great Russian psychologist Pavlov. Animals have certain natural responses. For example, if you put meat powder in the mouth of a dog, saliva forms. This can be measured very precisely; you can drip carefully measured amounts of meat powder on the dog's tongue and measure the number of drops of saliva. There are other stimuli that do not naturally cause a dog to salivate, for example, a musical tone. What Pavlov found was that by repeatedly pairing the neutral stimulus, the musical tone, with the meat powder, the dog would begin to produce saliva at the sound of the tone alone, without the meat powder. The dog had been conditioned to respond to the tone. It had formed a habit. This is what the formation of habitual tendencies looks like in Western experimental psychology. There are many demonstrations of such learning that have stood the test of investigation to this day. And there is a kind of truth to them. Creatures, including humans, do learn in this way. Pavlov himself was not a behaviorist; he wanted to account for his findings physiologically. However, this was the kind of work that behaviorists took over as proof that you do not need to hypothesize either a body or a mind; you can just chart the relationship between carefully controlled laboratory experiences and behavior that follows them.

All very well, you might say, but each experience that the organism encounters is new; it is not identical to the experience through which it first learned. For example, if the dog learned to connect one tone with meat powder and then it hears a different tone—it has been trained on bong and then hears a lower-toned bong—what is going to happen then? The explanation, first demonstrated by Pavlov, is through a concept called stimulus generalization. This involves a very interesting issue—the problem of similarity. I think that all philosophical and psychological systems in the world that get down to the nitty-gritty of how creatures perceive and learn, at some point run into the problem of similarity; that is, we see things in the world as related to each other and as similar to each other in varying degrees, and how can that be? In conditioning studies, the idea was that since anything an organism encounters in the world is similar to something else, then the response that the organism emits will reflect the similarity of what it encounters to what it has previously learned. In the case of the tone this works very beautifully. The closer the tone is to the one that the animal was trained on originally, the more drops of saliva it will produce [see figure 7].

So far so good, you may say, but the whole experimental setup seems to imply a passive organism. The dog just stands there in

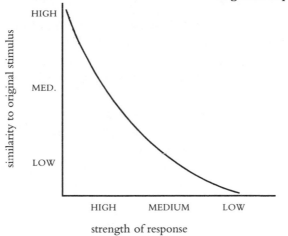

FIGURE 7

a harness and has meat powder or tones, or whatever, applied to it by the experimenter. In the natural state, motivated creatures roam around actively initiating interaction with their environment. This active type of situation is used in the second type of conditioning, operant conditioning, which was worked on most extensively by the American psychologist B. F. Skinner. Suppose you want to teach a rat a new response, such as to press a bar. You put a rat that has been food deprived for a certain number of hours, let's say twelve hours, into a cage that has a bar in it. Notice that you can't say the rat is hungry; hunger is a mentalistic concept that you cannot observe. You can only observe the amount of time that it has been deprived of food. The responses that a rat will emit in such a situation include a large number of bodily activities, such as running around the cage, rearing onto its hind legs, sniffing, and so on. Rats do not normally press bars to obtain food, but the food-deprived rat will eventually hit the bar in the course of its activities, and a pellet of food will appear. Food is its reward, but behaviorists call it a "reinforcer," to get rid of the mentalistic word "reward." It eats the food and then continues running around the cage. But in less time than before it will hit the bar again and get another pellet of food. Eventually it will learn to stay at the bar and press it continuously. You can discover all kinds of lawful relationships using this design. For example, you can chart the rate of bar pressing as a function of the number of hours of food deprivation [see figure 8]; the longer the rat has been deprived, the higher the rate of pressing the bar. Skinner felt that all behavior could be described as simply lawful relationships like this one between the input and the output.

The behaviorist approach did not deal only with learning. Suppose a creature has already learned something; what happens then? There is the issue of memory—or to use a less mentalistic term, retention—and its opposite, forgetting. You might think that studying memory would tempt one to put something into the black box, since if you are talking about the organism retaining something, it is tempting to think of its retaining and storing it in some place. But one need not fall victim to this temptation. Suppose I'm trying to learn Tibetan vocabulary words and I sit down and memorize, and at the end of the day I know a list of one hundred words. The next day we test me to see how many words I still know, and we discover I've forgotten eighty of them. The day after, I've forgotten still more, and in thirty days, maybe I remember only two. So forgetting curves can be as lawful as learning curves [see figure 9]. Here we have the number of items retained as a function of time since learning. Such forgetting curves can be replicated with many people.

So in all, behaviorists were very encouraged that, in these ways, they could have a complete objective psychology without recourse to the mind.

DALAI LAMA: I have encountered this whole approach before, speaking with scientists in America about how they're basically trying to understand the human mind. They ignore the human mind and deal with dogs or other animals. From the beginning I found that very peculiar.

ROSCH: Humans are very complex. You may have heard the story about the man on his knees under a streetlight groping around on the ground. A passer-by asks him what he is doing. He says, "I have lost my key."

The passer-by asks, "Where did you lose it?"

"Over there in the bushes."

"Then why are you looking here?"

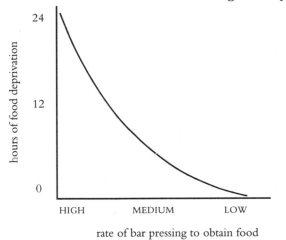

FIGURE 8

"Because there is more light here!" [laughter]

Just as Buddhism would claim that what it says about mind is true for all sentient beings, not just humans, so psychology wants to discover universal laws. For example, I have heard many Buddhist teachers say, "All sentient beings seek to gain happiness and avoid suffering." A behaviorist might say, "That is a very reasonable first hypothesis; now all you have to do is define your terms operationally, that is, in terms of objective experimental procedures." Pretty soon we will be talking about learning to press a bar to obtain food or to avoid electric shock. Another parallel with Buddhism is the need to simplify situations. Meditation itself, at least formless meditation, can be considered a very stripped-down, very simplified situation. Such training is considered necessary if one is to begin to see and work with mind. We cannot just start out being aware of what mind is doing in everyday complex situations. So the problem with behaviorism is, maybe, that it had the wrong simplified situations. Perhaps it excluded the wrong things.

Critiques of Behaviorism

Behaviorism is gone now, at least in its overt form. It ran into both internal and external problems. These issues are very rele-

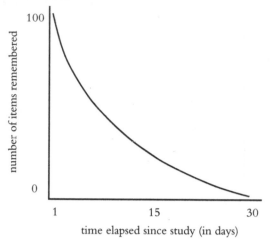

FIGURE 9

vant to some of the reasons for the demise of behaviorism. Internally, behaviorism turned out to be self-contradictory, or at least circular in its definitions. In the basic behaviorist model, you must be able to define and measure the stimulus independently of the response. That is, in some sense you must be able to define and measure the external world independently of the perceiving behaving organism. But in many of the experimental paradigms central to behaviorism, it is doubtful that one can do this. For example, in stimulus generalization, how do you know what things are similar for an organism *except* by measuring its stimulus generalization gradients? In operant conditioning, how do you know what a positive or negative reinforcer (reward or punishment) is? Psychologists initially tried to define the reinforcer as something that satisfied biological needs, but the problem is that there are many reinforcers that satisfy no biological need. Rats with plenty of food will still explore mazes; monkeys will solve problems just to be allowed to solve more problems; a child put in a room with toys will play with them with no obvious biological reason. You have to take into account an organism's definition of the world in defining your stimulus or reinforcer. This may seem like just a technical problem internal to behaviorism, but actually it is much broader. From the Buddhist perspective, one might say that the behaviorists had ignored, to their peril, the two-way interdependence between the organism and its world. So the need to consider mind seems to come back in.

External to its own system, behaviorism ran into even more problems. Animals, including humans, observed in their natural habitats do not do things the way learning theory in behaviorism said that they should. Take as an example humans learning their native language as tiny children. Language is very complicated. The behaviorist model was that it is learned through stimulus-response bonds, the child's mother providing positive and negative reinforcement whenever the child emits a word or a grammatical combination of words. When it finally occurred to a psychologist to look and see—to go around and actually record the interaction of mothers and their little children speaking in their naturalistic settings—it turned out that mothers never do that, never! They do not explicitly teach language. From the time the child utters its first word, the mother treats it as meaningful speech and talks back and forth with the child as though communicating with another human being. Mothers only correct factually false, not linguistically immature, statements.

Perhaps the most important reason for the end of the dominance of behaviorism was that it was displaced by another way of doing psychology. I think that these ideologies, these paradigms or ways of proceeding in science never go away just because of devastating criticisms. People have to find another way of doing things that seems more satisfactory. In psychology, people got the idea that you could take certain mental phenomena, things that had been in the black box, and develop clever methods for investigating them experimentally. That way you could make them real as scientific objects. Let me show you how that was done for one example: mental images.

A mental image is surely a prime example of a mentalistic concept that is not publicly observable. Neither I nor anyone else can look into your head at your mental image and say what it is or isn't. So we can't have observer agreement. For behaviorists, mental images are clearly in the black box. Now let's see how a scientist goes about turning a mental image, say, the image of an apple, into something real, a truly existing thing.

Let us say we seat a person in front of a screen and ask him to press a button every time he sees a faint flash of light on the screen. The flashes are so faint that he almost cannot see them. We measure how accurate he is at detecting the flashes of light. Now we ask the person to form a mental image, say to image an apple as vividly as he can and to hold the image while he is doing the same task of detecting flashes of light. We find that he is less accurate at detecting the light when he is imaging than when he is not imaging. Now let's get even more ingenious and compare images in the different sensory modalities. Suppose that while the subject is detecting flashes of light you instruct him to have an image of an auditory sound. You tell him to image a train whistle or a dog barking. What is found is that an auditory image interferes less in detecting a visual signal than the visual image did.

DALAI LAMA: My question is, What if we reverse the experiment? Right now we are concentrating on flashes of light, but what happens if we have to concentrate on something like a sound? Then, which interferes more, an image of a sound or an image of an apple?

ROSCH: Ah! Your Holiness, you have the mind of a scientist! That is exactly what was done; that's the second half, in fact the whole point, of the experiment. Subjects were asked now to detect a faint click in the ear instead of a faint flash of light. How much does a visual versus an auditory image interfere with detecting the click? You probably guessed what happened. In this case, the auditory image interferes more than the visual image. Now we have an interference effect that is modality specific—a mental image in the same sensory modality as a stimulus interferes more with perception than an image that is in a different modality. So you can begin to see the kind of case that needs to be made for mental images if they are to count as legitimate objects of scientific study; they affect learning, interfere with perception, and are even modality-specific in that interference.

DALAI LAMA: This is very close to the Prasangikas' view that no matter whether it is valid or invalid, the image that appears to a consciousness is there. For example, you can have an image, or appearance to the mind, of the horn of a rabbit. Although there is no such thing as a horn of a rabbit, there can definitely be the image of a horn of a rabbit, and the cognition that has focused on that appearance is in fact a valid cognition. So that appearance exists whether or not it represents or corresponds to any real phenomenon. The cognition is valid with respect to its image.

ROSCH: Yes, interesting; but I think there is also a difference. The experimental psychologist is still not allowing people's knowledge of their own mental phenomena, such as their images, to be admitted as evidence. The psychologist is not interested in people's relationship to their images or in the appearance of those images to consciousness except insofar as that can be measured by the kind of objectively verifiable external evidence that I have been describing. So, here the image as a mental thing is not valid unless it gives rise to some measurable lawful behavior such as in these experiments. Simply, people having images or knowing that they have images doesn't count.

DALAI LAMA: I think that many differences will arise depending on how concentrated you are on the image that you are holding, for example, that of the apple. It may not be the same with all the subjects. Stability of the mind is a crucial factor. There may be some who have such strong stability of mind that they will not perceive anything from the visual side, the visual stimulus. Other people may see most of it. There would be great variability. But this is, of course, assuming that you're dealing with people who have done some meditation. If everyone has done no meditation, then you would get more similarity.

ROSCH: This is why there is the need in psychology for statistical analysis, mathematical ways that have been developed to take into account variation among subjects.

Cognitive and Information-Processing Psychology

Behaviorism completely dominated psychology from 1920 until fairly recently. In the late 1950s and 1960s, some of the flaws in behaviorism began to become apparent, and also researchers gradually began doing work, like the work I described with mental imagery, showing that mentalistic concepts could be treated in a rigorous nonmentalistic way. During the same time period, there were contributions to the field from a variety of sources: information theory, linguistics, and computer science. In 1967 a psychologist named Neisser published a book entitled *Cognitive Psychology,* which gathered together much of the new work that was being done. It served to identify a new field in the making and to give it a name. Now also the name *information-processing psychology* is often used. (I should remark parenthetically that all this time, of course, there was also psychiatry and psychoanalysis, but those were different disciplines, separate from experimental scientific psychology.) It is only in the last fifteen years or so that the cognitive psychology/information-processing approach has taken over from behaviorism. And it has really taken over. Journals and buildings have been renamed. New scientific societies have been formed. It has been a kind of sociological revolution.

JEREMY W. HAYWARD: I think it is really important to understand how powerful behaviorism was. It may sound like a joke, but it wasn't. A whole generation of children were brought up and trained with an educational philosophy based on behaviorism. The people who are now adults were trained on behaviorist ideas.

ROSCH: Yes, and all the modern psychologists with gray hair, we were brought up on that. And it's important to understand that for what comes next, because the modern form, from the Buddhist perspective, may not be all that different from behaviorism. I would like now to turn to this current form.

Figure 10 is a typical representation that might be found in any textbook of what mind looks like in present information-processing psychology. You can see that it is still a box with input and output, but now inside it you have smaller boxes, inside of which there may be yet smaller boxes. The ideal is to be able to take the mind as a whole that shows intelligence and explain it in terms of parts, or mechanisms that are progressively less intelligent, more mechanical than the whole. It is an information-processing view, because it represents the flow of something called information from the external world into the senses and, mediated by attention, into the very short term, short-term, and long-term mem-

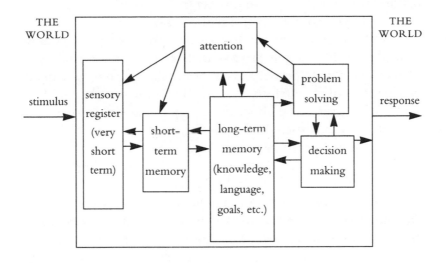

FIGURE 10   The Information-Processing Model

ories, thence to be used in solving problems and making decisions, finally resulting in behavior again in the external world.
Information also flows back through the system; for example,
knowledge and expectations from long-term memory influence
attention and the information that will enter the senses.

The form of the chart is that of a computer model. Now you
might say, "Oh, those Western psychologists. When they finally
stop using animals to try to understand the human mind, then
they use computers!" But consider that in order to conceive and
talk about the mind, all psychologists have to use analogies,
metaphors, and pictures taken from the natural and human-
made phenomena available to the people of the time. What else
can they do? The Greeks used metaphors from their elaborate
waterworks. Presently our model of mind is the computer. Buddhism also does this; think of all the agricultural images. "If you
plant rice seeds, you get rice not barley." One could imagine a
future world in which people grew up never having seen a plant
but very familiar with computers. You might have to say, "If you
put in a mail-sorting program, it sorts mail; it won't fly an air-
plane!" At the same time, the choice of analogy may influence the

psychology. Perhaps we can discuss this more in relation to the presentation on computers and artificial intelligence.

Now let's look at how information comes into this system from the world and gets processed. Because I understand Your Holiness wanted to hear about memory, I'm going to talk about this in terms of the memory system. But before starting on that, we should be very clear about the metaphysics of this system. It is completely dualistic. Out here is the world [see figure 10]. It is an independently existing, stable, nonmomentary world. Inside the diagram is the person, the mind, the information-processing device that also exists independently, is stable and nonmomentary. There's absolutely no doubt in any psychologist's mind that the world and the person exist independently of each other. No matter how interactively you describe their relationship, it is a relationship of two independent entities, each of which lasts through time in its own right. The mind considered as an information-processing device has the task of getting information about the outside world into itself, storing that information, and using it. The point of the memory system is to represent (re-present) the world and store it inside the mind.

Very Short Term Memory

Memory is usually treated as though there were three systems (although there is dispute about this): very short term memory, short-term memory, and long-term memory. We should start with the first. Very short term memory is also called iconic memory, or the sensory register. The idea is that information from the world, let's say the letter *A* or a chair, enters through the sense organs, in this case the eye, and is then held for a very brief period, about a quarter of a second, in storage in its "raw" form. Why do psychologists suppose this? As you might imagine by now, there are clever experiments that seem to argue for the existence of such a store. Let's say that a subject we have sitting in front of the screen of a computer sees an array of letters of the alphabet, *A, Z, P*, and so on. Let's say there are twenty letters arranged in front of the subject in rows, four letters in each row. The letters are on for only a very brief period of time, say 50 milliseconds (there are a thousand milliseconds in a second). At that kind of time interval, the subject just sees a flash of letters. Then the array of letters is turned off, and you ask the subject to tell you what the letters were. The subject can only remember about four letters.

Now let us say that we do the same experiment except that 100 milliseconds after the array of letters has been turned off, we give the subject a cue indicating which row of letters to report. There might be a tone that indicates which row, or an arrow might be flashed on the screen, pointing to the place where the row was when the array was on. The subject can now report every letter in the row that is indicated! More experiments can be done to see how long the cue can be delayed with the subject still able to report the indicated row correctly. This varies somewhat with the physical parameters of the experiment, factors such as the brightness of the letters, but in general it is found that the cue needs to be presented within 250 milliseconds (one-quarter second) of the stimulus in order for a complete report to occur. The logic of the experiment is this: In this experiment the array of letters was the world. The world has been turned off before the cue appears, so the subject can't be actually perceiving the letters. Yet it seems to the subject as though he is still perceiving them, and he is as accurate as though he were. Therefore, there must be a brief storage system, one that lasts under 250 milliseconds, in which visual information is held, within which one's attention can be directed to parts of the information, and from which the information disappears after that brief storage period.*

Short- and Long-Term Memory

The memories that we have discussed so far all lasted under a fourth of a second. Some information from very short term memory that has not been erased or lost and has been the object of attention moves on to short-term memory. Short-term mem-

---

*This material was presented in the context of a discussion in which the Dalai Lama and the geshes asked a number of leading questions. The dialogue has been condensed here for simplicity. It is continued in the section "Self, Selflessness, and Sense Consciousness" on pages 107–125.

ory lasts up to twenty seconds, and there are experiments, which I will not go into here, to demonstrate this short-term memory.

Most of what the average person, at least the average Westerner, means by memory is neither a sensory register (very short-term memory) nor short-term memory; it is long-term memory. Maybe we need to use the English term in translating this if there's no Tibetan equivalent for memory conceived as a long-term storage system—the way Sanskrit or Tibetan terms are used to translate Buddhist ideas for which there are no English equivalents.* Long-term memory lasts anywhere from half a minute up to the rest of your life. In the information-processing system, it is long-term memory that contains most of what we mean by a person—one's autobiographical memory, knowledge, habits, motives, and so forth. There is a persuasive—though of course debated—argument that there are actually two very different memory systems in what we call long-term memory; memory for events and memory in the sense of all the knowledge that the person has acquired. Knowing the meaning of the word *cat* is part of our acquired knowledge, whereas memory for the fact that the word *cat* occurred in a word list that one has just heard in an experiment is memory for a particular event. Memory for autobiographical events, for example, that the neighbor's cat scratched you when you were six years old, can have both an event and knowledge component; the incident may be recalled as a particular event, but it also affects your knowledge about cats, telling you that they can be dangerous.

Much of the experimentation done by the behaviorists and postbehaviorists, particularly when they studied human learning and memory, was about event memory. One very interesting debate has to do with the theory of forgetting. Remember that we are thinking in terms of independent, stable storage structures in the mind, like a warehouse or a bank. There is no idea of subtle impermanence, not even much of an idea of gross impermanence. In this storage-bank perspective, it is forgetting rather than memory that needs explanation. Why should anyone ever

---

*The last remark refers to a comment by B. Alan Wallace in an earlier discussion to the effect that in Tibetan there is no term for memory in the sense of a mechanical storage system.

forget anything? There were three major theories of forgetting. The first was that items in memory decay over time. It is like putting food in the refrigerator; you can lose the food because it decays. The second is that items are pushed out of memory by new information. You are putting cans into the refrigerator, but it gets too crowded, so as you put new ones in, they push some of the old ones out. The third is that there actually is no forgetting, items stay in memory permanently but you lose access to them. The cans are still in the refrigerator in perfectly good condition, but you can't find some of them anymore. In spite of a great many very ingenious experiments, it has never been possible to prove one of these theories over the others.

DALAI LAMA: There are different ways of forgetting. Sometimes there is something that you forget but when people remind you, you immediately remember. But sometimes it takes time for you to remember. Even though people remind you, you don't remember. And then after a while you say, "Oh, I remember." It shows different levels of forgetfulness.*

ROSCH: Yes. It is such phenomena from everyday life—that you have forgotten something and then you remember it—that makes it reasonable to propose that items are not really lost from memory (memory considered as a storehouse), but that you have just lost access to them. The trouble is that when such observations are made into a theory of memory in the Western sense of memory as a storehouse, then it can never be disproved. Every time you remember something that you had previously forgotten, it counts as proof of the theory. But when you cannot remember something, even if you never remember it your whole life, you can always say that you have just lost access to it rather than that it is gone from your memory. One of the important canons of scientific investigation is that theories be disprovable; you have to be able to state the conditions under which the theory could be found to be false as well as those under which it could be found to be true. The reason I keep talking about method is

---

*The reader might bear in mind in connection with the Dalai Lama's remark that there is no special term in Tibetan referring to memory as long-term storage.

because if you get the flavor of the way cognitive science is done, its methodology, it helps to understand it more than study of any particular bit of its content.

Actually not all theories of event memory treat memory as a bank in the same way. You spoke of different levels of forgetfulness, and there is, in fact, one memory theory that says that there are not different memory storage systems but only different levels of processing the memory material. Another theory, called the theory of constructive memory, argues that material in memory is always being changed, reconstructed, to fit with our knowledge, motives, and all the rest of our memory.

Now we come to the aspect of long-term memory that is one's knowledge—all of the knowledge that an individual has acquired. This is often called semantic memory because much of the work, many of the seminal experiments that were performed, concerned knowledge of the meaning of words in the language or knowledge acquired from reading meaningful material. The question is how such knowledge is structured in memory. Much of the work is done in the form of computer models that are meant to be validated by showing that they can actually run on a computer (Dr. Greenleaf's presentation should have more to say about this) or in the form of computerlike models meant to be tested by experiments on humans.

Finally we have a field of research that concerns specifically human kinds of knowledge. Here is one example of the kind of theory and experimentation done in this field. In our knowledge of the meaning of nouns, there are class-inclusion relations. Thus a canary is a bird and a bird is an animal. Some of the attributes of canaries are specific to canaries—for example, a canary is yellow; some attributes are shared with other birds—for example, a canary has wings; and some attributes are shared with all animals—for example, a canary has skin [see figure 11]. This is part of the logic of our zoological classification system and the logic of our language. The question for the psychologist investigating semantic memory is whether the memory system for this knowledge is structured and stored in this same way—a class-inclusion relationship with its attributes—yellow stored with canary, wings with bird, and skin with animal. The theory is that figure

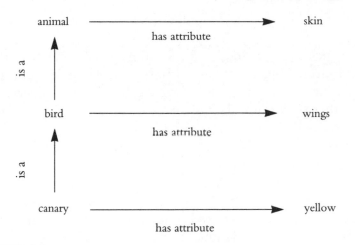

FIGURE 11

11 has some kind of reality within the memory of the subjects and that it takes the subjects real time to move their attention around in that memory structure. Were that the case, it should take them more time to answer questions about whether a canary has wings than about whether a canary is yellow, and more time still to answer a question about whether a canary has skin. To test this, the subjects sit in front of a computer screen on which statements of this type appear, and they must press a key as fast as they can to indicate whether each statement is true or false (true statements like "A canary has wings" and false statements like "A canary has fur" are both presented). The variable being measured is the subjects' reaction time. The finding is as was predicted; the logically further away the attribute is from the attributee, the longer it takes subjects to verify the statement. Although the interpretation of this particular experiment has been hotly debated, it is by experiments such as this that psychologists feel they can gain some access to the way knowledge is structured and stored in the mind. Models of knowledge more elaborate than this one can include people's knowledge of their own society, plans, goals, and anything else you feel needs to be incorporated into a model of human knowledge. The only provision is that you be able to specify the model in such a way that

it can either be run on a computer or be investigated experimentally.

In conclusion, we might, for a moment, consider the information-processing system as a whole. You will notice in figure 10 that the various boxes inside the big box are all connected to each other by arrows. This shows the recognition in information-processing psychology of the interrelatedness of various cognitive processes. Thus, attention is required to get information into the sense organs in the first place, to get information from the sensory register into short-term memory and from that into long-term memory. This direction of flow is called "bottom-up." In turn, higher-level processes from long-term memory direct attention and influence the lower-level processes—for example, more information can be held in short-term memory if the items are meaningful. This shows top-down flow. So both bottom-up and top-down processes are going on all the time. All of these processes influence people's decision making and, hence, actions in the world, which in turn will influence the kind of situations they will be in and the information that will be available to come in through the sense organs.*

---

*Dr. Rosch's presentation originally ended with some issues of comparison between Buddhism and cognitive psychology. This part of her presentation begins the following conversation.

Self, Selflessness, and Sense Consciousness

A Conversation

Cognitive Psychology and Buddhist Thought

ELEANOR ROSCH: I would like to indicate some issues that might spark a discussion of the relation between cognitive psychology and Buddhism. First there is the general issue of methodology. This raises the question of the role of meditation in connection with acquiring knowledge of one's own mind. Then, in terms of content, I would like to touch on some major points of the three yanas in Buddhism* and raise questions about their connections with the information-processing model. I am particularly interested in what Western psychology might incorporate from Buddhism so that psychology can be about real minds rather than hypothetical pictures of minds.

In discussing introspectionism we saw that in present-day psychology, as in behaviorism, introspective knowledge of one's own mind is not admissible evidence in studying the mind. In a sense this shows wisdom. Left to one's own top-down processing, one will see only what one's desires and preconceptions lead one to see. So something akin to meditation and to mindfulness and awareness in daily life is needed, some method for taming and training the mind so that it can be an instrument of knowledge about itself. There is absolutely no sense in Western psychology or medicine that meditation can be treated as an instrument of knowledge, and the kinds of research that are done on meditation would certainly never lead to the discovery that it could. Most research treats meditation as though it is a pill,

---

*See note on page 2.

something to provide relaxation. The type of meditation used is usually Transcendental Meditation,* since all meditations are considered equivalent. A typical experimental design might be to compare physiological measures of a group of people who have been instructed to do TM for twenty minutes with those of a group who have been instructed to relax in some other way, such as listening to music. If no difference is found between the groups, it is concluded that meditation is ineffective. A second type of research on meditation simply tries to prove that meditation does something, anything, by demonstrating that one or more meditators from some tradition can do something that people normally cannot do, such as control their breathing or block out sensory stimulation. The researcher may be an advocate of meditation seeking to prove that it is legitimate or may take a condescending attitude toward it—an attitude that the backward people who invented the technique just happened on something that is effective. Either way the meditation is taken out of context. A third type of medical research is practically oriented; it seeks to find new ways to engage the mind in the healing of the body. Thus subjects might be taught to visualize killer cells attacking the site of their infirmity. All of these techniques incorporate a kernel of truth: most meditations probably include some pacifying action; some meditations obviously do train meditators to do things that untrained people cannot do; and minds certainly influence bodies. But none of this will help the modern Western psychologist develop a genuine and powerful view of real minds. Western psychologists need to have access to their own minds.

Self and Selflessness

ROSCH: Next we have various issues of content. We could start with the self. For Buddhism a central issue for the mind of

---

* Transcendental Meditation is the name given to the particular method of meditation taught by the spiritual school founded by Hindu guru Maharishi Mahesh Yogi. This meditation, which involves at least in some phases the repetition of a short mantra, or verbal phrase, is particularly popular in English-speaking countries. It is often simply called TM. This type of practice differs, both in technique and purpose, from the mindfulness-awareness type employed by Buddhist practitioners.

any sentient being is the mistaken belief in a self and the clinging to that when in reality there is no self. If you look at the information-processing diagram we have been using, you certainly do not see a self. What you see is many separate boxes, separate processes. So one reaction that an interested Buddhist psychologist might have to this is to think, "Ah, that is like analyzing the self into the five skandhas, the five aggregates, and finding no separate self—very enlightened!"* But, equally, you do not see no self there either. What is, in fact, happening is that Western psychologists simply have no inkling of the importance of the self, let alone its nonexistence. This relates to the issue of method discussed earlier. Without access to one's own mind, one cannot begin to see the self referentially in all of one's processes—thoughts, emotions, everything—and without seeing that that self-reference is there, one cannot begin to understand conceptually what is meant by saying that all that is not based on a real self.

DALAI LAMA: On the issue of the identification of the self or the self-clinging attitude, the importance of this identification has been mentioned in Tibetan texts such as Shepa's *Great Exposition of Tenets*. He says that first of all you have to identify the self, the innate notion of self that everybody has. This could be done only from the point of view of one's own experience on an emotional level.

ROSCH: Yes, that is what is lacking in Western psychology.

DALAI LAMA: We're really concerned with the innate sense of self and not something you're fortifying by means of reasoning or philosophical study. What's really important is the innate sense of self.

ROSCH: Yes, but that is something you cannot understand if

---

*One of the most fundamental teachings of the Buddha was that there is no coherent or essential self, or ego. When we investigate, he said, what we find instead is the activity of the five skandhas (Skt., lit. "aggregates" or "heaps"). These are form, feeling, perception, (conceptual) formation, and consciousness. Some Buddhist schools, including the Prasangika Madhyamika school advocated by the Dalai Lama, subscribe to the idea of the "mere self," which has a conventional reality based on the force of conceptual designation.

you are alienated from your own mind. There is a minor theme of study in personality psychology and in cognitive psychology called the "self concept." It is about the development of people's concepts of themselves. But no one who does work on this seems to realize either that there is not an actual self—or how important people consider this issue of whether or not there is a self. Perhaps in a culture that already has some deep idea of a self, like an atman,* it is easier both to direct people to the sense of self and to challenge it.

FRANCISCO J. VARELA: But wouldn't you say, Eleanor, that if pressed with this question, many Westerners would say: "Oh, self is the conscious perception of something. My self is my capacity to see this, to talk to you, to recognize—that kind of reflective awareness."

JEREMY W. HAYWARD: I think that if you ask most Western people walking down the street, "Do you think you have a self?" they would say, "Yes, of course I have a self!" They would say either, "It's my mind," or, "It's my heart," or, "It's my soul or my memories." Most people do believe they have a self, even if they are not Christians or scientists.

ROSCH: Yes, and the scientists who are taking the bottom-up approach are the ones who say, "But so what?" So far I have been talking about the relation of self to the information-processing approach in a somewhat bottom-up fashion—the flow of information comes into the system from the world through the senses and into the short-term memory. This is called bottom-up or low-level processing with the idea that the sensory register (or very short term memory) is the bottom or the lowest level of the system. As we move to the right in the diagram (figure 10), we get what are called higher levels. For example, a psychology class entitled "Higher Mental Processes" would include topics such as problem solving but would not include perception. Actually the distinction between problem solving and perception may not have to do with the mental level either. To say "bottom-up"

---

*The idea of a real eternal self, or *atman,* akin to God, is a basic tenet of most forms of Hinduism.

means that the process is dependent on, under the control of, information coming from the world into the organism, whereas "top-down" indicates that the process is more controlled by information coming from the organism, from its long-term memory, motivation, knowledge, plans, and so on. It is not that top-down processes are assumed to be independent of physiology. It is from the bottom-up point of view that you don't see a self anywhere in the cognitive system. But what if you take a top-down approach?

Average Westerners, like everyone else, do have a sense of self. If asked about it (and I have questioned many students), they will discover that it is vague and will struggle to define and defend it. The dissection of mind as done in behaviorism, information-processing psychology, or for that matter, in the Abhidharma, precisely violates this vague sense of self—which may be one reason why these approaches tend to be seen as so objectionable by nonprofessionals. Psychologists, too, often become distressed with the fragmented view of the person generated by the bottom-up approach and may seek to emphasize top-down processes—the way in which people's concepts, beliefs, desires, and goals affect their perception and other lower processes. One way to integrate the person as an information-processing device is to put an additional box into the diagram at the right side, the higher-processes side, labeled "supervisor," with arrows to all of the other boxes. Another way is to talk about the whole person and emergent properties of the whole person. An emphasis on the top-down approach may seem "wiser" and more human in many respects, but it tends to deny the power of analysis and to reintroduce the idea of a self as a real thing.

DALAI LAMA: Do emotions like hatred, desire, and so forth, come in anywhere under your experiments in cognitive psychology? I'm not talking about any subtle levels of emotion but just the grosser levels. Because, if you accept the fact that emotions arise—like desire, wishing and so forth—there is no way you can explain this apart from the notion of self. Something that is desirable to *you, you* wish for it, *you* desire it. Something that is repulsive, *you* don't want, *you* feel hate toward it. The whole event of desire for this and aversion toward that doesn't arise apart from the notion "*I* like," "I don't like."

ROSCH: Yes. That is what I mean by the information-processing approach being so slippery; it doesn't have to acknowledge that. There are many ways to get around it. We can just put in another box, labeled "emotions," with arrows to and from long-term memory, perception, attention, and so on. Let's see how this might work with an example: You see a bear coming at you. First stimuli from the bear have to come into your sense organs and be held in very short term memory. Then you have to recognize the bear (for simplicity, I left out another box, called "pattern recognition," that should go on the left-hand—lower-level—side of the diagram.) The pattern has to connect with the knowledge about bears that is stored in your long-term memory, about what bears can do and also what you can do about what they do. You have to make a decision, and then act—run away. Somewhere in this process you have a connection with the emotion box—it is now called "hot cognition"—that's fear! There is a great deal of dispute about where in this process the emotion enters. One venerable theory is that you don't have emotion until you see how you've acted; in this case it is a response to seeing that you are running away. Another new controversial theory is that you feel the emotion even before you have recognized the stimulus. So you see, by using the information-processing approach, you just don't have to confront the notion of a self if you don't want to.

THUBTEN JINPA [interpreter]: It is necessary to distinguish between the innate notion of self and the innate self-grasping attitude. We say, "I am going." This shows that there is such a thing as an authentic sense of self called the mere self, which is not a mistaken sense of self. Then there is another notion of self that is mistaken, that is grasping at some inherently existent self. So these two should be distinguished.

DALAI LAMA: Even with the notion of grasping at an inherently existing self, there are different types. One conceives the aggregates (skandhas) as something separate from self and the self as the supervisor. But then there is another notion of self that identifies the self within the aggregates, not as separate but as something among the aggregates. Then, even with the notion that holds self as supervisor, there are two types. One regards the self as totally independent of the aggregates, as some kind of supervisor that is totally unrelated to them. The other one identifies the self with the aggregates but at the same time regards it as the supervisor. It's among them and yet it's a little bit more important. An example given is that among the merchants, there is the chief merchant, who is not different from the merchants but at the same time is the supervisor. Between these two, it is the second one that is innate. The first of these, where you have the sense of self as the supervisor separate from the aggregates, is only learned; you don't have it innately. The second one, where you have the sense of the supervisor among the aggregates like the chief merchant among merchants, can be innate. Then there's something more subtle than that, which is simply the grasping to inherent existence. There are three levels.

Just as when Buddha taught the four noble truths he taught them on the basis of things that mattered to sentient beings, in the same manner when he presented the view of emptiness as the ultimate nature of phenomena, he divided phenomena into two categories: the person, the agent, on one hand, and the thing that the person relates to, the environment or external phenomena, on the other. Not only are there two different categories of phenomena, the person and the external phenomena, there are also two different types of misconceptions with respect to the nature of phenomena: misconceptions with respect to the nature of the person and with respect to the external phenomena. The means to overcome these two types of misconception is to realize self-lessness,* which is the ultimate nature of these two types of phenomena. Therefore there are two selflessnesses, selflessness of person and selflessness of phenomena. Generally speaking, comparing the two, the realization of the selflessness of the person is said to be easier than realization of the selflessness of phenomena because of long familiarity with the actual self, the person. When

---

*Selflessness (or egolessness) here, in the Buddhist view, can be regarded as a specific case of emptiness, that is emptiness of self.

you're just thinking, "I'm going to stay here," "I'm going to go," then to your natural mind—that is, one that's not a learned mind with a whole bunch of theories that you've learned from psychology, or whatever—what does your self appear as, just naturally, spontaneously? It appears as "I," as an owner. Then mind, body, and speech belong to that "I." To a certain extent that's true. You can say, This is my body. Without "I" we cannot say that this is my body. So there is "I." When we're showing affection, kindness, not toward the body, not necessarily toward the mind, but toward the human being, that's the "I" in that other human being, isn't it? What is your innate sense of "I," whether it's in yourself or in other people?

What Is the Nature of Mind Itself?

ROSCH: Mahayana Buddhism raises the next issue—that of duality and nonduality.* In Western psychology, duality is supposed—the world is inherently existent and separate from the person, and vice versa. This is not even a belief or an explicit metaphysic, because no one has conceived of any alternative viewpoint to it. What is offered as an alternative, a paradigm shift, is generally a minor move within the system itself—for example, the argument, often attributed to "Eastern" thought, that since we know the world only through our minds (our preconceptions, desires, conditioning, interpretations), there can be no objective knowledge of the world. Within the information-processing framework, such arguments are no challenge at all. Information-processing psychologists say, "Of course! There is always top-down processing going on. We can give you lots of demonstrations of that. We already know that. So what?" And they are perfectly right. It seems that this kind of partial challenge to the dualistic view doesn't basically affect it. How can one do cognitive psychology based on a view of world and person codependently arising at each moment? This is simply a view in which

---

*One of the basic tenets of Mahayana Buddhism is the nonduality of subject and object, mind and world.

there are no representations—only presentations. After all, the arising, the phenomenal world, remains lawful in both cases.

The issue that is most central, most important, to many schools of Buddhism is the realization of the very essence of mind. This principle is called by various names: beyond mind, no mind, primordial mind, one's original face, true nature, that which is unfabricated by mind, great perfection. In the Western way of seeing things, such matters are in the category of religion, never science, and cannot enter at all into any psychology.

DALAI LAMA: There are two general areas for which dialogue or cross-communication between Buddhism and psychology could be very valuable. One is in the investigation of the nature of mind itself, of the thought processes, conceptualization—simply straight investigation into the nature of mind. The second one is investigation of the nature of mind specifically in relation to therapeutic purposes, dealing with people who are subject to some mental imbalance or dysfunction—how to bring them to better health.

The main purpose or objective of Buddhist theory and practice of psychology is to utterly dispel the mental distortions, or *kleshas,* most importantly, attachment or anger.* Mental imbalance, dysfunction, and so forth arise principally as a result of the mental distortions of attachment and/or anger. So, while on the one hand the major project in Buddhism is to utterly eradicate the *kleshas,* there is a kind of secondary therapeutic side project. I feel that a lot from Buddhism could be of use in therapy. From my own experience, I have found that some people with certain mental disorders or who may be imbalanced because of drugs, by being introduced to Buddhist concepts and practices their mind gains a greater balance than it had previously.

In terms of the first of these two areas—the investigation into the nature of mind itself—probably there is no one who has a broader explanation than the Buddhists. However, the presentations of the mind and cognitions and so forth that one finds in

---

*The *kleshas* are usually enumerated as a set of three: attachment of passion, anger of aggression, and ignorance; or as a set of five: anger, pride, passion, jealousy, ignorance. Occasionally a sixth is added to this last set.

Buddhist texts are not done from the same point of view as the experiments that you have conducted as a psychologist. So we have a lot to learn from the psychologists. It would also be valuable to try to compare the results that you have gained from these experiments with the presentations of Buddhism.

Now, from the point of view of a Western psychologist, how would you prove the presence of something called awareness, the instrument of knowledge?

ROSCH: Well, you see, that is exactly what Western psychologists do not know how to demonstrate, if we stick to the rules.

DALAI LAMA: As a psychologist you are actually dealing with matters of cognition and awareness. So without identifying what you are dealing with, how can you have a science? Psychologists do have a distinction between matter and cognition, or something that is cognition and something that is not cognition, do they not?

If the examination of the mind, of cognition, is done only through the behavior that is the result of it and there is no way to directly examine the mind, then that is one thing. In that case, techniques might be helpful that provide a possibility of directly examining the mind. This is explained in the Buddhist texts, and also by other systems where there is a meditation on mind, and where identification of one's own mind is explained.

One way of defining cognition in Buddhist terms is as an agent that has the capacity to arise in an aspect corresponding to the object that appears.* This is just one definition of the mind or cognition. Mind is not like matter, of which you can just have a visual image and meditate on it. But one way, one technique, to identify mind is to withdraw your mind from focusing on external objects. Then what is left is mind. If you use mindfulness, this allows you to prevent your mind from being distracted by external objects. Then you can meditate on your own mind. At the beginning it might be difficult, but later when you find that your mind is distracted again, you reinforce this mindfulness, and when you are again distracted, you again reinforce mindful-

---

*This is discussed further in "Perception and Consciousness," pages 190–212.

ness. After a while, you will get to an experience of clarity and lucidity. At that point what remains is simply a sense of lucidity and clarity like pure water, such that if that clarity encounters an object, then it arises in the aspect of that object. Otherwise, it simply has this pure luminosity or clarity to it. Specifically with respect to this training, the most important thing is time; it simply takes time. But as a result of this training, gradually the experience becomes clearer and yet clearer. This is the process by means of which one sees the nature of the mind.

What Is the Basis of Continuity?

ROSCH: Another content area one might want to consider in comparing Buddhism with cognitive psychology is that of karma and continuity. In Buddhism, although there is not a real self, there is not only a vitally important sense of self but there is also a causal continuity in one's experience—that is karma. Learning and memory in Western psychology are all about causal continuity. But it is undoubtedly not exactly the same sense of causal continuity. So this might be an impetus for discussion.

VARELA: I think at this point it is clear that even in science in the West, this whole issue of self is very vague and shifty. There is no clear doctrine even within science. Generally, people have a certain feeling about this question. When you tell them that Buddhism does not believe in a self, they say, "That's silly. I can remember when I was little." In other words, they have recourse to a notion of memory and continuity through memory. But at the same time there always seems to be a certain degree of unsatisfactoriness to those kinds of answers, that is, answers that say that the apparent continuity of memory is the cause of the apparent continuity of this "mere self."*

I can say I'm here, but in the West there is also a very commonsensical idea that the reason the mere self is solid or has a reality to it is the fact that I can refer to that mere self with a sense of time, years. I can say not only that I am Francisco, but that I was

---

*See note, page 109, and remarks by Thubten Jinpa and the Dalai Lama, pages 112–14.

here yesterday and so on. For forty-one years, in some sense, I've had the same mere self. Normally when people hear the Buddhist teaching of nonself, they ask, How can that be? If there is no self, how can you explain the fact that there is continuity? It would be interesting perhaps to know—do you see this continuity only in the sense of episodical memory, event memory?

DALAI LAMA: When Buddhists speak of the nonself doctrine, they do not refer to the mere self, because mere self is there. Just as you can see that this body was physically different when I was young, in the same manner you can also refer to your mere self at the time of childhood. Self is a designation that is made on the basis of the continuity of the aggregates. Just as your physical body is the continuation of the physical body of the child, in the same manner there is a self that is designated on that basis that retains continuity.

I think clarification is needed for the Buddhist term *mere self.* When we speak of mere self in Buddhist philosophy, this term *mere self* does not exclude any and all kinds of bases; it excludes only the *inherent existence* of the self.

VARELA: What kind of basis could be given for the mere self? How is it explained that even if it is not substantial, it has a continuity? Now, I say I have a merely designated self called Francisco. Why is it that two seconds later I don't have a merely designated self called Thubten Jinpa? What is the explanation for this? In the West we would tend to think that it is due to the fact that memory accumulates, and it is on the basis of that recollection of memory of a causal sequence stored in the brain somewhere that I can say that's me. So the question is, If this is the Western explanation, what would be the equivalent explanation in Buddhist philosophy?

DALAI LAMA: The Buddhists might give a similar answer. The continuity of your body is not the continuity of Thubten Jinpa's body. How can you be Thubten Jinpa? That's one answer. Another answer is that you have this old, past history, your memory, and so forth, but that doesn't mean that your memory is self.

At this point it's important to be familiar with the Buddhist concept of how conceptual thoughts, as opposed to direct perceptions, function with respect to an object. When conceptual thoughts operate with regard to an object, they tend to do so by means of exclusion. This is a major facet of Buddhist epistemology. How do you identify something? You identify it by a process of "not this, not this, not this. . . ." Thus you cognize what remains after this by a process of exclusion. Even one entity, like a book, has many different aspects. For example, this is just one book. But there is the impermanence of this book, its quality of being a product, its being white, and so on. When the conceptual mind cognizes these aspects, it does so in a very selective manner. Therefore even though the mere self of a person is one entity, nevertheless within that you can distinguish many different aspects. Take, for example, myself. There is a self that is a monk, a self that is Tibetan, a self that is from the Amdo [region of Tibet], and so on. There are many different selves. And some preexist others. For example, the self that is a Tibetan existed earlier than the self of the monk. The self of the monk is acquired only when someone becomes a monk. When you search, you find that actually this one entity of the self has many different aspects.

VARELA: Is there then another self that says I am all of these selves together? Somebody that can say, "Yes, I'm Chilean and a scientist," and so forth, Who is that? I don't have to imagine anything in saying there is somebody like that. As His Holiness was talking, saying, "I am a monk; I am a Tibetan," etc., who was talking then? Who is that? The one who says, I am this, I am that, I am that. Who is that?

JINPA: That's the self!

DALAI LAMA: For example, you lose your temper with yourself. There are two selves [the angry one and the object of the anger], but actually it's the same continuity of the self. These two different selves are designated as separate on the basis of the time they occur.

B. ALAN WALLACE [interpreter]: One thing that may not be clear here is that for Buddhism, the mere self is able to perform functions. Just as the pen is able to perform functions, so can you and I perform functions, even though we are mere selves, merely conceptually designated. In English if you say it's merely conceptually designated, it implies that it has no power.

DALAI LAMA: Another concept that might be necessary to be familiar with here is the concept of generality. When you see a vase somewhere, you label it. You know that it's a vase. You see it. If you go somewhere else and you see another vase, immediately you say, "Oh, that's a vase." Why do you get this understanding? Why do you know that is a vase? The vase you are seeing is not the one you saw before. Why do you see that it is?

In order to understand generalizations, you have to understand abstract phenomena. For example, you know that this table is not a person, so from that point of view there is something nonpersonal about this table. This nonpersonal aspect is not concrete, not solid, but because you can realize it, it's there. You can apprehend the fact that it is not a person, but you cannot grasp it.

There are many of these kinds of phenomena that are mental constructs, that is, they are abstract or merely designated. Generality falls into this same category and applies to the kind of innate notion of self that you have, not designated on the basis of particular instances but rather on the basis of the continuities: that I, the previous I, the next life's I.

HAYWARD: For me the mere self is almost indistinguishable from an inherent self. Now you have this mere self; this self is a man. The same self was born in England, has lived for forty-seven years, is for now living in Dharmsala. Now all you need to add is rebirth after the death of this mere self and you have a soul!*

DALAI LAMA: When you use the word *soul,* this actually raises a different issue altogether. Merely the word *soul* doesn't matter. It's not the mere term that has to be refuted but rather the theory that comes along behind it. When people present this existence of soul, they normally tend to associate it with some kind of self that is permanent, partless, a single entity. That's really unrelated to the Buddhist view.

HAYWARD: That is why I used the word *soul.* The way you

---

*Dr. Hayward is questioning the validity of the mere self on Buddhist grounds. The Buddhist doctrine of egolessness is considered very definitely to rule out the existence of any kind of soul.

were describing mere self, it sounded like I have the same self as I did forty-seven years ago. It's me, this me. That begins to sound permanent.

DALAI LAMA: Here the important point is that there is continuation, yet what is continuing is momentarily changing. Consider the I when I was ten years old. If the two, the self I have now and the self of the ten-year-old, are exactly the same, one and the same, then the ten-year-old would be an old person and the old person would be a ten-year-old child. It doesn't make any sense. Then you will have to say the person who died was a person who was the same at the time of the birth.

HAYWARD: So it's not the same self.

DALAI LAMA: No, it *is* the same self, but it is momentarily changing. It has the same continuity, the same continuum. One entity, the same entity, which is momentarily changing, and yet meantime there is a continuum.

VARELA: It's the same in the same sense that a scientist would say that this body is the same although all these molecules have changed.

DALAI LAMA: Yes, that's right!

VARELA: So the pattern is the same. This pattern, the pattern of the body, is nevertheless gone when I die, is it not? What about the pattern of the mind?

DALAI LAMA: Death involves the grosser level of the body. The subtle body still will be there.

VARELA: All right, this is where I want to go now. For a Western scientist, what we have just said is fine and good. Now I want to get to the subtler, as you say, levels of continuity. Now, suppose I die. Western science would say that the pattern we have called self is gone forever; there's nothing left. Buddhists say, No, there's something left. How do we describe that continuity now?

DALAI LAMA: Here the question of subtleties of the mind comes in.*

---

*Questions of the relation between mind and brain and the subtle levels of mind are taken up again later, in "Consciousness, Gross and Subtle," pages 146–65.

Sense Consciousness

DALAI LAMA: Now I should like to ask, Is the sense register, or what you call very short term memory, on the sensory level or on the mental level?

ROSCH: This is a question that arose in the study of very short term memory and was investigated experimentally. Actually I think that any time you have a model of the mind that is divided into different compartments or stages, then whenever you find out something about the mind, there will be a learned dispute about which compartment or stage to put it in. We find this even in Buddhism. According to the Yogachara school, there are eight consciousnesses. When the idea of bijas (seeds of future actions) came up, then there was a dispute about which consciousness contained the bijas. In cognitive psychology the question about whether something is sensory or mental is usually phrased, "Is it peripheral or central?" The terminology implies either an actual or a hypothetical physiology: Is it in the sense organ or in the brain? Here is the type of experiment that was done to answer this question for very short term memory. The same experiment can be done that I described before, with the rows of letters and arrows that flash, except that here we separate the information given to each of the two eyes. The row of letters is shown to one eye and the cue indicating which row to report is shown to the other eye. If the very short term memory, the sensory register, were in the sense organs themselves, then the subject should not be able to do the task under these conditions, since the information and the cue are coming into different peripheral organs. What is actually found is that the subject can do the task just as well as though all of the information had been given to both eyes. Physiologically, this argues that the memory is stored in the brain at least as far back as where the fibers from the two eyes meet. So the conclusion is that the memory storage is central/mental rather than peripheral/sensory. [There is some discussion among the Tibetans.]

JINPA: We're having a debate about whether or not there are two visual perceptions. His Holiness' point of view is that since there are two different causes, the two visual sense organs, therefore there should be different visual perceptions based on these two different visual organs.

VARELA: That is interesting. They're different up to a point and then they come together. You can mentally ascertain that there are two visual perceptions, and then they come together. For example, one of your eyes is more dominant. This ocular dominance is well known; it shows that the two function independently. But at the same time the fact that you can see in three dimensions implies that these two perceptions come together; otherwise you would see two different images. So you have two separate images and then the two join. Therefore, it's not contradictory to say that they're separate and that they come together.

GESHE PALDEN DRAKPA: The sense organ might be deep within the eye; however, Geshe Yeshi Thabkhe feels that it might be on the surface. His reason is that when you have a very bright light, like sunlight on snow, sometimes it destroys your vision. This suggests that your vision must take place on the surface, where it is vulnerable, because if it's way back in the innards of the brain, then why should light that doesn't hit inside the brain damage it?

ROSCH: The geshe's idea about the bright light has been applied in an experiment, although I am not sure what he means by "sense organ." (By the way, you people are rapidly recapitulating the development of this field.) If you follow the array of letters by flashing a bright light, it erases the memory. The subject cannot recall any of the letters. It is not a very bright light; it doesn't injure the eye in any way, but if it flashes for only about two hundred milliseconds, it removes the memory.

DALAI LAMA: This is really an important experiment to know about. As a result of being shown this bright light, you are not able to recall when you're asked. Can you recall afterward?

ROSCH: No, you can't. It's gone. You can never recall it. There are many other ways besides a light to erase a perceived stimulus from memory. This field of investigation has a name; it is called backward masking. You also get erasure, for example, if you use a circle that surrounds a single letter as your cue after the array is turned off. Subjects can direct their attention to the location indicated by the circle, but they have no memory of which letter was in that location. It has been erased. Backward masking is a very active research area with some three thousand experiments done but not much agreement on explanations, though most of the theories are physiological in nature.

DALAI LAMA: This phenomenon cannot be explained mainly on the consciousness level. When you show this bright light and it affects your memory, it happens on the basis of the sense organ. Since these experiments take place on a very gross level of mind that depends very much on a physical basis like sense organs and so forth, it cannot be explained on a mental level.

VARELA: I'm not sure that I understand what you mean by mental level in that sense.

DALAI LAMA: I mean those deeper levels (or you could say more primitive, I don't know), more subtle consciousness that is more independent of sense organs. If you are operating on a rather gross level of mind and then all of a sudden you plunge into a deeper, subtler level of consciousness, lapses of memory also arise. In this phenomenon, is there some fainting on the part of the subject when you show this absolutely bright light, some kind of surprise? Do you black out for a very short time?

ROSCH: No, no, it's not that sort of a bright light. It's just bright enough to erase everything.

DALAI LAMA: Are there any differences on the part of the subjects, such as that some are more attentive? Statistically speaking, does it make any difference whether some of the subjects are clearer minded while some are more foggy minded?

ROSCH: No, it makes no difference.

DALAI LAMA: When we are dealing with these sensory perceptions, we are dealing with rather gross levels of mind that are very much dependent on physical matter, that is, the kleshas and the sense organs. I find it's very difficult, almost impossible, to separate them from the physical basis, the sense organs. They're almost like the energy of these cells.

VARELA: In fact one can see this while looking at the activity of one cell in the cortex. What seems to happen to the energy of the cells is what you suggested a moment ago. When you show the letters, the cells in the cortex hold the image for a little bit, but when a flash of light comes in, they have a new activity. They undergo a reset. Therefore that internal retention is lost. So it is the same phenomenon as you mentioned. It really doesn't depend on the subject. It is, just as you said, a sort of very basic or low-level phenomenon.

DALAI LAMA: Let us take a purely hypothetical instance (there is no question of this actually being able to be done): Imagine there being no brain, no stuff back there, just simply the eyeball. Given that, would there be any kind of visual impression or any kind of visual experience at all?

ROSCH: No.

VARELA: You see, Your Holiness, this is the whole point—that mind and brain do not function as separate things. They have to be together.

Artificial Intelligence

NEWCOMB GREENLEAF

I am a computer scientist and some people might think that I have come to the wrong conference, because here we are discussing mind and life, and I work with machines. Indeed there is a very emotional debate in America, and I suspect all over the world, concerning the relationship of human beings and machines. It is, of course, a very old debate that has been rekindled by the presence in our midst of these new complicated machines, the computers. Some people are very offended at any mention of machines in the same breath with human beings. They feel that to compare a human being to a machine in any way takes away from the sense of the preciousness of being human. On the opposite side are those who say, "Of course, it is completely obvious that the mind is a computer or that the brain is a computer!" Or if they are being a bit more careful, they say the mind is *like* a computer or the brain is *like* a computer. My talk will in some respects try to illuminate this controversy.

Indeed there has already been a lot of computer talk here in the other presentations. Professor Varela spoke of the "programs" in the brain. This is not a word from biology; it is a word from computer science. Professor Rosch talked about "bottom up" and "top down." Where did she get these words? Not from psychology but from computing. Our language is becoming full of computer words. All sorts of people use computer words to describe all sorts of situations. It is perhaps particularly relevant to talk about computers here, because we're talking about mind. This is so, because one of the major efforts of computer scientists is to make the computers so smart that they will be smarter than we are! Twenty-five years ago, many computer scientists said very confidently that in a few years computers would surpass human beings. But this has not happened yet. No one really knows when or if it will happen, but everyone has an opinion.

What Is a Computer?

I'll talk a little about what a computer is and then talk specifically about attempts to make the machines as intelligent as or more intelligent than we are. Of course there are many ways to describe this effort, and most computer scientists like to stay away from words like "consciousness" or "understanding." They are rather like behaviorists. They like to talk about intelligence because they believe that intelligence is something that can be demonstrated and measured, and they want their machines to show intelligence in a demonstrable, measurable way. They would like their machines to demonstrate greater intelligence than humans, and indeed to do better than humans at tasks that humans do.

DALAI LAMA: Until now, in what kinds of fields have computers proved more efficient than humans?

NEWCOMB GREENLEAF: Well, computers originally were made to do mathematical computations, and they are very good at this. But in the area of what we now call "artificial intelligence," extremely efficient programs have been developed, which I will talk about later, for example, to help doctors do medical diagnosis or to do legal research for lawyers. Computers also control our airplanes when they are flying, and they control many of our industrial plants. While there are benefits from this, there are also great risks, and many difficult issues are raised. Computers have been implicated in some major industrial accidents. But we should not blame the machine. Rather, it is the fault of the people who believed that the computer could be trusted, that they had programmed the machine in such a way that it was smart enough to handle any situation that came up. Suppose a computer program helps a doctor decide on a course of treatment for a patient, and then the patient dies. Who is responsible, the doctor or the programmer?

We had an example on October 13, 1987. The stock exchange in New York went boom, way down! Why did it do that? In large part because many people with lots of money who were investing very heavily in the stock market were using computer programs to decide what to buy and what to sell. All of a sudden things happened so that everybody's program said "sell." Everybody sold, and the stock market crashed. In this case the cause was greed; they believed their computers would make them rich!

There are always two aspects to a computer. There is the "hardware," which is the physical object, not so much the box but the components inside the box. And then there's what we call the "software," or patterns of activation inside the computer. There are two parts to the software. There are the programs, which are the sets of instructions of what to do. They control the action of the computer. And there is data, the information that is being acted on inside the computer.

The hardware units that the user interacts with directly consist of the input device, which is the keyboard, in the case of Dr. Livingston's computer here, and the output device, which in this case is a display screen. Inside the box the most important units are the memory cells, where the programs and data are stored, and what we call the "CPU," which stands for central processing unit. The CPU is really where all the action takes place, where the computations and comparisons are made, where the programs are actually carried out. But if you look inside the box, you won't see any action at all, since it takes place on a microscopic level inside chips containing many thousands of transistors.

If the computer is a robot, the output might be physical motion and the input might come from a video camera or from the robot's touching things. So we see here a very close analogy with what Professor Varela described as the fundamental elements of the brain. The sensory surface of the computer is the keyboard (or other input device), and the motor surface (which in this case does not really move) is the screen (or other mode of output) by which the computer communicates with us, gives us its results.

There are essentially two different kinds of programs. Some are special-purpose programs like the word processor that Dr.

Livingston has in his computer. With the word-processing program in his machine, his computer becomes an ideal secretary. It takes dictation; it writes his letters. He has to type on the keyboard, but it creates the data that will go into his letter and allows him to edit it in any way he wishes, to change it, and make his letter or his book say just what he wants it to. It is an ideal secretary, an excellent servant, so useful that he brought it all the way to Dharmsala from San Diego. But this program is a special-purpose one. It will only be a secretary. It will not do mathematical computations; it has only a limited calculator. He can't make it do anything he wants. It is basically a word processor with maybe a little bit of extra capability.

It also has an outlet so that it can be hooked up to a telephone to deliver his letters or a book to a remote station where whatever he sends can be printed out. Or a printer can be directly hooked to this machine so that its output is not limited just to the screen. In any case, he is using a special-purpose program for preparing documents. There is a vast array of other special-purpose programs. All businesses in America have accounting programs. Architects now often use computers to design buildings.

In addition to all the special-purpose programs, there are also what are known as universal programs, an idea that goes back to Alan Turing, a pioneer in artificial intelligence and computer development, in 1935. Universal programs are generally called *programming languages*. They allow the people using the computer to write any kind of program they wish so that the computer will execute it. A programming language is a program that runs another program. It allows you to write any special-purpose program you can imagine. Of course, you can't simply say, "I imagine a program that will be infinitely intelligent or will be an enlightened being." You have to imagine it at the level of very fine detail. You have to devise formulations that say: in this case, do this and this, in that case, do that. If you can imagine it at that level, then you can write the program, and the universal machine will execute it.

There are many, many different programming languages. Some of the most famous are Fortran, Lisp, Basic, Pascal, but there are literally thousands more that computer scientists have invented. The disk that Dr. Livingston put in his computer has a word processor on it. If he had brought a disk containing Lisp or Pascal, then we could sit down and write any program we wanted to on his machine and then run our program. The only limitations would be the limitations of the size of the machine, the amount of memory, and the amount of time that we are willing to wait for the output.

Inside the box, there are basically two kinds of things. There are the memory chips that store both the programs and the data. If you are using the computer as a word processor, then the memory contains both the word-processing program and whatever you have written, both of them in the same memory area. Then there's the CPU, the central processing unit, which carries out all of the actions. It takes things out of memory and puts them back in memory. It receives input from the keyboard and sends output to the screen. It carries out arithmetic computations, and it compares things. It also executes the program; that is to say, it goes into the program stored in memory and takes out the next step, executes that, and then takes out the next step and executes that, and so on. There's only one CPU, and so we see immediately that this computer is completely unlike the human brain! The human brain has billions of neurons, and they're all working at once. Here we have one central processing unit. At any given instant something is happening only in one place, so the whole computing process takes place one step at a time. For very complicated programs, this creates a bottleneck. Because so many steps must be carried out, execution can be very slow, even though the machine in a way is incredibly fast. This machine does many millions of tiny operations per second, but many operations are needed for something as simple as adding two numbers. If you have tremendously complicated problems, difficulties arise, because there is only one place where things are actually happening.

Nowadays a great deal of research is being done in computer science in what is known as parallel processing, which involves many CPUs. Maybe each one has its own memory, or maybe they all use a common memory. There are big debates over which arrangement is best. How should the multiple CPUs be connected together? How should each or all be connected to the various other elements of the computer? Building a parallel computer is an extremely complex and difficult problem, and it is even more difficult to program it! One of the major areas of computer science research nowadays is building parallel machines and learning how to program them. The idea here is that each of the CPUs, maybe fifty thousand of them, is busy most of the time, so there is a tremendous increase in the power of the machine. But only for some special kinds of computations have we succeeded in harnessing the power of a parallel machine.

Programs

Now I want to turn to programs and give a simple example. To make matters more concrete, I would like to talk about a program that would not really be inside a computer but is similar, is analogous to such a program. This is a program for making breakfast—a breakfast program for an American breakfast [see figure 12]. Two fried eggs and chilled orange juice. One approach, which would be called "bottom up," deals with the simple or primitive actions that must be carried out. It just describes in sequence all the things you have to do to make this breakfast. You get the orange, you squeeze the juice, you chill the juice, you get the two eggs, you get the pan, you crack the eggs, you fry the eggs, and then you serve the breakfast.

Now we're going to look at essentially the same program in a "top-down" version. In "top down" you start with the overall role. We want to serve breakfast. Within that, there is the notion of a server. What does the server do? Well, the server calls the chiller and the fryer. What do the chiller and the fryer do? The chiller can't do anything until he has the squeezed juice. The fryer can't do anything until he has the pan and the eggs, so the chiller calls the juicer and says, "Get me some juice." The fryer calls the cracker, the agent who will crack the eggs, and calls the pan, saying, "Bring me the pan." Now the pan is just a pan. It does not contain a process, so there's no need for anything more to be done there. We get the pan, but the juicer says, "I need an orange," and the cracker says, "Bring me two eggs." Once we have the eggs and the orange, then the juicer and the cracker can do their work, providing us with juice and two cracked eggs. Then the chiller and the fryer can do their work, and we will have two fried eggs and some chilled juice. Now, finally, the server can do his work, and we can eat our breakfast! That is top down.

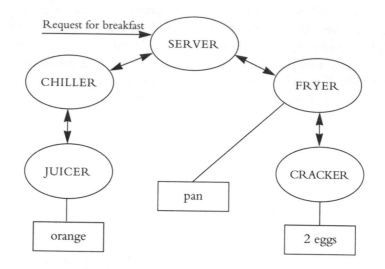

FIGURE 12

This top-down approach is a general programming strategy, but it also gives you an inkling of one basic strategy for creating artificial intelligence. When you have a complicated task like serving breakfast, you break it up into little simple actions. You have an agent that performs each of these actions. Now this really is how many computer scientists think of the mind, and something similar came out in Professor Rosch's talk yesterday—that inside our mind we may have thousands of agents that relate to each other in many different ways. One term that has been used for this is "society of mind." All these agents inside our mind are relating to each other, issuing requests and commands and so on, and everything is going on at once. The result is mind.

It is the software of the brain in a sense. Some people have said that this is not a society of mind, it's a bureaucracy of mind, because these agents only do one thing. If you ask them to do something else, they'll say, "No, it's not my job!"

What Is Intelligence?

Now let's turn to the question of intelligence. What requires intelligence? A very interesting thing has happened because of the computer and attempts to create intelligent machines. We have really had a complete revolution in the way we view intelligence. If twenty years ago you asked, "What is the essence of intelligence?" you probably would have received the response that it is logical reasoning. Playing chess, being able to do mathematical computations—these were seen as the signs of great intelligence. But having vision, understanding stories, common sense, even a child has these! This is not intelligence.

Now we try to program computers to do these things. Computers are good at logical reasoning and wonderful with mathematical computations. We have computers that play chess very well (I'll talk about that some more in a bit). When these things had been achieved, twenty or thirty years ago, many leading researchers came out with very optimistic predictions: "In a few years computers will be smarter than we are because we've already done the hard things. All that is left is the easy stuff, which even a child can do." Then they began to look at the easy stuff and discovered that it's not easy at all!

Let's consider vision. It's incredibly difficult to get a computer to see. You can hook a TV camera to the computer, but all you have is a field of little dots of color. That isn't seeing at all. If that were all we had, we would not be able to look at our world. When we see, we see people. I see Francisco Varela. I notice that he is different from the couch. Even though the top of him is purple and black and the bottom of him is gray and the gray is almost the same color as the couch, I know that the bottom of him that is gray is not part of the couch, but rather it's part of him! It's horribly difficult for a computer to take a scene from a TV camera and try to make sense of it. When the computer does manage to make sense of the scene, it takes a long time to do it. This is an area of very active research, but computer vision is still at a very primitive level. To see the world, we need to understand the world, and there is so much to understand.

Take the task of understanding stories. How does a child understand a story? A simple story about a dog and a boy and a girl. You read a story to a child and then you ask some questions. What happened? Why did the girl and the dog do this? Where did they go? It turns out to be terribly difficult to write a program that can understand the kind of story that a child understands. We're still not very good at it. Some progress has been made, many different approaches have been taken, but still our computers do not have the ability to understand the stories that a child understands. You can load into the computer a lot of information about dogs and children and play. But each piece of understanding seems to require further understanding, and the task is never done. The poor computer is, in a way, very isolated from the world.

ROBERT B. LIVINGSTON: It didn't have a mother.

GREENLEAF: It didn't have a mother, and it doesn't have a body—perhaps that's more important. A robot, you might say, has a body, but it's not at all like our body. We'll talk about a robot further on, but as for this poor computer here, the only way it can sense the world is through a keyboard. It's very, very limited in terms of its relation to the world. Researchers are trying all the time now to make machines that will sense the world more. But when they succeed, there is another problem. With the TV camera looking out and little sensors on the robot's arm, an enormous amount of data starts coming in. How can you deal with this data?

Or the robot may have a microphone that picks up sounds. Understanding speech is also something that computers are just awful at doing. This——computer——can——understand—— me——if——I—— talk——like——this. If I talk normally, running words together, the computer has no idea what I'm saying. It can't tell where one word ends and another begins.

What has happened here really is a total revolution, a turning upside down of our notion of intelligence. Now when we ask about intelligence, we think about the intelligence of a child. This is the key to intelligence. If only we could make a computer that was as smart as a five-year-old, that would be a tremendous achievement! So the word *intelligence* has acquired a completely upside-down meaning in relation to the meaning it used to have.

Four Strategies for Artificial-Intelligence Research

Here is a very rough list of different strategies that can be employed in artificial intelligence. One is *exhaustive search,* in which we don't try to imitate human intelligence, but rely on the strengths of the computer, on its speed and accuracy. We build its intelligence out of these strengths without worrying about how human beings are intelligent. The computer will think of so many things in such a short space of time that it will be intelligent. This is the approach used in making machines that play chess.

Another, very different approach is to imitate an expert, to create an *expert system*. For instance, since Your Holiness is an expert on the path to enlightenment, we computer scientists will come in and start asking you many questions in a very systematic fashion. We will write down rules for what one must do, in all circumstances, to become enlightened. We will make a huge system of rules, thousands and thousands of rules, and then this program will tell us how to get enlightened! That's a bit of a silly example, but this is really how it works for doctors, lawyers, and so on.

A third approach uses the *society of mind* view of how the mind works, which we heard from Professor Rosch. Think of the mind as a big box, and then inside it there must be smaller boxes, and inside of those there must be still smaller boxes. Each of these has its own special role. The breakfast example is like this. We have the server, the chiller, the cracker, the fryer, and so on. All of these relate to each other, but the mind, of course, is vastly more complex. It has thousands and thousands of agents relating to each other. So we build a program that has all these agents as little programs inside. Each agent is rather dumb, but if all the agents interact properly, the hope is (and it really is at the moment a hope and not much more) that intelligence will emerge.

Then, finally, a fourth approach is to say, "Who knows what's in the mind, but regarding the brain, there we have some real knowledge. We can see the neurons; we can see how they're connected. Maybe we can make an intelligent machine by imitating the brain."

While the four basic strategies for artificial intelligence (AI), are sometimes placed in opposition, a person working in an AI lab is not generally committed to a single strategy but uses whatever works best in a particular situation. A single program could combine elements of exhaustive search, of an expert system, of imitating the mind, of imitating the brain. Generally anything that will work is fair game, but nevertheless there are different trends.

A Game of Chess

Let me talk about the game of chess for a moment. Chess is played with sixteen pieces per side on a board with sixty-four squares. A great deal of effort has been put into making computers play chess. One of the first tasks taken up by AI researchers was to write a program that could play good chess. Now you could imagine a very simple way of doing this. The present position in the game is stored in the computer's memory. When it is the computer's turn to move, you can examine each of the possible moves that can be made. In a typical position there might be thirty legal moves. For each of these, the opponent could make roughly thirty different moves, and so on. These possibilities can be represented in a "game tree," which bears a faint resemblance to a real tree [see figure 13]. Trees in computer science always grow upside down so the branches are going down. The "root" is at the top and represents the current situation. Each box represents a position of the pieces on the board from which there will usually be about thirty different branches representing possible moves.

Now, in order to play good chess you would have to look quite far ahead. It's not enough just to look two or three moves ahead. This won't do at all. You have to look ten, maybe fifteen moves ahead. Well, unfortunately, the further ahead you look, the number of alternatives increases in a fashion we call "exponential." That is to say, there are thirty boxes on this level, and on the next level there will be thirty boxes coming out of each of the thirty boxes here, that is, thirty times thirty. On the level after that it will be thirty times thirty times thirty. Down ten levels you have thirty raised to the tenth power. This again is a staggeringly large number. Even a terribly fast computer is not going to be able to examine all these possibilities. Quantities that grow exponentially are inherently unmanageable.

By the way, I might mention that the idea of exponential "ex-

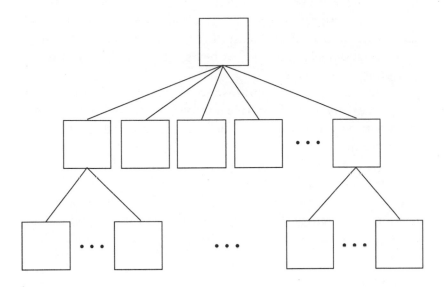

FIGURE 13. A representation of a small portion of a game tree for the game of chess. Each square represents a position on a board. From a typical position there will be about thirty possible moves. The tree illustrates the exponential explosion that is encountered when a program attempts to examine all possible moves to any depth.

plosion" is actually a very old one. There's an old story involving a chessboard and grains of rice: You put one grain of rice on the first square, two on the next square, and four on the next, each time doubling the number of grains of rice. Eight, sixteen, thirty-two, and so on, and finally you must put two to the 63rd power grains of rice on the last square. If we write this number in our usual notation, it is 9,223,372,036,854,775,808. Of course this is an impossibly large quantity of rice.

The "brute force" strategy for playing chess is to look at all possibilities for many levels. Since this strategy is prevented by an exponential explosion, it is necessary to "prune the tree." The program must decide which positions are not worth exploring further, so all such branches can be removed from the tree. This means that the program must be able to evaluate positions to see if they are promising. If enough branches are pruned off, your machine can look far ahead into the game and will be able to play very good chess. Much research has gone into developing strategies for pruning the tree so that machines can play good chess. Now I can go to a store, at least in America, and buy a little machine for about fifty dollars that beats me every time. I'm not a very good chess player.

Although the chess programs are now so good that they can beat almost anybody, they have not quite surpassed the top level of human performance. It has been speculated that part of the reason for this is that because of these programs, the human players have improved! The human players use the machine to analyze positions and to understand things they did not understand before. In any case, for whatever reason, we have yet to develop a program that comes close to beating the world champion even though it can beat 99.9 percent of the players in the world.

The Expert System

The next strategy I want to talk about is the strategy of the expert system. In the United States at least, this is where a great deal of money is being invested. Companies are starting up all over the place, trying to make expert systems. We have mentioned how these are used in medicine and law. A very active area in the use of expert systems is petroleum geology. How do you know where to drill to find oil? Nowadays you might ask an expert system. In all cases, basically the same strategy is used. People who are known as "knowledge engineers" interview an expert, or many experts. They have a technique for finding out just how an expert makes decisions. What would you do in this situation? What further information would you require, or how would you make your decision? They compile thousands and thousands of rules, and then they have a kind of program in which all these rules can then be used to imitate the expert.

I saw an amusing example when I visited China. It is a software system for Chinese medical therapy, an expert system for imitating an acupuncturist. Patients go in and discuss their symptoms with the computer. "What is wrong with you?" "I have a pain here in my hip." Then it would ask other questions, such as, "Do you ever feel hot?" I don't really know what kinds of questions would be appropriate to ask in this situation. But a knowledge engineer has worked with an acupuncturist, and this program will say where to insert the needles. I don't know much about acupuncture, but this program works well enough that they are proud of it and show it off.

Often many experts are interviewed, and when people talk about the advantages of expert systems, they point to this as one of the sources of power. The idea is that if you interview many, many experts, you have all of their knowledge, and your program will then be more powerful, will have more knowledge, than any individual human being could have. Of course, one of the problems is that the experts do not always agree, and then what do you do?

Another thing that can happen is that information can be put into the expert system directly from some kind of sensory piece of apparatus. For example, in a diagnostic program, information can be put in without the doctor actually having to provide the information. You can have a piece of apparatus that takes pulses, that senses how hearts are beating, or measures the electrical activity in the brain. This data can be fed directly into the computer and analyzed there, rather than having the intermediary of the doctor looking at the test data and then putting it in. In this way, a huge amount of information can go into the computer because it can come directly from monitor devices on the patient. There is tremendous potential here, and a great deal of research going on. By and large, such systems are still not used very much. Generally a doctor in America will not consult expert systems. There has actually been a lot of frustration coming from people who have tried to get doctors to use them. One thing that has been discovered is that doctors hate typing. Dr. Livingston seems to be an exception to this, but by and large, doctors will do anything to avoid having to sit down and type at a keyboard.

FRANCISCO J. VARELA: I think we need to make a clear distinction between a data base to which a doctor can go for information, and an AI project that attempts to capture the expertise of many doctors. The former is clearly useful. We don't really know about the latter. Is it as good as a doctor, or maybe even better? So maybe you can comment on how successful the AI projects have been as opposed to the more straightforward data bases?

GREENLEAF: If you are dealing with a specific disease, then

some of the expert systems apparently perform, on the whole, quite well. But if you simply have no idea what's wrong with a patient, then the expert system is pretty much at a loss and is likely to make very bad mistakes. In fact, in general, expert systems have proved somewhat of a disappointment, because the knowledge base that they're working with is always limited. As soon as something happens outside the data and the rules that have been specifically put in, the systems go wildly wrong. Whereas when we human beings make mistakes, we tend not to make such bad mistakes.

Similar situations occur when computers run industrial plants or fly airplanes. Maybe the computer does better as long as things go normally, but when an exceptional condition occurs, the computer can make worse mistakes than a human being ever would.

For a while there was a great deal of hope that expert systems would prove to be the dominant method in artificial intelligence. Now not many people believe that anymore. Some still do. Certainly expert systems have their uses, but other approaches are now by and large being favored in artificial intelligence.

The Society of Mind

Another approach, as mentioned, is the society-of-mind approach: to build a system in which there are lots and lots of what are generally called agents. These agents are just simple little computer programs that are connected to many other similar programs. The breakfast program we saw earlier is a good example of such a program on a very simple level. There are a bunch of agents in there: the server, the chiller, the fryer, the juicer, the cracker, the pan, the orange, and the eggs. Each of these has its very limited simple function; each is connected to others in a very specific way. When an outside input comes in and goes to the server and says, "Bring me breakfast," then the server calls the chiller and the fryer and so on as we saw before, and the result is a breakfast. The idea of the society-of-mind approach is that the whole mind is like this, that we have within our mind thousands of agents, each of which is connected to others in various ways, and that in our thinking this is really what we are. We are just a bunch of these agents hooked up together in various ways.

Yesterday the question was raised, Is there a self in there? Is there a sort of agent, "me," who is the boss of the whole thing? There's some debate on that in the computer world. Some people want to put in a big boss who runs everything, but on the whole I would say, most of the people who work in the society-of-mind approach to artificial intelligence take the stance that there is no central headquarters. There is no overall boss. There is no agent who I would say is me. I am the totality of the agents, perhaps, but nobody is running the show. The show simply goes on. When breakfast is being prepared, the server may be in charge, but later, for a different task, some other agent would take over. Sometimes agents cooperate, sometimes they fight. Sometimes they are in a struggle, and there will be another agent who will adjudicate the conflict, who will judge which agent should be followed, and so on. So you get a vast network of agents. This view seems to have some form of egolessness in it.

So far I don't know of any society-of-mind-type AI program that has been spectacularly successful. But many people are working on this approach. Will it someday produce intelligence? We don't know. This brings us to our fourth basic strategy for AI: imitating the brain rather than the mind. Workers in this area build networks of processors known as *neural nets,* which learn from experience. To illustrate, let me use the situation of breakfast again. Imagine a network with the server on one side and the orange and the eggs and the pans on the other side. If we ask the server for breakfast, this will activate the network. At the beginning the network is set up with amounts of activation assigned somewhat arbitrarily, so we should expect the breakfast to be a fiasco. Probably the eggs will go on the floor, the orange will go out the window, and the frying pan will hit you on the head. And you say, "No, no, that's terrible; do it differently." But first you describe exactly what should have happened, and the network will adjust the strengths of connections between the various processors to make a better outcome more likely. There are various systematic ways to do this. Next time maybe at least the orange gets squeezed, but then the juice gets poured on the floor, an egg gets cracked, the pan gets thrown out the window, and again you describe what should have happened and again the network is adjusted. Over time the network will be greatly changed, and if the process works, it will eventually produce a rather good breakfast.

Well, of course this is not a realistic example. Let me give you an example on which neural nets have actually been rather successful. A major question in artificial intelligence is, How can the computer recognize the letter *A*? If you make all of your *A*'s exactly the same—the same size, the same thickness, with the same orientation—then it's not too hard to write a program that will recognize that. But the problem is that we don't make our letter *A*'s all the same. Let us take a standard letter *A*. We can get the computer to recognize it, but then it looks at another one and sees that it is different. Well, that's not an *A*; it's different. Take another one. That's not an *A*; it's different. And so on, with any number of letter *A*'s. Yet a child, or probably even a pigeon, will be able to recognize all of these as a letter *A*. Pigeons are quite good at this. Computers are absolutely terrible! However, this is an area in which neural nets have proved to be quite successful. In this case the input would be a pattern that could be sensed with a video camera; for the output, the computer would have to ask, Is this an *A*, or a *B*, or a *C*, or a *D*, or none of the above, none of the letters? It is with this kind of thing that neural nets have recently had some fairly spectacular successes, which has made them the fashionable approach to artificial intelligence. Now when you pick up the popular magazines you no longer see articles on expert systems, you see articles on neural nets.

VARELA: An interesting example of a neural net is this: Suppose you want the computer to be able to take a book and read out loud, for example, for a blind person. While this has been very difficult until recently, neural net computers do it now. To start with, you show the machine the kinds of texts you want it to read, such as, for a blind child, children's stories. So the computer will start reading aloud like this [makes incoherent sounds]. What you do is act as a teacher to the machine. Every time it tries to say "the dog" and botches the job, you say, "No, no, no, no. It's "the dog." The way you teach is by forcing the right pattern into the machine, and that propagates inside the machine by some specific rules. It propagates back from the output. You do this over and over and over again. What is interesting—and this is reality, not science fiction—is that overnight the machine learns. The next day a new person comes into the room and the computer can read, "The-dog-is-going-with-the-boy." The machine can actually learn. This is now a product you can buy. You show the machine some kinds of text for a few hours, and then after that the machine can read.

You are forcing the machine to imitate you. You act as a tutor. It has to have a tutor. No tutor, no learning. The tutor can be effective in training the machine to read the story of the boy and dog, but once it has learned that, it can read any other story. It has actually learned how to do that kind of reading.

LIVINGSTON: Now there are also neural nets that will decipher speech. They are still fairly crude, but they are reasonably good. They can decipher the speech of a child or an adult or a person with a foreign accent reasonably well. Now there are also inexpensive programs for blind people to use. They can speak to the machine what they want to write. They know that it is going to make many mistakes. The machine will then read back what they have written, including commas, periods, and so forth. And if it encounters a name that it is not familiar with, it spells it. As the machine goes all the way through the text, the blind person makes corrections and changes the text as desired. So blind people are no longer dependent on a screen for word processing.

VARELA: The key thing here is the basis for learning, which is what the expert systems don't have. The expert systems have many rules, but that's all. A neural net is more like a living thing in that, if exposed to the proper environment, it learns.

B. ALAN WALLACE [interpreter]: The first one has an inflexible program, and the second one has a flexible program.

VARELA: Yes, right. Of course, it is not general, because this network will only learn how to read a limited kind of text. It won't know what to do if you make it read in mathematics. But it's fairly flexible and is a lot better than anything we ever had before.

DALAI LAMA: You mentioned this program that lets you teach the computer to read. Let us say it learns to read after five repetitions. Would other machines learn with the same number of repetitions?

VARELA: Basically, yes. All machines will learn in the same number of tries. It is a standard time that depends on the quality of the program for backward learning.

DALAI LAMA: But once they learn, they don't forget?

GREENLEAF: Oh, no.

ELEANOR ROSCH: In fact, one machine at Stanford, which was taught English by an American, was given French and read it with an American accent! [laughter]

Computers in Society

GREENLEAF: I've now covered the four strategies for making machines intelligent. Finally, I would like to leave this area and say a few more words about computers in a more general social context. Many important social issues are related to the use of computers. For example, President Ronald Reagan is a great believer in what has come to be known as "Star Wars," or the Strategic Defense Initiative. The idea is that we will put out into space a whole bunch of computer-controlled weapons that will protect us from the Russians. How will they do this? Well, as soon as the Russians start shooting their missiles at us, these weapons will register that fact and shoot the missiles down and protect us. We are spending a great amount of money on this project. This project is based on the belief that computers can be made as smart as we want them, that we can actually make computers that will go out in space and will know that one thing it senses is Russians shooting at us while another is a volcano or a meteor, or just a computer malfunction.

One problem with this idea is that computers almost never work right the first time! In fact, "debugging" is a word that we use a great deal. When you write a computer program, you expect it to do one thing and you run it and it does something else. Then you go and look at the program you wrote and look for "bugs," or mistakes, and correct them and run it again. After a while it runs correctly most of the time. Then you decide that there are not too many more bugs and start selling it. But in a large program, there will always be some bugs remaining. This is true even with something familiar like a word processor. The situation will be incomparably worse in situations in which we have very little experience, like sitting in outer space watching for a Russian missile. We have no way to remove the bugs from such a program. The only way we could do it is to ask the Russians to shoot a lot of missiles at us and see what happens. So the tremendous reliance on computers is totally misplaced here, and yet people still cling to their beliefs that we're going to be able to make these computers so smart that they will protect us.

We have great problems in our schools with teachers who are not good, in part because we pay our teachers very little. It has been said that we really do not need to get good teachers, because in a few years we can replace the teachers with machines, with computers, and these computers will do a wonderful job of teaching our children. One no longer hears much about this, but fifteen or twenty years ago we read all the time about the wonderful teaching machines that would take over our schools from the teachers. The faith that the computer would save us hindered our efforts to get good teachers.

We very often encounter in society the belief that the computer can save us, and generally this is a misplaced belief. The computer can be a tremendous servant, a tremendous tool. When we use the computer to help us, then it is fine, but when we think it is going to be able to save us, then we make a terrible mistake. There's a great danger in relying too much on computers.

DALAI LAMA: Very nicely said.

Consciousness, Gross and Subtle

A Conversation

On Artificial Minds

DALAI LAMA: What is the basis of the computer scientists' certainty that computers will sometime in the future be smarter than human beings?

NEWCOMB GREENLEAF: Well, I would say there are perhaps two bases. One is what I would call scientific arrogance. [laughter] It's the notion that science can do anything (and this is a deeply held belief in the West), that science will eventually solve any problem. So we have the idea that making the computer smart is a scientific problem, and eventually science will solve it! It's as simple as that. I think another source of this belief, though, is in our popular culture—science fiction. I don't know if Your Holiness saw the movie *Star Wars*. In this movie there were two robots, R2-D2 and C3-PO. They were wonderful characters! And they had personalities. They were smart, they were lovable, and yet they were machines. A whole generation of people saw this movie when they were children, so they take it for granted that this is reality.

DALAI LAMA: So actually there is no sound basis for that kind of optimism?

GREENLEAF: Some things have been achieved, and I have talked a little about some of the achievements, but by and large the field has been characterized by very optimistic predictions that have turned out to be wildly wrong! People predicted ten or twenty years ago that in ten years computers would be smarter than we are. People have now learned some from experience. They don't make these predictions, at least in public, quite so often anymore. [laughter]

JEREMY W. HAYWARD: What argument does the best and most convinced AI expert give for the belief?

GREENLEAF: What they usually say is not exactly an argument for their belief, but a sort of pragmatic thing. They say, "We're trying to do this. Now if we didn't believe we could do it, we would get discouraged and quit! So you people who are saying we probably can't do it are pessimists. We are the optimists; otherwise we would just be depressed!" [laughter]

DALAI LAMA: That's right.

HAYWARD: I think an important part is the argument of reductionism. Because the mind can be reduced to the brain, the brain can be reduced to biology, biology to chemistry, chemistry to physics, and physics is mechanical, therefore anything that the mind can do can be done by machine. Therefore some kind of computer should be able to think.

GREENLEAF: Good point, yes. I think that would be very much the argument that, after all, what is happening in there must be computation; what else could it be? It must ultimately be physical things acting in accordance with laws, and all you have to do is find the laws and you'll be able to have an intelligent machine.

FRANCISCO J. VARELA: As a matter of fact, there's a famous quote from one of the founders of AI, who said that the brain is just a computer made out of meat.

GREENLEAF: Yes, and that argument is actually carried further. Surely what is important about the brain cannot be that it is made out of carbon and oxygen and hydrogen and so on. What is really important about the brain can only be its structure, its logical structure—how the neurons are connected and how they fire. So if we can imitate that in the computer, then it doesn't matter that it's not made out of meat. If we can imitate that, then we will be imitating the brain, and since the mind is just the brain, we will have the mind.

VARELA: Which is like the current belief of neuroscientists that for every behavior, there is a circuit of neurons that explains why that behavior arises.

ELEANOR ROSCH: One of the first psychologists to represent the knowledge in long-term memory in the present kind of format said that any engineer could design the human back better than it is designed by nature (many people have back trouble), and therefore surely a computer scientist can design a better mind.

GREENLEAF: That is definitely scientific arrogance at its most blatant.

DALAI LAMA: The person who initially makes the program for playing chess needs to know how to play chess, of course.

VARELA: But does the person have to be a good player?

GREENLEAF: Probably a good player, but not a world-class player.

DALAI LAMA: So if you could have a mediocre chess player who makes a program for the computer, and the computer could come around and beat the mediocre player and much better people, doesn't this suggest somehow that the computer is thinking? Does it or does it not, that's the question.

GREENLEAF: Well, what the computer is doing is looking at this game tree, and every second it evaluates thousands of positions. Is that thinking? This is not the way human beings play chess. Because we do not have the ability to look at hundreds of thousands of positions in a very short time, human beings play chess very differently. Actually we don't understand how the great chess players play chess. They seem to perceive the board as alive with potential, to perceive it in almost a yogic fashion. But when you are actually playing against the machine, it seems almost inevitable that you will perceive it as thinking, even if you know better.

VARELA: But what is interesting is that His Holiness' question is exactly the point of view of a computer scientist: "If we can make a computer beat somebody, if it can become better, it means that we're getting somewhere, that we're providing the machine with something like—

DALAI LAMA: If you have a certain program and you ask questions within that program, it can give an answer. If you ask questions outside the program, then probably it can't answer. I'm wondering whether there is a parallel here: If a mediocre chess player writes a program, you can expect the program to respond within the capacity of the mediocre player. But what if the computer can come back with answers, in other words, chess moves that are beyond the programmer's level? This seems to be very interesting. It raises issues.

GREENLEAF: It *is* very interesting. The reason the program can do better than the programmer is because the computer can examine hundreds of thousands, maybe even millions, of different positions in a relatively short time. The programmer can't do that even though he knows what he would do if he could.

THUBTEN JINPA [interpreter]: What do you actually program? The moves of the chess pieces, that's all? That the knight goes this way and so on?

GREENLEAF: Yes, and eventually the machine makes a decision. It goes through this tree.

DALAI LAMA: It's like a calculator? You just press a number and then put the sign of multiplication?

GREENLEAF: That's right. You make your move and type it into the computer: "Pawn to king four," or something like that. You also tell the machine that it has a certain time, say ten seconds, to make its move. On that basis it will look down the game tree as far as it can in that amount of time, pruning as it goes, and then it will make a decision on what is the best move, based on its evaluation of the hundreds of thousands or millions of positions that are examined.

I might mention another game, the Chinese game of *go,* which is now played mostly in Japan. I don't know if Your Holiness is familiar with it. It is a game on a much larger board, using little black and white stones. A large amount of effort has been put into making a machine that will play *go,* and so far the best programs play a very mediocre game. *Go* is a much more difficult game for a computer to play than chess. This is partly because there are so many more possibilities in *go* but also because the patterns that an expert *go* player senses are much more subtle. *Go,* in a way, is more like a dance, whereas chess is more like a battle. The essence of a good *go* player is very hard for a computer to capture.

ROBERT B. LIVINGSTON: Newcomb, isn't it also true that

in chess there are very explicit rules, and quite a number of them? In *go,* there are perhaps fewer rules but many more potentialities in the field. The computer does best when there are very rigid and comprehensive rules. For example, in real life we have some rules, but they're fairly loose, and people change the rules as they go along, and so it's an unpredictable game.

VARELA: It's probably true for the same reason that computers are good at mathematical computations but very bad at vision.

Could Computers Have Consciousness?

VARELA: So, Your Holiness, at least for Westerners, it seems convincing that artificial devices can perform some cognitive acts, like learning how to read or how to pick things up, which is the reason we wanted you to hear a presentation on artificial intelligence. It is extremely important to know that in the West, when trying to understand mind and the brain, people use the results of artificial intelligence research as confirmation of their theories. In physics in the past it used to be that if I had a theory, I could prove it if I could predict something. In cognitive science, more and more, the convincing argument is that if you think you're right, you should be able to build a machine that bears out your theory. Say, for example, if I think I know how movement works, then I should be able to construct a machine that moves. It's a different sort of argument; and this field of artificial intelligence is being used as a way of proving or validating what we say about mind. The question I have for you is, What would you say is the status of these machines with these little bits of cognitive capacity? Is there any kind of mind there? Is there any kind of real perception there? How would you go about comparing it to ordinary human mind, or any animal mind for that matter?

DALAI LAMA: We can't say it has a consciousness or cognition, I think, because the concept cognition has to be based on a continuum of cognition from the previous moment; it is not something derived from matter. So, for example, as in the previous discussion, if there is no reference to any subtle or extremely subtle consciousness, then there's no question of a gross consciousness arising from within the absence of subtle consciousness. I was thinking whether certain physical substances, as a result of some kind of interaction, can have a relative level of cognitive feeling—not actual cognition, but some facsimile of it. I'm really not able to clearly decide what is the case.

In our tradition, in some cases the power of mantra can create situations where things act as though they have cognition. Or there are certain types of wheels with certain mantras on them that you use for black magic, where certain kinds of artificial animals—like a frog or scorpion—act as if they are real animals. When you cut their bodies you see the mantra wheel inside. The question is, Is this a real sentient being, or not? I don't know; it seems only a facsimile of a sentient being; it does not have the subjective cognitive powers.

VARELA: How could one go about deciding that question, Your Holiness?

DALAI LAMA: It's very difficult. I can't decide. There's a certain plant, a small form of flower that catches flies. Whether this plant has real cognition or not, personally I can't decide. In the traditional texts, there are mentions of different types of hell-realm beings in the form of plants, things like that. Therefore I can't decide.

VARELA: The argument in scientific circles is that if ever we have a machine that can imitate the human being to the extent that it can fool you, that is, could sit here and talk with you and drink water and so on in such a way that you couldn't tell it was not a human being (not because of its skin and appearance but because of the way it interacts with you), then that would be convincing proof that we have synthesized mind. This is actually known as the Alan Turing test, a criterion for deciding when the AI enterprise has been successful.

GREENLEAF: There are several things wrong with that view. For one, we are terribly easy to fool. There is a famous example of a very simple computer program that carried on a conversation with people while imitating what is known as a nondirective psychotherapist. This is a very simple program, though doubtless intelligent. It would say to me: "What is your problem, New-comb?" Then I would say, "I feel very angry today," and the machine would say, "Why do you say you feel angry?" and so on. It had very simple strategies for making responses. People would relate to this machine, and soon they would be telling it secrets that they had never told anybody!

DALAI LAMA: In terms of the actual substance of which computers are made, are they simply metal, plastic, circuits, and so forth?

VARELA: Yes, but this again brings up the idea of the pattern, not the substance but the pattern.

DALAI LAMA: It is very difficult to say that it's not a living being, that it doesn't have cognition, even from the Buddhist point of view. We maintain that there are certain types of births in which a preceding continuum of consciousness is the basis. The consciousness doesn't actually arise from the matter, but a continuum of consciousness might conceivably come into it.

HAYWARD: Does Your Holiness regard it as a definite criterion that there must be continuity with some prior consciousness? That whenever there is a cognition, there must have been a stream of cognition going back to beginningless time?

DALAI LAMA: There is no possibility for a new cognition, which has no relationship to a previous continuum, to arise at all. I can't totally rule out the possibility that, if all the external conditions and the karmic action were there, a stream of consciousness might actually enter into a computer.

HAYWARD: A stream of consciousness?

DALAI LAMA: Yes, that's right. [His Holiness laughs.] There is a possibility that a scientist who is very much involved his whole life [with computers], then the next life . . . [he would be reborn in a computer], same process! [laughter] Then this machine which is half-human and half-machine has been reincarnated.

VARELA: You wouldn't rule that out then? You wouldn't say that is impossible?

DALAI LAMA: We can't rule it out.

ROSCH: So if there's a great yogi who is dying and he is stand-ing in front of the best computer there is, could he project his subtle consciousness into the computer?*

DALAI LAMA: If the physical basis of the computer acquires the potential or the ability to serve as a basis for a continuum of consciousness. I feel this question about computers will be re-solved only by time. We just have to wait and see until it actually happens.

The Origin of Consciousness

HAYWARD: But may I ask, still on this stream of conscious-ness, What is the refutation of the appearance of a new moment of consciousness?

DALAI LAMA: Then there would be a beginning to a contin-uum of the consciousness.

HAYWARD: Why could there not be one?

DALAI LAMA: In general, of course, we speak of the universe as being without beginning. Between the two positions, that things arose without any particular cause at all and that con-sciousness has beginningless continuity, although the latter one may not solve each and every question, it definitely has fewer log-ical inconsistencies than the former.

HAYWARD: Well, the scientists take the view that conscious-ness arises from a material cause.

DALAI LAMA: Buddhists cannot accept this. You have to di-vide the cause into two: the main or substantial cause and the cooperative cause. Matter can only be a cooperative cause, never the main or substantial cause for consciousness. This is very much related to cosmology. According to the Buddhist view of evolution, there is an infinite universe. In Buddhist cosmology, any world system will go through phases. Sometimes it is de-stroyed, sometimes it arises, sometimes there will be gross mat-

---

*In the tantric Buddhist tradition of Tibet, it is regarded as possible for an accomplished practitioner to transfer his consciousness into the body of an animal that has just died if the body remains essentially intact.

ter, sometimes no gross matter, but really there is no beginning or end to it. And there is always subtle consciousness.

So what is a sentient being? A sentient being is an entity designated upon the basis of a body and mind, and fundamentally what is referred to by the mind here is the extremely subtle mind.

HAYWARD: Which is continuous through all the cycles?

DALAI LAMA: This is correct.

Same Body, Different Person

LIVINGSTON: I'd like to ask you two questions. The first concerns transplanting a heart, and the other, transplanting a brain. The first one is realizable, and the other is absolutely theoretical; I would like your answer to both questions. Suppose one of your colleagues had a very bad heart attack and you were told that he could have his heart replaced with another heart. This can and is being done medically now, and it could be done here. If the transplant were done, would the individual be the same after the heart transplant?

DALAI LAMA: Yes. One point that might be interesting to take into account is that in the Buddhist system we have the theory of the indestructible drop (*thigle*), which is said to be at the place of the heart.* Now this heart should not be identified with the physical heart that we normally speak of in medical terms, but "heart" here has a different connotation. Sometimes "heart" is used to mean a central place. It should be taken here in that sense. In this case, if you take out the organ of the heart, then there's no complication. If you identify what's spoken of as the heart in Buddhism with the organic heart, then there is a big problem in changing it, that is, in doing a transplant. So it's clear that I prefer the interpretation in which nothing of really profound significance happens to the individual by removing this organ or replacing it with another.

LIVINGSTON: Yes. So as long as the thing is physiologically successful, it is the same individual?

---

*See pages 78–79.

DALAI LAMA: Yes.

HAYWARD: May I clarify that? Is that because from Your Holiness' point of view the real heart, the indestructible drop, is not changed? The physical heart is changed, but the essence is not changed?

DALAI LAMA: That's correct. The indestructible drop may not be transferred. But then there is another type of practice in which a complete change in the body takes place. It's like a resurrection in another body. There's a transference of consciousness into a newly dead body that has not decayed yet. In Tantric practice, this does happen. In this case, there is a total change of the body, the physical body. Both of these two bodies are said to be totally different, but the life span of the person is said to be one. It's very mystical, but imagine a person, a Tantric practitioner who actually transfers his consciousness to a fresh corpse. His previous body is dead; it has left and is finished. Now he has entered the new body. So in this case, you see, he has a completely new body but it's the same life, the same person.

LIVINGSTON: You are answering the brain question already! You are saying that if you transplant the brain, it is equivalent to a body transplant, right? In other words, say, your brain troubles you and you need a new brain and you get a brain, still in good shape, from a dead body (I mean the person technically died from other causes but the brain is intact), and you transplant it. If it were possible, then it would be, in effect, the individual's brain that would be continuous. So it is as if this brain has a new body.*

VARELA: Your Holiness, before you said that the continuity of the self is based on memories, which are supposed to be brain phenomena. We have changed the brain now, so there is no memory; how can the person be the same? I'm just referring to something that was said before, the continuity of the self.

---

*It appears that Dr. Livingston assumed that consciousness is equivalent to brain, so that when His Holiness spoke of the Tantric practice of transferring consciousness, this meant there is a brain transplant. His Holiness in fact appears to have meant that consciousness is transferred by meditative practices to an entirely new body (with, of course, its own brain.) This is clarified in the following discussion.

DALAI LAMA: The meditator who through a Tantric technique transfers his consciousness into a dead body hasn't actualized the clear light state of death. This means he has not gone through the process of death. Because of this, he is able to retain the entire knowledge that he has gathered during his lifetime. Memory is definitely not brain; it's really different.

But here we are dealing with a mere hypothesis from the Buddhist point of view. So it has to be experimented with; what could happen has to be checked! [laughter] But we would say that since we transplanted the brain in order to save that person, we can say that it is his brain after the transplant.

LIVINGSTON: But I'm still not clear. I think I hear what you're saying, but I want to be absolutely clear. Who is where?

DALAI LAMA: If you transplant B's brain into A's body, then that brain actually now belongs to the A person. Although this brain didn't belong to him previously, after the operation we would say that it belongs to the A person, the one who's receiving the transplant.

B. ALAN WALLACE [interpreter]: So this really is different from Western neurobiology.

LIVINGSTON: I'm not dismayed and I'm not disappointed, I'm thrilled. [laughter] I think it's very important, because even though it's hypothetical, it tells me something about where you think the self exists in the final sense!

DALAI LAMA: During conception, even the physical substance on which that self is conventionally based—the egg and sperm—belongs to someone else—the parents—still you can say that it belongs to that self also. The body comes from someone else, but as soon as the consciousness enters in, it's that new person's body, embryo, fetus, or whatever you want to call it, even though prior to that it wasn't. So I find a parallel here in that the physical constituents of the embryo come from two different people, that is, obviously, the parents, but as soon as the consciousness enters into the mixed cell, that cell now belongs to that consciousness. But there is a very easy way to resolve this whole question: we will have to wait until such a transplant takes place! [laughter]

Levels of Consciousness

LIVINGSTON: May I ask a little bit more? We talk about A as a person who receives the brain, right? For a moment, let's talk about B, who donates the brain. Where are his experiences; where are his memories while he's alive?

DALAI LAMA: The Buddhist view is that when all this knowledge is stored, it is stored in the form of some kind of imprint. Only when the imprints are activated and result in actions does this work via the brain. Therefore, since human beings employ consciousness through the brain, because the consciousness is filtered through the human brain, then it is human mental activity, but the consciousness itself is not [human].

HAYWARD: Then what is the imprint imprinted on?

DALAI LAMA: If you take the Prasangika position, it would be the mere I, whereas if you're from one of the more basic schools like the Yogachara, then the imprint is established on the stream of consciousness, mental consciousness, not the brain.

The best explanation is from the point of view of the highest yoga tantra.* Here we divide consciousness into three levels: gross, subtle, and very subtle. As we discussed earlier, the grosser the levels of mind, the more they are dependent on the body. The subtler they are, the less dependent they are, and the very subtle consciousness is independent of the body. We have this very subtle consciousness that is called clear light, clear-light mind. The grosser levels of mind that arise through the interaction with brains, neurons, sense organs, do so because we have this source that is the very subtle consciousness. So there is a great distinction in that in Buddhism the gross levels of consciousness are emergent properties of the subtle clear light, whereas for you people, for science, it normally emerges out of the brain. Just as all the grosser levels of mind arose from the very subtle consciousness, they would also eventually dissolve into the very subtle consciousness. So it's like the source of all the grosser levels of mind.

Therefore we can say that the storehouse in the consciousness

_____

*See note, page 81.

on which all the imprints are made would be the very subtle consciousness, this clear-light mind. It retains stored memories.

LIVINGSTON: The clear-light mind stays in body A that receives the brain from B. Is that right?

B. ALAN WALLACE [interpreter]: That would be right. Whereas in the case that His Holiness gave before of a person transferring his consciousness into a fresh corpse, this clear-light consciousness is what's being transferred, and that's why you say the same person has gone into the other body. Even though the brain is different, it's this continuum of the subtle clear light, or the very subtle mind, that has been transferred; therefore you say the person has gone over.

HAYWARD: What you would call the clear-light mind, subtle consciousness? Is this the *kun zhi?**

DALAI LAMA: Although in certain tantric texts it's called *kun zhi,* it is very different from the Yogachara explanation. The Sanskrit term is *alaya vijñana.* This is sometimes related to the very subtle clear-light mind, but it's a different concept. The difference is that the Yogachara *alaya vijñana* is separate from the sixth mental consciousness because they have eight categories of mind, whereas the tantric system has six mental consciousnesses. You have five consciousnesses that are sensory, and the sixth is included in mental consciousness. Subtle consciousness is included in this sixth one but is not identical with it. Another difference is

---

*The *kun zhi* (*kun gzhi*), or *alaya vijñana* in Sanskrit, is the eighth, or "foundation consciousness," in the Yogachara system of eight consciousnesses. It is often referred to as the "storehouse consciousness," because according to the Yogachara school, traces of previous karmic action remain imprinted there and become seeds of future actions. The seventh consciousness (Skt., *manas;* Tib., *nyon yid*) is the cloudy mind that instigates subjectivity or self-consciousness. It carries an embryonic sense of duality between subject and object. The other six are regarded as sense-consciousness. Five are the consciousnesses related to the usual five senses. The sixth consciousness (Skt., *mano-vijñana;* Tib., *yid*) is the aspect of mind that coordinates the data of the sense-consciousnesses so that, for example, the smell, shape, and color of an apple are all related to the same object. His Holiness the Dalai Lama refers to this system in the next paragraph but then explains tantric variations on it.

that according to the Yogacharins, the fundamental storehouse consciousness is always [ethically] neutral.

It's also very important to know that this term *clear light, ösel* ['od gsal] in Tibetan, has been used in many different contexts. In the Sutras it refers to emptiness, the ultimate nature of the mind. In the *Uttaratantra* text, this term has been used to describe the luminous nature of the knowing activity of all minds; and in tantric practice it means the very subtle consciousness.*

So, there are three levels of mind: the gross, the subtle, and the very subtle. The very subtle level is clear light. The subtle levels of mind refer to what you experience after the experience of clear light when you go through the dissolution process in dying.

How do we distinguish between these three levels of mind? The gross level of mind is the sensory perceptions. The subtle level refers to what the texts technically call the "eighty indicative conceptions." This is difficult to explain. The first class of them is indicative of an aspect of the experience of the dissolution process that happens at the time of death; it also includes negative emotions like desire, hatred, and so forth, that is, the kleshas. The six root kleshas (the six root mental distortions) are included in this second category, the subtle mind. Among these eighty indicative conceptions, there are thirty-three that indicate the nature of the white appearance, a stage in the dissolution process of dying, and forty conceptions that indicate the nature of the red increase, which is the second stage of dissolution. So there was a certain vision or appearance and now it increases. Then there are seven for the third stage, which is called the deadly attainment, or black near-attainment. It's called near-attainment because it approaches the actual experience of the clear light.

HAYWARD: May I clarify one point? You're describing these in terms of the process of death but they are nevertheless all the time present?

DALAI LAMA: Yes. In these four stages of dissolution, the early ones are grosser compared to the later ones. Therefore,

---

*The *Uttaratantra,* despite its name, is not a tantric text but a Mahayana treatise on buddha-nature, the awakened state of mind that is said to be the basic nature of all sentient beings.

when these different emotions, the eighty conceptions, arise, indicative of the four stages of dissolution that are to come, they also differ in that the grosser require more movement or energy. Just as there is a difference in subtlety at the time of the dissolution process, there is also a difference in energy, which is the mount or vehicle of the consciousness of the eighty conceptions. Gross ones such as a strong desire for something or strong aversion to something, those that require very forceful emotion on your part, are associated with the first two stages of the white and red. And those that are neutral are associated with the third stage, the black near-attainment. So there are these three stages of dissolution: white appearance, red increase, black near-attainment. And then the final clear light is the fourth stage. Another way of referring to these four stages of dissolution is as empty, very empty, greatly empty, and completely empty. The meaning of "empty" here is that each level is empty of the grosser levels of the preceding experience. These four stages comprise the process of dissolution that takes place after dissolution of the physical elements—earth, water, fire, and air.*

So before you go through the first stage of subtle dissolution, white appearance, the karmic links between your physical body and the gross levels of mind have already been severed. Your physical body can no longer function as the basis for your gross levels of mind. So, clinically speaking, the person is dead at the point when air dissolves into consciousness, just before the white appearance. Until then, although the karmic link between the body and the mind has been severed, the self of the person is still within that old body.

The body may not decompose when the person is in the clear light. Some people can remain in that stage for a week, or some, twenty-two days. This has actually happened in India. For example, the late Kyabje Ling Rinpoche, my tutor, remained for

---

*According to the Buddhist tantric tradition of Tibet, everything is composed of the elements of earth, water, fire, air, and space. At the time of death, the elemental basis of life in a physical body dissolves as follows: earth dissolves into water, water into fire, fire into air, and air into space, or consciousness.

thirteen days in the state of clear light. His body remained very fresh. This consciousness, the very subtle consciousness, is the self or consciousness and carries on into the next life. Consciousness is already completely independent of the body. Therefore, it can move.

VARELA: Where is the memory of that consciousness, Your Holiness?

DALAI LAMA: Memories that are based on a grosser level of mind, and therefore body, are already gone. But the more subtle memory is retained. More subtle memory that is related with more subtle consciousness carries on. Certain meditators, through the power of their meditation, are able to bring the grosser levels of mind down to a more subtle, deeper level. They are able to activate the subtle level. Then they begin to have a more heightened awareness in which they can see events of their past life. This shows that if one is able to bring one's level of mind to a subtle state, one is able to link this life with the past and the future.

This explanation has been based on the system of the highest yoga tantra. I have encountered many meditators, all of whom are tantric practitioners, so this explanation is given on that basis. But there are others who give an explanation from a Sutrayana point of view,* who without undertaking any tantric practices are able to attain a heightened awareness through which they are able to experience events in their past lives or have precognition. This is done on the basis of the sixth mental consciousness, of the grosser levels of mind. How is this possible? I can't explain it clearly. I don't know.

LIVINGSTON: Maybe I could ask you, Do you think it is possible that I could have a clear-light mind?

DALAI LAMA: According to Buddha, in tantric explanation, every person, every living being can have the experience of clear light at the time of death, naturally, but this experience could be brought about through meditative techniques as well.

LIVINGSTON: Now let's go back to A and B. I believe that A

---

*See note on page 42.

needed a brain because his brain was damaged and B had a brain that he couldn't use in the long range because his body was damaged. Imagine that we do the transplant and it is successful. The connections go and this person lives and becomes active and may be able to meditate and do other things. If I understand you correctly, the self is the one who received the brain, A. Now if for the moment we talk about B, who had clear-light potential at least, what became of his clear-light potential when the brain was transferred to A?

DALAI LAMA: One point you have to consider is that how long the person remains in the clear light of death is partly determined by what kind of condition he had at the time of death. For example, if someone has an accidental cause of death, the processes of dissolution take place very quickly, in split seconds, just as in that experiment with the flashing letters the mind worked in split seconds. But if the person undergoes a natural death, the clear-light experience could be long. So if the person donating the brain is not dead when the operation is taking place, he could have the experience of clear light as well, for example, if his breathing processes have just stopped but his body still hasn't decayed. One point to remember is that the experience of clear light takes place in the heart, not in the head.

Dualism, Subtler and Grosser Bodies

VARELA: How do the subtle levels and the grosser levels communicate? You said that the subtle level's continuum could enter into a body. That seems to me not to be very explicit. How would that happen? To a Westerner it sounds like dualism: there is body and something comes from outside and enters it. It doesn't sound very satisfactory.

DALAI LAMA: You have to understand that the very subtle mind is not isolated from body because there is a very subtle body conjoined with the wind [*prana*].

VARELA: How does that body relate to gross body?

DALAI LAMA: They are of one nature. From the point of view of its function, it is called very subtle wind, energy, while from the point of view of its measure of clarity, it is called very subtle mind. Before this very subtle mind enters into conception, we already have a subtle body of the intermediate state, the bardo.* It's called subtle compared to the gross body of right now, the current way we are alive. You may call it subtle compared to this, but there is a body. This body is a complete being, a complete form; it has its own speech, its own form—everything is there. And it also goes through a death process. The moment this very subtle mind enters the next body is the point at which the physical aggregate of the previous being, the bardo being, also ceases. The death of the bardo being is simultaneous with conception as a human being. There is also an experience of the clear light at that point, and this clear-light experience is called the clear light of the reversal process. From the clear light you have the subtle mind of the black near-attainment, then the red increase, then the white appearance. Then everything becomes grosser, grosser, grosser until birth.

HAYWARD: So is it the exact reversal of the process of death you discussed before?

DALAI LAMA: Yes, just the reversal.

JINPA: A major author of Tibetan textbooks at one of the monasteries, Drepung Monastery, says that there are two levels of person, a subtle person and a gross person. Based on the very subtle body and mind, there is a subtle person, and based on the gross levels of body and mind, there is a gross person. Then the question arises, If that is the case, are these two different persons? He answers no, because when the gross levels of minds are active, the subtle levels of mind don't function. They stay in a latent state. When the very subtle levels of mind and wind, energy, are active, then the gross levels of mind and energies remain latent. Therefore, there are not two persons and there is no discontinuity. Another interpretation is that this very subtle mind and body

---

*According to the Tibetan Buddhist tradition, there are six intermediate states, or bardos, one of which is between death and rebirth. The very subtle mind wanders in this bardo, undergoing various experiences, conjoined with a bardo body that is also subtle in nature. Being insubstantial, it can fly, pass through walls, and so on.

is continuous, always functioning. It is always there whether the person is having an active experience of gross levels of mind or not. So there are two ways of understanding this; it's very difficult.

DALAI LAMA: So for us, these phenomena might belong to the third category that is very concealed. If you don't accept the theory of reincarnation, then there are many things in the world that you can't logically explain. They have to be regarded simply as miscellaneous accidental events. If you say things just arise without any particular cause, then there isn't any reason why anything couldn't arise out of anything.

VARELA: On the other hand, in what you just said it is very important to me that these are very subtle phenomena and that therefore the connection between the grosser and the subtle levels is very difficult to ascertain. This is why for the Western ear it sounds like dualism, like mind and matter, separate forever, but in fact that is not really necessary.

DALAI LAMA: On this point, it might be quite interesting to note that according to the Kalachakra text there are discriminations of different levels of elements. There are the five external elements and the five internal elements; and within the five internal ones, there are two levels, a gross level and a subtle level. Then the text speaks of a very subtle wind that is technically called "life-supporting wind," which has the nature of five colors, five colored light rays that are of the nature of the five elements. The fundamental source of all the elements is this very subtle energy that is of the nature of the five elements. This produces the subtle levels of energy, subtle levels of elements within the body, which in turn causes the grosser levels to arise. These in turn have relations with the external elements.

HAYWARD: So each arises from the other? The very subtle, of course, is the clear light. This is continually present, and out of that at birth arises the subtle consciousness, and out of that arises material, sensory consciousness?

DALAI LAMA: That's right.

VARELA: In fact if one examines closely, it's like there are many, many subdivisions. It's like a continuum going from gross, to less gross, to slightly less gross.

DALAI LAMA: Yes.

HAYWARD: So you could you say that all of these levels of consciousness, gross, subtle, are all contained within clear-light consciousness like a seed within—?

DALAI LAMA: Yes, imprints in the form of a seed. A text of the Sakya tradition* speaks of this very subtle mind, which is the mind of clear light containing all the resultant qualities of Buddhahood in potential form and all the characteristics or realizations of the path as qualities and all the characteristics of ordinary levels of cyclic existence in the form of characteristics.

This explanation of the external elements has been spoken of in relation to individual beings, but then we have this environment that we all perceive in common. This could be looked at as the environmental effects of karma, the common effects that we experience together. There are two types of karma. One is very individual and the other one has fruits that can be experienced in common, as collective karma. When the second type of karma comes to fruition, it is not only in our own being but also in the environment that we all experience.

---

*There are four major traditions of Tibetan Buddhism. In order of age, these are Nyingma, Sakya, Kagyu, and Gelug.

Development of the Human Brain

ROBERT B. LIVINGSTON

Evolutionary Importance of Cooperation

There are two aspects to human brain development that I hope to elucidate. The first relates to that marvelous moment in evolution when the human brain underwent a spectacular, almost explosive expansion—when we emerged as a species in the Western way of thinking about these things. The second aspect relates to the spectacular development of the human brain in the individual from embryogenesis through early childhood.

In utero, the developing brain is the largest, most rapidly growing organ. It constitutes the greatest obstacle to safe childbirth. After birth, the brain doubles in volume in six months and doubles again by the fourth birthday. These evolutionary and developmental processes constitute our greatest human legacy. They are perhaps the most remarkable phenomena in the history of life on earth.

It is easy to understand how a bigger brain with more neurons and more opportunities for decision making, for thinking things through more completely, for greater mindfulness, could provide evolutionarily selective advantages for faith, mutual trust, cooperation, and altruism, as well as for territoriality, distrust, competitiveness, and combativeness.

My impression is that evolution has been misrepresented in the West by exaggerating the selective advantages of competitiveness and combativeness. Evolutionary and developmental evidence clearly indicates that most organisms, of whatever complexity, even single-celled organisms, cannot thrive and may not even survive without participating in cooperative behaviors with other forms of life. We have tended to downplay cooperation as contributing to evolutionary development while tending to exaggerate the role of conflict. Perhaps conflict is more dramatic and memorable.

DALAI LAMA: Is there some relationship here with the notion of struggle in the Marxist sense?

ROBERT B. LIVINGSTON: Yes, yes, I want to speak about this. Franco-American cultural historian Jacques Barzun wrote a book suggesting that predominant public attitudes in the West have been deformed by misinterpretations and misemphases related to the writings of Darwin, Marx, and Freud. And many other social commentators have said this too. Barzun's thesis is that the lessons we have drawn from Darwin have greatly exaggerated competition and conflict. Darwin himself did not use the phrase "survival of the fittest." Those are the words of Herbert Spencer, who was not a scientist. Rather, Darwin consistently expressed a balanced view of the relative importance of interdependence and cooperation among species as compared to aggression and competition. Overemphasis on the Spencerian way of thinking has led to widespread assumptions that evolutionary selection depends predominantly on interspecies competition, conflict, and conquest.

It is helpful to reflect on how much evolution can inform us about cooperation and to recognize how overemphasis on competition can misguide our assumptions. Here is my own favorite example: The lupine, a blue wildflower common in alpine meadows, is often found on mountain slopes where few or no other alpine flowers grow. With unconscious bias, it was assumed by early botanists that this flower's isolated existence was due to its behaving like a "lone wolf"—hence the name *lupine,* which means "wolflike." Lupines were suspected of keeping other plants away by stealing nutrients. Subsequently, it was discovered that lupines had evolved selective advantage by acquiring the ability to survive in mineral-impoverished regions. After death, lupines leave a residue of concentrated minerals that make it possible for less capable plants to grow there. Calumny imposed on the lupine by attributing wolflike traits to it happens to be matched by late recognition that the wolf is more cooperative than combative in its environment. This is an example of "double calumny" from unwarranted biases concerning evolutionary balance between cooperation and conflict in both plants and animals.

Between the higher apes and earliest humans there was an increase in brain size by a factor of two; it doubled quite suddenly, quite abruptly. To accomplish this it was necessary for babies to be born very early, premature as compared with other great apes. Premature birth, with the brain continuing to grow after birth, was necessary if humans were to acquire large brains without necessitating considerable change in the female pelvis to accommodate major prenatal brain development. A long period of postnatal brain development entailed a long childhood. This meant a long period of interdependence between child and parents. A long period of rapid brain growth was needed to reach the full brain size, and this meant that there was time and opportunity for interdependent communication between parents and child. This allowed for the evolution of language and culture.

What about conflict and competition in evolution? With the emergence of language and culture in this long childhood, it was possible for the child to adapt to the environment, that is, to the physical environment and to the social environment, and this meant that the parents could control how much education the child had for compassion, conflict, or cooperation, for solving problems without harming other people or other animals. This was a great opportunity, the full potential of which has not yet been realized. This is why I am full of joy to meet with you—because I think we can talk about the educatability and adaptability of the infant brain in terms of resolution of conflict and avoidance of suffering and harm.

This is as much as I will say about evolution. I leave the evolution story to tomorrow's presentation.

Fertilization

The nervous system is built for action, and this action system goes into effect long before birth. Nervous system actions, throughout one's life, are continuously aimed at securing internal satisfactions. The noblest action of a human, such as the actions of a bodhisattva,* I presume, are also aimed at obtaining internal satisfactions. The gulf between ordinary and saintly lives is likely to lie with how those internal satisfactions are reinforced throughout infancy and childhood, as is the case with the cultivation of other social attributes and skills.

In general, actions to obtain internal satisfaction have been shaped and organized by evolutionary selection so as to ensure the well-being and survival of the species. We can trace goal-oriented actions all the way back to before fertilization, when sperm are swimming up the maternal genital tract and the gigantic ovum (about one thousand times the size of an individual sperm cell) has emerged from its follicle and is lazily floating down the estuaries of the fallopian tube. The egg is relatively big because it has to nourish the embryo for some time until a placenta can be established. There are lots of sperm, lots of the male material, and each one is, in effect, competing for the opportunity to enter the egg. When one succeeds in coming close to the outside of the egg, it enters. The head of the sperm has all of the contents necessary for the act of fertilization.

Sex cells, ova and sperm, arising from the parental ovaries and testicles, each contain twenty-three chromosomes. These chromosomes contain the genes responsible for inheritance from each parent. Each parent contributes twenty-three chromosomes that combine to provide forty-six paired chromosomes in the fertilized ovum.

Now let us figure how many possible combinations of genes there are for each new individual. Each sex cell receives half of the total of forty-six matched, paired chromosomes that both parents carry in their nonsex cells, as well as in each of their sex cells until the final cell division. At the final division, either one of each pair goes in one cell, and the other one of the pair goes in another cell. So these twenty-three chromosomes are sorted randomly and there are 8.39 million (2^{23}) different eggs and 8.39 mil-

---

*A bodhisattva, the model figure of Mahayana Buddhism, is characterized by the six "transcendental virtues" of generosity, patience, discipline, exertion, meditation, and knowledge of the nature of reality.

lion different sperm. This means that there is a tremendous possible variation for each parent's contribution. Throughout her lifetime, the female will produce only about 400 of these chromosomal selections. In his lifetime, the male produces a few thousand multiples of each selection among the 8.39 million possibilities. The process of fertilization combines these two lotteries in the production of an offspring. The child will therefore be one individual selected by chance out of 70.37 trillion (8.39 million × 8.39 million) possibilities provided by those parents!

DALAI LAMA: Is it so that before the sperm enters the egg there is no possibility of birth? And once that entrance has been made and the sperm has gone into the egg, is it absolutely certain that an embryo will develop, or is there still some element of uncertainty?

LIVINGSTON: Giving birth without sperm is called parthenogenesis. Evidently this does not happen in humans. A woman apparently cannot produce progeny without benefit of sperm. Nonetheless, parthenogenesis can be readily induced in frogs by pricking the eggs with a needle or by imposing other mechanical perturbations. Even with proper exposure to sperm, there is no certainty about fertilization. Even after a sperm has successfully fertilized the ovum, there is no certainty of successful embryonic and fetal development. Each of a long succession of events throughout the reproductive process remains problematic and uncertain, even in presumably normal circumstances.

DALAI LAMA: If that is the case, is a third cooperative cause necessary for the actual development of the fetus?

LIVINGSTON: From the Western scientific point of view, there are many cooperative causes necessary for the actual development of the fetus.

DALAI LAMA: Is the sperm composed of many cells or is it like the amoeba, which is composed of only one?

LIVINGSTON: Each ejaculation contains millions of sperm, but each individual sperm, consisting of head and tail, is one independent cell. The sperm—its head, body, and tail—are all one cell.

DALAI LAMA: So, for example, the color of the eyes, the

shape of the nose, and so on, such things are determined by the genetic code of the chromosomes?

LIVINGSTON: Yes. Each person, as you know, is the creative consequence of the union between half male-contributed and half female-contributed chromosomes. Some inherited traits will be expressed through genes passed along by the female and others through genes passed on by the male.

DALAI LAMA: But if the embryo receives proper nutrition, care, and so forth, then what level of detail is determined by the natural genetic code?

LIVINGSTON: I'm confident that there are some tissues in which the requirement is exactly provided, but there are some others that are not at all entirely determined. As we have indicated, each fertilized ovum, and consequently each newly created individual, is one out of 70.37 trillion choices! That is a big number! Why, 70 trillion is twenty times bigger than the United States debt! [laughter] I reckon that this number is larger than the total number of humans that have survived to reproductive age and succeeded in reproducing offspring since the beginning of the hominid line. You can certainly look around this room and say confidently that there are no duplications here. You can look over the whole world and say confidently that there are no duplications there. This, I believe, is a very important observation. [His Holiness chuckles.]

DALAI LAMA: Does a deformed embryo occur as a result of a deformation or a fault in the sperm? Or at a later stage, as a result of later circumstances?

LIVINGSTON: It can be a fault of the sperm, or a fault of the egg, or a fault of the processes of the individual baby. It can also be the fault of the mother's uterus, or placenta, or endocrines. Many things, you see. Really I feel every birth is a kind of miracle, because there are so many chances for error.

Importance of Care During Pregnancy and Early Years

Now I should like to explain a bit more about human brain development. At birth the average human brain weight is about 350 grams. In six months, the infant's brain has doubled in volume. This is like adding a host of new components and doubling the numbers of connections in a computer. The consequences are not simply additive but multiplicative—with vast expansion of perceptual, expressive, manipulative, and cognitive powers. All that is required for doubling the brain volume in six months is tender loving care and mother's milk! By the end of three years, the child's brain has doubled in volume once again. After that, the brain increases in size by only a few percent, until about age twenty, when the brain stops growing.

JEREMY W. HAYWARD: Does this actually mean that if a child is deprived of care that the brain doesn't develop?

LIVINGSTON: Yes, precisely. This brings up a very important point. Touching is life supporting to the newborn. If a baby is not touched and cuddled and rocked tenderly and spoken to, it will not live. It will suffer depression and may sicken and die simply because of a lack of touching and tender loving care. If the mother is undernourished during the three months or so before she gets pregnant, throughout pregnancy, and throughout breast feeding, she will be unable to transfer to the child—via the placenta and breast milk—sufficient nutrients to support the rapidly growing tissues of the child's body and brain. Her undernourishment will prevent the child from being able to live up to its genetic potential, to express itself fully in body and brain growth.

What is uppermost, I think, in our minds is the fact that more than two-thirds of the world's children do not live up to their genetic potential because of undernourishment and disease interfering with their growth and development, with their play and experience. Probably you could say 100 percent of the children do not live up to their genetic potential because of some neglect of promise or potential the child has. So the best way parents can contribute to the furtherance of their genetic abilities, their genetic prowess, is by cultivating the opportunities for optimal interaction with their children. If children in some part of the world are passive and dependent and weak, it brings us all down; and the history of the world shows us that great people and great contributors to the world can emerge from any culture. They have only to utilize this 70.37-trillion-odd chance of being great, and then the parents have to ensure that this reaches its full potential.

When children are born, they have almost all of their neurons—more than 90 percent—and those neurons are vital. They have the capacity to live for the full lifetime of the person, and they will not reproduce. After birth, there are many millions, perhaps a couple of billion nerve cells that develop in the first year of life, and after that there's no more bloom of new nerve cells. The nerve cells in the first year of life are very interesting, because they are small neurons; and in fact, neuroanatomists originally thought they were glia cells, not neurons. These small neurons have a different way of behaving. They develop into the brain and are influenced by the activities of the environment in the brain, and they make connections here and there according to what is going on. There is no predestiny for these neurons; they make connections that depend on what the children are experiencing, and this means that the children are building brains that are unique to their already individual experience. It's already unique but the children are making it more unique.

I mentioned that the brain doubles in size during the first six months, and this doubling is based on extending the size of individual cells and the number of processes they go through and the number of connections they make, and enriching the connections again in accordance with experience. So there are new cells, and also many old cells, that are modeling the world, creating a world view for this child. This goes on, and by the fourth year the brain has doubled once again.

In terms of this development, the period from conception to the fourth year is very precious. During this time, children can learn any language and will learn a language if exposed to a culture that has a language. By adolescence or thereabouts, it is more difficult to learn a language. If they have not learned a language by then, it will be very difficult. At that time, a language is learned by using the previous language as a tool, and for the rest of one's life one learns new languages on the basis of the languages one already knows. One carries into later life the shape of early language—the expression, the tone, and other characteristics that are already formed. In addition to learning language, one creates a total world view, a total environmental adaptation that is social, physical, and biological. At about the time of adolescence one becomes relatively more rigid, less adaptive. It is harder to adapt to an entirely different environment, and one uses the reference point of the previous environment as a model for further adaptation.

I am trying to portray very briefly the emergence in the uterus, in early childhood, and in adolescence of a combination of brain, mind, and self—personhood. The newborn baby, for example, begins to differentiate itself from the environment, to differentiate itself from its mother, to differentiate itself as a body with tangible movable parts, and so forth. The baby in the uterus and the newborn have a very high metabolic rate. This corresponds to the amount of work that is done by the brain, which is in an organ system that is already burning metabolically at a very high rate. In the adult, the rate of brain activity, measured metabolically, is ten times that of any other tissue in the body at rest. In fact, the brain burns ten times as much oxygen and produces ten times as much carbon dioxide as the rest of the body. Even athletes who exert themselves to the maximum can only reach about sixteen times the average metabolic rate, and they cannot sustain this very long—maybe for two hours in something like a marathon race. This means that the brain is running a marathon or a half-marathon all of one's life, waking and sleeping. It's a very busy tissue.

Now here is something interesting: At the time of adolescence, for reasons we do not know or understand, this rate of metabolism in utero and childhood—which is twice the adult rate, meaning twenty times the rate of the adult resting body—comes down to the adult rate. So, some time around adolescence, the rate of brain activity comes down to the half-marathon level of exertion, and we don't understand that. But I think something very significant is happening in the trajectory from the fertilized egg to adolescence that we should pay more attention to!

This is the story as we have visualized it so far: The sperm have moved from the vagina, through the uterus, and up the fallopian tube on both sides, and on one side there is, fortunately, an egg. By the time a sperm gets to the uterus, the egg has already formed a little ball with the yolk side and the outside of the egg, which then implants itself in the wall of the uterus, which is just exactly right for its being received. So, now we can talk about the development of the embryo.

When and Where Does Consciousness Enter the Embryo?

In an early stage, the conceptus—as seen by microscopy—reveals a cluster of tiny cells that are similar in appearance. These initially undergo synchronous cell divisions that are manifested as a progressively expanding, undulating spherule. It undulates in synchrony with "spasms" of simultaneous cell divisions.

Particular cellular differentiations and specializations among the dividing cells are established according to instructions that are read out from selected segments of the genetic code as successive stages of embryonic and fetal development unfold. At an early stage, the conceptus resembles a miniature mulberry. The outer surface of the spherule that lies opposite to the yolk sac—a developing remnant of the ovum that is designed to contribute part of the placenta—begins to spread out. Cell divisions are now, by virtue of their multiplicative expansion, very numerous and getting out of synchrony. As more cells are added, they form a flattened surface in the depths of which can be seen, at first, two and then three germ layers.

Early Embryonic Development

Now I would like to call for two successive demonstrations that you and I can cooperate in. These will illustrate two fundamental developmental events: early embryonic development and early brain development. First we will illustrate development of the embryo as a whole. Then we will illustrate how the nervous system organizes itself for behavior within the developing embryo.

I will now ask you if you could put your hands out like this, with the left hand below the right. Now I will put my right hand between yours. [Dr. Livingston and His Holiness put their hands together.] Now our three hands are compactly resting on top of each other. By putting our hands together, we have established a three-layered system, isn't that so?

When the embryo starts to develop, the first sign of its differentiation forecasts the relations that will obtain among the nervous system and other organs in the body. The initial step involves formation of three microscopically distinctive layers. Two layers appear during the second week, and at the outset of the third week, when the conceptus is beginning to implant itself into the walls of the mother's uterus, the middle layer appears. During the third week of existence of the conceptus, while it is establishing its intrauterine home, we can distinguish all three layers you and I are demonstrating. This layer, your left hand facing downward, called the *endoderm,* faces into the yolk sac. It will develop into visceral organs: lungs, gut, pancreas, liver, kidneys, and so forth. The middle layer, the *mesoderm,* represented by my right hand, has to do with formation of the *notochord,* skeleton, and muscles, as well as the heart, blood vessels, and so on. The upper layer, the *ectoderm,* your right hand, faces toward the future outside world. It has to do with production of skin, hair, nails, teeth, some thin bones on the crown of the skull, and the entire nervous system, spinal cord and brain, and peripheral nerves, including neuronal components of the sense organs [see Figure 14].

In response to molecular signals from the mesodermal notochord, the ectoderm forms a *primitive streak,* which is instructed by the *notochord* as to its lengthwise orientation and to which end of the streak is going to form the brain. The notochord is unique and common to all vertebrates. It is an elongated elastic rod that establishes midline and dorsal-ventral orientations, and the direction of the head of the embryo. The notochord says, "Your head sits on one end, and you sit on the other!" More concretely, the notochord forms the vertebral bodies and bones at the base of the skull. It survives in the adult as the elastic cushions, the intervertebral disks, which lie between the vertebral bodies.

B. ALAN WALLACE [interpreter]: This will come up again later in the talk I'm sure, but His Holiness is recalling Buddhist medicine, in which the bone, the marrow, and the semen come

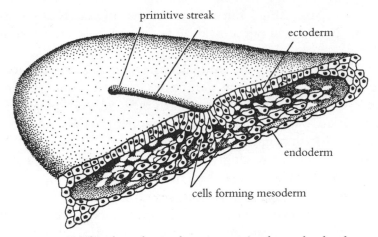

primitive streak

ectoderm

endoderm

cells forming mesoderm

FIGURE 14. The three-layered geometry in the early development of the embryo.

from the male side, the male constituent, whereas the blood, flesh, and skin come from the female constituent at conception. It would be interesting to see how this relates then to Western developmental anatomy.

LIVINGSTON: When we talk about the correspondence between Buddhist insight and Western neuroscience, I must emphasize that Western scientific interpretations are, by and large, more descriptive than explanatory. And they are always incomplete and uncertain. While we in the West think we are progressing rapidly, and especially recently, I can say with personal conviction that over the course of forty years of teaching several neuroscience disciplines in several universities, I have found that everything I carefully learned and taught has undergone changes, mostly in radically revolutionary ways, even recently. I have felt obliged by these experiences to explain to my students that 50 percent of what I tell them is wrong, and that I can't for the life of me tell them which 50 percent! [laughter]

Nervous System Organization

The second thing I want to talk about is how the nervous system organizes itself for behavior, and I want to do a demonstration with you again. Would you put your hands out exactly as you did before? Now I will put a hand between and these are squeezed down.

As I already noted, the entire nervous system originates from the ectoderm. We shall now demonstrate how this one germinative layer provides for development of the brain and spinal cord. The primitive streak that was formed under the influence of the notochord soon begins to form a *neural groove*. Both sides of this groove become increasingly thick, and like two approaching waves, these swellings meet and are zipper closed along the top to form a neural tube [see figure 15].

Continuous within the walls of the neural tube are three layers. The inmost layer, represented by your left hand, is called the *matrix layer*. It lies next to the fluid-filled central canal, which runs the length of the neural tube. This is the liveliest layer, being the generative source of all the neurons, each of which, after many genetically specified cell divisions, migrates to a specified location in one or the other of the three layers.

In the mature nervous system, the matrix layer provides for nervous governance of respiratory, circulatory, digestive, excretory, and sexual systems. This includes the central and peripheral (sympathetic and parasympathetic) divisions of the autonomic nervous system. The cells of the next layer, the mantle layer, form nervous system centers, which in cooperation with the visceral innervation systems just described, control expressive and emotional behavior. Then comes the outer, marginal layer, signified by your right hand. This supplies neurons for the cerebral cortex and other highest level systems and particularly the recent evolutionary contributions to brain organization.

DALAI LAMA: This is not a matter of the skin of the central channel is it? It's not like layers of skin?

LIVINGSTON: Although the original germinative layer, the ectodermal layer, provides skin, hair, nails, and related epidermal tissues through its contribution to the neural tube, it is wholly dedicated to forming the nervous system. As the three layers in the neural tube become structurally and functionally differentiated, they have only remote resemblance to skin.

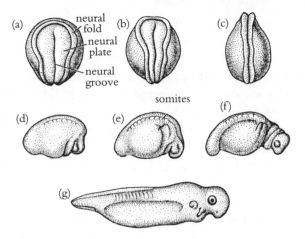

FIGURE 15. Formation of the neural axis in the early stages of vertebrate development.

DALAI LAMA: Is the neural tube hollow inside?

LIVINGSTON: Yes, and it's filled with cerebrospinal fluid, a very interesting fluid. I think this will become clear when you see the motion picture we're about to show that depicts the structural organization of a whole adult human brain. [The film, *The Human Brain: A Dynamic View of Its Structures and Organization*, copyrighted 1976, shows microscopic reconstruction of human brains from fine sections.]

DALAI LAMA: When an embryo develops into a proper body, does it start from the place of the heart or somewhere else in the center? The Buddhist texts speak of a nucleus where the consciousness first enters it, and this is the same nucleus where consciousness eventually dissolves at the time of death.

LIVINGSTON: I do not know where it might be appropriate to assign a locus for entry of consciousness into the conceptus, or where one might want to locate its dissolution at the time of death. Perhaps the ectodermal flattened surface. I should think it might be oriented according to which part will be the head of the embryo and that has not yet been established. My conception, from a Western neuroscientific point of view, is that consciousness is an emergent property that depends on the existence of a sufficient aggregation of appropriately connected nerve cells.

Western biologists talk of genetically specified destinies of cells: certain cells, by some kind of agreement among themselves, become dedicated as skin or brain cells. Some are destined to become heart and cardiovascular and skeletal muscles, and so on, and others are destined to become visceral. This dedication occurs fairly early. We don't know what controls this. Once the destination is chosen, then the three groups work in harmony. Each goes about its business—the upper one, to make an elaborate brain and spinal cord; the middle segment, to make the heart and the skeleton and muscles; and the lower part, to make the viscera and so on. And this goes on in harmony; there is a lot of signaling between these three tissues to communicate which stage each is in. I think this might be quite important in that it brings about a relation of the gut and the brain and the heart.

My view is that, beginning roughly between gestational weeks twenty-two and twenty-six, the fetus manifests outward signs that by inference imply that its still quite primitive nervous system may be developing glimmerings of what I would call primitive awareness. If some kind of subtle awareness exists prior to that time, it is too subtle for present physiological discriminative procedures to detect. From the Western neuroscientific standpoint, I see no appreciable evidence for any—even primitive— awareness earlier than the twenty-second week of gestation. This issue is profoundly important from a medical-ethical point of view.

Around week six, the first motility, the first movement, of the embryo begins to occur. This movement is purely muscular. The embryo has no nervous system yet; it has a beginning nervous system, but this is not connected to the muscle. So the muscle is spontaneously active, and the embryo shows little twitches or discharges, really very small. And at approximately seven and a half weeks, the nerves reach the muscle and this twitching stops. The muscle becomes quiet, subdued, when it receives its innervation, and from then on the muscle does not move unless the nerve stimulates it.

At the beginning the pattern of movement is always total, always integrated. Later on, at about week eight or nine, there begins to be a kind of movement that goes down the axis of the spine from the neck or head. Then innervation begins, not only motor nerves to the muscles, but also sensory nerves from the nervous system to the muscles. At about eight weeks, then, there is the first chance for some kind of reflex. The first response to a stimulus comes when a light hair is touching the cheek or mouth, in which case the fetus turns its head away. This is a definite response. It begins with the face and involves first neck turning; this is a total-body response, so it will go down the rest of the body with a swimming motion. Around this time the fetus has a structure that is identifiably human. There is a big head and some body, and an attachment to the placenta. The limb bud is only a little button, so there's no hand formed, and the leg hasn't even started to have a bud.

About week nine, there begin to be some coordinated movements, which seem to be not just motility but some kind of central-nervous-system-controlled activity that is integrated and involves individual body parts; this is different from the overall swimming movement. There is head movement or arm movement and a beautiful stretch, or there is jaw opening. Later, about nine and a half or toward ten weeks, breathing movements begin, although not in the usual sense because the baby is in a bath. Then, at week ten, the first yawn occurs. Maybe it gets a bit of—

DALAI LAMA: Clear light.*

LIVINGSTON: Clear light, yes. [laughter] The heartbeat begins between the fifth and sixth weeks, but at first it is just the contraction of a tube. There isn't really a heart with chambers yet. About the seventh or eighth week, this tube begins to be a heart and begins to pump circulation to the embryo. The head end of the neural axis and the heart are reasonably close to each other. The heart drifts down into the chest a little later, so there's a communication between brain structure and mouth at this point, and that forms the pineal gland in the brain stem.

After yawning, in another week there is swallowing and sucking, so the baby is preparing for maintaining itself. About week twenty-two, there begins to be primitive electrical activity

*See "Sentient Beings," p. 81, for a discussion of when, in everyday circumstances, one may experience clear light.

which, very coarsely, resembles the electrical activity of the adult. There is some electrical activity earlier, but it is episodic and transient and not well organized. But at this point there is an EEG, and this goes through successive stages so that by somewhere between, say, thirty-five and thirty-nine weeks, the child begins to experience the active-eye-movement type of sleep as well as slow-wave sleep. One might presume the child has an opportunity for dreaming during the late periods of pregnancy. At this stage an organizing central-nervous-system-control begins in the brain stem and then exercises itself on the spinal cord and muscular system; it controls the head and arm movements, stretching, jaw opening, breathing, and so forth. It must control these, because the cortex doesn't begin to develop until much later, about week twenty-two. Then it becomes very rapidly organized, but it takes time to start developing, because its development has to fit into an elaborate sequence.

The Early Brain's Control of Perception

There are two types of cortex that are the highest level of cortex in some lower animal forms. I won't describe them in detail, but the oldest is called archicortex, of which the hippocampus is a member. Next to that is a very expanded development, called the mesocortex, which just means "middle cortex." This cortex has a great deal to do, along with the older cortex, with visceral control, control of all the organs of the body, and with expression of emotion. A third type of cortex, the neocortex, is a new appearance in mammals. The neocortex is quite different. If you open the head and stimulate a waking individual in the unanesthetized state in different brain areas of neocortex, the person sees a flash of light, hears a tone, feels something on the surface of the body, or moves a limb, all in nonvolitional perceptions. If you stimulate either the archicortex and its hippocampus or the mesocortex, then the individual always says, I feel terrible, or I feel joyful, I feel sexy, or I feel elated, or something like that. The difference between the neocortex and older cortex is the difference between something that is kind of analytical and detached and something that is very intimate.

What I want to point out now—and if I succeed in communicating this, then I have earned my ticket—is that the brain stem and its associated structures can exert control down on the motor system and also on the sensory system at each of its relays on the way to cortex, including affecting cortex itself. The reason I emphasize this is that the brain controls not only motility and motor activity, but also controls sensory input. This means that the brain sends out messages to sense organs like the ear, the eye, the nasal passages, the skin, and muscle tissue that has sensibility; these messages from the central nervous system function as controls on the sense organ itself, on the retina, on the cochlea, and so on.

This is very important for epistemology because the behavior of this system is to improve performance and to shape experience in accordance with past history, expectation, and the purpose of the organism. That is, when a visual image is being formed, or when a sound is being processed, or touch, olfaction, and so forth, as these messages come in from the very beginning of the stimulus all the way through to wherever it may ramify in the brain, there is a capacity for the brain to control what gets formulated. This means that every experience we have is conditioned or shaped in accordance with our past history, our expectations, and our purposes. So, in Western science there's no pure vision, pure hearing, or pure olfaction. All these are influenced by the brain. We wear lenses, invisible to us, that separate us from reality. We cannot take these lenses off; they get changed over time if we find some consistent noncorrespondence, but it's a very slow process.

The following demonstration is not compelling but is exemplary of the simplest kind of experiment that one can do. First, you make a "T" and measure it to make sure the horizontal and vertical legs are exactly the same length. Then you show this to a group of people and ask if they think one of the two legs is longer or that they are equal in size. Usually three groups of people emerge. Some will insist very strongly that the vertical leg is longer. Others will insist that the horizontal leg is longer. And a small group will say that they are the same length. It doesn't matter if you try to measure it for them. They are still compelled by this very simple experiment. If you go to the Netherlands and test people there, about 92 percent of them would tend to tell you that the horizontal leg is longer. The distances they travel in their flat country are always horizontal. If you go to Switzerland, about 92 percent of the people will say that the vertical leg is the longer of the two lines. Their environment causes them to see distance more in terms of up and down.

So as I said, perception gets formulated in accordance with the history, expectations, and purposes of the organism. What I'm trying to get across is that the nervous system is built for action. The motor cells begin to contract even before they have innervation, before nerve connections to them have been established. Innervation comes to the motor cells before they have sensory control; the central nervous system controls both sensory and motor controls. The action of the nervous system is goal directed, and the goal is internal satisfaction.

The action of the nervous system consists of motility, which is essentially the relaxation or contraction of muscles, and secreting or not secreting. Motility has three categories. One is *visceration,* that is, control of contraction or relaxation or secretion of the gut, the lungs, the liver, the kidney, the sex organs, or the sweat glands, for example. The next step in motility is *expression.* This is motility expressing outwardly the person's internal moods and feeling states: emotions, gestures, attitudes, social signals, and so on. We experience emotions that are so intimate and private that we often don't stop to reflect on how importantly communicative they are. We manifest perfectly natural bodily attitudes when we are joyful, depressed, or suffering. For example, we may explode with dramatic body attitudes and gestures and vocalizations when we happen to hit our thumb hard with a hammer. We may stimulate strong emotions, or stimulate their nonexistence, but unless we are consummate actors, the underlying truth is likely to be readily apparent.

By bodily attitude I mean what I'm doing now. I'm erect, upright. You know I'm probably watchful, otherwise I might fall down. I'm always in a catastrophic situation because I'm always falling. I'm always correcting with my muscles to adjust against a fall, and this bodily attitude, the skeleton itself, is telling you something about me. It's very important nonverbal communication. I'll give you an example. Have you seen films of Charlie Chaplin? He knew how to do this perfectly, superbly, so he didn't have to do much facial expression. He kept his face quiet and communicated with bodily action. You knew even when you saw him in a silhouette in the distance that a woman had rejected him, or he had lost a job, or something terrible had happened. Or you knew that he and the woman were in love and the job was secure and he was a happy fellow! So this is bodily attitude, which also includes emotion. Bodily expression happens through blushing, heart-rate change—it can go up or down or become irregular—respiration, which can change in the same way, as can the gut and the sex organs, and so forth. Then there is anger, anxiety, fear, depression—the whole list of the negative emotions. And there are the exalted emotions, including love and compassion, empathy. All the things that are human expressions and that relate to cooperation and conflict are included here. Much of this nonverbal signaling takes place when you're negotiating with somebody, or teaching somebody, or learning from somebody.

Effectuation is the third kind of motility. This is what a person or any organism does to the social or biological or physical world. The Great Coral Reefs are the biggest monuments in the world. They're the most dominant feature contributed by life, living forms, in the world, and yet we think of corals as low life forms. They have developed probably the biggest cooperative enterprise in the world, and it involves not just the corals themselves, but also other creatures, such as a type of bacterium that stabilizes the coral near the surface so that it's protected against wave action. And there are many other interdependencies. I don't want to dwell on corals, but I want to say that life has much to show us about cooperation. A dog can build a cave to hide in, and so forth; a bear will maybe build some protective structure at the mouth of a cave, or something like that. These are effectuation. And with the exception of the cooperative coral, humans are the greatest effectuators.

Effectuation includes books or boats or buildings or bridges or contracts or constitutions or computers—whatever is designed and built. It also includes our reproduction. We change the world by producing children. Humans are always doing things. Everything that we see around us, even the agricultural contributions in this vicinity, are human-contributed. If you look down in the fields, you see the fingerprint of the dykes and waterways. Those are effectuation.

The Role of Feelings in Memory

Now I want to talk for a moment about these same brain mechanisms as they relate to learning and memory. We are already prepared for this. There is something about this emotionally active system, including the hippocampus and the archicortex, that is all the time monitoring the world. The hippocampus is receiving auditory, visual, somesthetic impulses, as well as very direct impulses from olfaction. So it knows what's going on in the world. But it's not organized toward effectuation. It's organized toward this internal experience of the I, the mere I.

When something biologically significant occurs in an individual, the hippocampus sends a message down into the brain stem to order that whatever patterns were obtaining in the brain at that moment should now be stored as information about what was going on in the world. This means that biologically significant events get transmitted to a brain stem system, which then says whatever was going on should be stabilized as a pattern. The ability of the brain stem to retain this pattern means that specific neural circuitry is not needed to produce it. It is like bringing out an image on a photographic plate by stimulating it repeatedly. It gets a faint print from the first experience. Next time it gets a stronger print. Or if it's a very important event, then there's a "now print" order right away. Your Holiness, I would venture that you would be able to tell us exactly where you were on November 22, 1963, if I remind you that Kennedy was assassinated on that day. You would know where you heard the information, who you heard it from. Is that true?

DALAI LAMA: Yes.

LIVINGSTON: So what happened in His Holiness' organization of mind and brain, I think, was that this was a biologically meaningful event to him as a person, and his brain automatically printed it. It printed everything. It printed the details of who the news carrier was, what kind of message came, what the form of the message was, where the knobs on the television were, Jacqueline Kennedy in black, everything. Many other images come up, and all these are surrounded with that experience. All this is dependent on the hippocampus. If the hippocampus were absent, this would not be retained.

This printing that is excited by the "now print" order or "now store" order goes down the spinal cord, goes up in the cerebellum, in the forebrain: it goes everywhere very quickly and retains the local pattern of activity in each place, a local history, which taken together with the other local histories makes a pattern.

DALAI LAMA: The factor that leaves a strong imprint upon the memory, is it related to feeling?

LIVINGSTON: Yes, exactly. To be remembered, an experience must evidently be related to personal feelings to warrant the hippocampal discharge. And, given the essential requirement that the experience has substantial personal meaning, that it arouses or alters personal feelings, the retained memory can be related to anything—something as theoretical as an abstract idea or as ephemeral as an odor.

WALLACE: The associated feeling could be happiness, sadness, or nothing?

LIVINGSTON: The associated feeling could be happiness or sadness or any other feeling state or mood. But probably there is nothing stored that is as neutral as nothing. Nothing is not memorable unless something powerfully emotional was an additional critical factor in the experience. For example, a door that does not open may have tremendous emotional impact, depending on the context. There may be fear that some violent person might enter through the door. In this respect, a nonevent, or perhaps nothing, could very well be memorable.

Associated feelings are very important. We know our state of hunger or our bladder or whatever quite readily. The physician, for example, asks how you are feeling. It's a very significant question. The patient may say, "I just feel tired today," and that may be an alarming sign to the physician. Or the patient may say, "I feel much better; I'd like to go home." Whatever it is, the patient has access to a self-image that is true. If he reveals it in truth, then he can be helpful to the doctor. What one person can describe to another about himself can contain all the information that relates to emotion and expression.

The brain is like a symphony, well tuned and well disciplined, and it works marvelously. It's always integrated. From the very beginning of embryonic life, it is totally integrated. So, for instance, when His Holiness heard about Kennedy's assassination, I'm sure he stopped what he was doing and changed his picture of the world, changed his thoughts and hopes for the future in significant respects because of that intelligence. He may have said, "I hope it is not true." But once an event is verified, all the switches are changed, and this is done by the kind of thing I'm calling a "now store," "now print" kind of order.

HAYWARD: Are you saying that everything is forgotten, nothing is stored in, let's say, to use Eleanor's concept, long-term memory, unless the hippocampus says "store"?

LIVINGSTON: It is not the hippocampus that gives this order; it is the brain stem. The hippocampus gives you value attachment to the different events, so it says, "Wow! That was significant! Store!" It's good to have such a thing, because if one doesn't have it, one isn't a person anymore, really. I know a neurosurgeon whose car slid off the road as he came home on a very rainy night. He fell over a cliff. He had brain damage that was located just at the hippocampus. Since the accident, he not only can't do neurosurgery; he can't even manage to have a relationship with his wife, because he forgets everything as soon as his immediate attention is interrupted or loses its focus. He remembers everything that was stored in the past—he remembers his roommate in college, his lessons in medical school; he remembers the patients he operated on. But from the date of that accident in the car, he has been unable to remember anything new. You can have a short talk with him, as long as he can keep the short-term memory going. But if you go out of the room and come back in even a few mintues, he remembers neither the content of the conversation nor your name. A small lesion in the brain resulted in the loss of his previously excellent ability to store new memories fully and lastingly. This man has suffered not just a loss of part of the hippocampus, he has suffered an irreparable loss of personhood, of humanhood. Because of his inability to store new experiential memories, he has lost his indispensible link with the human community.

Perception and Consciousness

A Conversation

From Sensory to Conceptual Consciousness

DALAI LAMA: In ancient India many Hindu philosophers maintained that the mode of conceptual thoughts engaging with objects was direct and nonselective. It's a matter of engagement through affirmation. It's a matter of the mind engaging with the object—"Ah, this is this"—by a process of pure affirmation rather than a process of "not this, not this, not this." The Buddhist logicians, on the other hand, maintain that the relation of conceptual thought and the object develops through exclusion. You perceive what something is by excluding what it is not.

JEREMY W. HAYWARD: If I look through the window and say, "I see a tree," in the first moment what happens is that I see something, then I name it tree. Is it correct from the Buddhists' point of view that there is a sequence, a small time interval, during which that something becomes "tree" in my mind?

DALAI LAMA: When you see something and you think it's a tree, there are two levels of discrimination, one being sensory and the other operating in the realm of the conceptual. When you first see an object like a tree, the first moment of awareness is sensory. In English you would say there is no consciousness; you're not conscious of it. But after that, perhaps a split-second later, you're conscious of it. Then you know it's a tree, and the mental consciousness is working. This mental consciousness can be active while you're looking at the tree, and also, even when you're not looking at the tree, you might be conscious of the tree. You can have an image of it. Between the two, there is a difference. The mental consciousness that you have of tree when you're actually looking at a tree is much more vivid than the one you have when you're not looking at it.

HAYWARD: The sensory level is not yet conscious, but how does it go from sensory to conscious? From the scientific point of view, there is a time between the beginning of treeness arising and the final tree. Even if I see the tree as continuous—treeeeeeeeeeeeeee—actually, in my perceptual system, what is taking place is tree, tree, tree, tree, tree, very fast. When light from that external reality impinges on the retina, some vague form occurs due to the operation of the retina itself. This vague form is then acted on, although it's still not conscious, and is either accepted or rejected by the brain. This is then further operated on, and some name occurs, at which point the experience becomes conscious. At that point it becomes the tree, while at the beginning it was that vague nameless formless object.

This is why I was asking about the time sequence. This vague whatever-it-is that hits the eye seems to go through several stages, until suddenly I see a tree. That process takes time.

FRANCISCO J. VARELA: From the point of view of neuroscientists, this is a matter of the emerging patterns in the human brain. It takes a little while for a pattern to emerge, and this little while is something like that [Varela snaps his fingers]. I think this is a question that has been of great interest to scientists; and also, this point connects with the meditative practitioner's discovery of the intermittency of the self in meditation. My self is not one solid thing but is composed of moments of experience. I see that and I see that and I see that. Perhaps there is a correspondence between the intermittency of self and the fact that, for the brain to construct a perception, it takes a little while, on the order of one-tenth of a second. I think Jeremy's point is that from the Western standpoint this process actually takes time, at least a fraction of a second. The question is, Between the moment my eye encounters a sensory moment and I can see patches up to the point where I discriminate an object, what is the process? Is that a unitary duration or can it be divided? Is there observation of that in meditation? What would be the shortest duration that we are capable of perceiving as "now"?

GESHE PALDEN DRAKPA: We can answer with certainty that there is a sequence that does occur in perception. Let's take the example of the visual perception of the color blue. The visual perception of the color blue occurs, but the perceiver has not yet ascertained it, so a mental ascertainment does follow that visual perception. It would be very rapid, a matter of two or three moments (moments in the Buddhist sense of extremely brief durations). But exactly what fraction of a second, this tradition does not say.

Ascertaining and Nonascertaining Consciousness

DALAI LAMA: There are two types of perceptions. One happens when you are distracted to a second object at the moment when you are already looking at something. At that time there is a perception of the first object, which is one type of perception. There is another type where you are actually paying attention to the object. Both are perceptions, but the second one is ascertaining and the other one is not ascertaining.

HAYWARD: In the nonascertaining one, there can nevertheless be action. The organism can act on the basis of that nonascertaining cognition even though is doesn't become conscious.

VARELA: This is factually true. For example, you do something, and only afterward there is a second moment in which you become conscious of your action, but the action is already done. For example, in driving my car, I often brake before I am conscious of doing so.

B. ALAN WALLACE [interpreter]: His Holiness points out that this comes from past conditioning. If you have never driven a car before and you see someone coming toward you, you don't have the response of hitting the brake immediately. Likewise with something coming toward your eye, you don't have to have a whole conceptual process to think to close the eye. This does seem to depend on previous conditioning.

THUBTEN JINPA [interpreter]: I think we have to make clear what we mean by consciousness, because in English it seems that when you say "conscious," there is some kind of mental conceptual ascertainment. When we use consciousness in the Buddhist context, the term is wider. Anything that is the subject of experience is consciousness, including nonascertaining awareness.

HAYWARD: Say I am sitting here and you are translating something His Holiness just said, so I'm very interested and paying attention. Now from the corner of my eye I see this glass and I take a drink, because my throat is dry. Then I put the glass down, all the while continuing to listen. Later on, I think I would like a drink, but I discover the glass is empty! As I was listening I never knew that I took a drink. Now, do you call that action conscious?

DALAI LAMA: It is conscious. But if you didn't know the glass was there in the first place, how would you do that?

WALLACE: His Holiness, Thubten Jinpa and I have tried to understand what you mean by conscious, and what we've come up with is *conceptual mental ascertainment*. Now this is very, very important.

DALAI LAMA: In Buddhist philosophy, when you speak of something being ascertained, you consider it to be identified; you know, you are sure, it is there. And that ascertaining awareness would seem to be necessarily mental and necessarily conceptual. Thus a conceptual ascertainment would seem to be equivalent to what you are speaking of as consciousness. Buddhists also speak of visual perception apprehending an object. But what determines whether visual perception knows the object or not is whether it's able to lead to or yield a mental ascertainment. With this criterion, you can have something that appears to visual perception without its knowing it, because this was nonascertaining awareness. Although it appeared to visual perception, later on you don't know whether you've seen it or not, because it did not yield the mental ascertainment. Therefore you would say that visual perception did not know its object even though the object appeared to it. The criterion is whether or not the visual perception yields an ascertainment.

A Buddhist Definition of Consciousness

ELEANOR ROSCH: I think it might be important to elaborate on the Buddhist meaning of consciousness, because it is not the same as what we mean.

DALAI LAMA: Yes, that's right. The Buddhist definition of consciousness, from one point of view, is a subjective agent that has the potential to arise correspondent to an object that appears to it. Through the force of the stimulus of the object, consciousness has the ability to arise in an aspect corresponding to the object.

ROSCH: But I thought the object and the consciousness were codependent? How can the object of cognition come before the cognition?

DALAI LAMA: The object's being dependent on the subject doesn't mean that the object is dependent on a subject that *precedes* it. It is important to make discriminations between two types of analysis—relative and ultimate analysis. The fact is that the object cannot withstand ultimate analysis and is ultimately unfindable.

The only mode of existence the object has left is that it exists by the force of designation, by the force of imputation, of consciousness. For example, when you see this as a cup and you use it for drinking tea, you do this by relying on the conventional experience; you don't question the validity of that convention. But this cup doesn't exist when you analyze it with the ultimate analysis. The only mode of existence it has is the existence it has by the force of conceptual designation.

Now, we could further analyze this as follows: Which conceptual mind designated it, mine or yours, in an earlier moment, in the next moment? Which cognition does it depend on? If you search whether that cognition was in an earlier moment or a subsequent moment or whether it's something that was coexistent with it, or whether it is my consciousness or your consciousness, again you are falling into the extreme of ultimate analysis, and then again you won't find anything.

ROSCH: Are you saying that in relative analysis, where there is a cup, this requires that the object precede consciousness?

DALAI LAMA: According to the Prasangika, it is sequential.

VARELA: Is it required to have a *thing* there already preceding the perception, a thing that later, in the second or third moments, we will call the cup? Because in terms of neuroscience, that is factually wrong. You cannot say that I will perceive yellow because yellow first arrives and then it's picked up by my brain. So I think we are trying to track to what extent in the Buddhists' [relative] description is the object already constituted? Or is it acceptable to say, as a neuroscientist would, that the object is an *emergence* of this interaction and is not in itself already constituted.

JINPA: But according to your presentation it sounds as though neuroscientists would say that you don't actually see the object. What you see is the picture of it!

VARELA: That is precisely correct.

ROBERT B. LIVINGSTON: It occurs in your head. Assuming that it occurs outside is called the "phenomenal fallacy."

DALAI LAMA: There is a lot of debate between Sautrantikas and Yogacharins about this question. Whether the appearance of the object is one with the object or whether it is something different; whether the appearance of the object is simultaneous with perception or is sequential.

VARELA: But then it is not considered a fundamental tenet that the object has to be already there preceding its cognition? Would it be acceptable, as it would be for a neuroscientist, to say that the object arises in the cognition, that it is not separable?

DALAI LAMA: Here our Buddhist schools have different views. One view that is common to all of the Buddhist schools (leaving aside the view of Vaibhashikas, which is very different, more realist) is that the appearance or image of the object has to be simultaneous with the actual cognition. And also it is of the same nature as the actual cognition. The difference is that when the Yogacharins identify what the image is, they say it is a product of one's own imprints, the imprints of earlier moments of consciousness. They refute an external reality, the external world, as independent of mind. Therefore, they say the perceptual image is a product of one's own past imprints. Other schools say the image is a projection of the object.

Although Prasangika Madhyamikas and Sautrantikas accept external objects or external reality, there is a big difference. When Sautrantikas explain external reality, they base their theory on the fundamental belief that there are partless particles.

Theirs is something like the reductionist philosophy with assorted elementary particles, some elementary basis that the entire world or universe can be reduced to. The Prasangika school speaks of external reality, but they say when you analyze it, there is no such thing as fundamental entities. They break down under analysis.

VARELA: Most neuroscientists would feel very comfortable with the idea that there is one level that you could call an inviolate essential level of physical reality. There is a world out there; then, in come living beings with different brains, and each one makes a different construction of this world, all of them slightly different pictures of the same thing. But we neuroscientists want to have a foundation. We want to be able to rely on the idea that all of those different constructions refer to the same ultimately inviolate level. That is the dogma, and it *is* a dogma; there is no absolute proof for it.

DALAI LAMA: I think there is a similarity between the Buddhist outlook and your point of view; even the Prasangikas speak of relating to an object through an image. This image is simultaneous with cognition, so that what you actually see is the image.

VARELA: That is the similarity. The difference I'm trying to point out, which I think is equally important, is that for the Prasangikas there is no external existence as such. By contrast, though the neuroscientists, too, would accept the simultaneous arising of the object and the perceiver, they would nevertheless hold to the reductionist analysis of external reality.

Is Perception of a World "Out There"?

WALLACE: There are people with amputated limbs, say, a hand, and where the hand would be they can experience pain? His Holiness finds this very unbelievable.

LIVINGSTON: That's right! They may not feel pain, but they may also feel pain. In other words, they can feel normal sensibility and even motion, or they may have no sense of motion. Any of these conditions is possible.

DALAI LAMA: Does the sense of pain or motion decrease over the years?

LIVINGSTON: It may, it may not. I've had people who have had a phantom limb for forty years or more. For instance, there was a man with his right arm missing. If you asked him where he felt the sensation of the missing arm, he could localize it in space. It was so real to him that if you asked him to make a motion that would make the missing arm, in his sensation of it, pass through the table, he would do it but it felt very strange to him, very bizarre, as if he were violating some law of physics, or something like that. It gave him gooseflesh or he would shudder and get frightened. It's very real.

DALAI LAMA: It's like during meditation, when you feel yourself going out of your body, sometimes you are surprised because you don't get obstructed by the door. It is quite similar to that.

VARELA: I would like to suggest an experiment we can do right now to show Your Holiness that you can have a phantom nose! Cross your middle and index fingers and then touch the tip of your nose. Do you feel two noses or just one?

DALAI LAMA: I was already prepared for that, so I was already thinking there wouldn't be one nose! Yes.

VARELA: You always find two noses. That's just an example of how one undoes the natural sensory situation. Perception changes and you can have something that seems very real because you feel it directly, but from the ordinary point of view, these perceptions do not correspond to the actual situation.

LIVINGSTON: Then there is another kind of phenomenon. If you tie a monkey's fingers together with a little bandage and then explore the motor cortex in the opposite hemisphere, you find that there is a change in activity of the neurons corresponding to the limitation of movement imposed by the bandages. If you amputate fingers, there is a migration of neurons to compensate for the gap in motor capability, and the monkey's brain has a different map of the changed hand. So the brain rebuilds itself in close correspondence to what happens on the periphery.

I'll give you another example of brain development in correspondence with the environment: The cerebellum in the newborn is much smaller relative to the rest of the brain in proportion to adult size, and it is my supposition that the cerebellum doesn't develop until the child emerges into the world because in the uterus there is flotation. There is very little inertial mass in the movement of the limbs, but when the baby comes out into the world, its limbs become wired to its growing cerebellum and this wiring becomes an accurate neurological map of the body and the gravitational field and the environment that the child is in. There's something else interesting here—that the brain undergoes this major growth, doubling in size in six months, and doubling again by the fourth year. We know from some experiments with animals that the environment, or the things the individual learns from it, do have an effect on the mapping or the organization of the growing brain. So it is my belief, though I don't have any evidence for humans, that this enlargement and organization is bound to the environment. If the environment changes radically later, there can be some readjustment, but in early life this binding is very close.

DALAI LAMA: Wouldn't there be some difference, then, in the brains of aborigines who lived a very, very simple life as opposed to those of, let's say, Westerners in a very, very complex society, very sophisticated? Would that have a strong effect on the brain?

LIVINGSTON: But the aborigines don't lead a very simple life, because they have to know the specific names, not the type names, of all the trees and bushes within about a hundred-mile range. They have to know them as individuals. They have to have a proper name for any persistent foliage, tree, bush or whatever, so they have a tremendous memory challenge. They have a very difficult life! Now this is very practical. They have to learn the names of things so that if they're told to go someplace, they can find their way by the proper names of these trees and plants and bushes and so forth.

VARELA: Here's an example to illustrate further the point that perception is bound up with motor interaction with the environment. This is an absolutely fundamental point about how neuroscientists understand perception that is not often brought out. The experiment was done some time ago and in it two small newborn kittens were taken and kept in the dark. When a cat is born, its eyes are closed—it has no vision. These two kittens were only taken out into the light in an empty round room painted with stripes. This was their whole world. One kitten was allowed to walk around normally. The other one was strapped into a little cart where it could not use its feet. The one who could walk would pull the confined one around in the cart so that it, too, experienced passive motion around this round striped universe. So as their eyes began to open both kittens were exposed to an identical environment. The only difference is that one was walking around on its own four feet and the other was moving around passively, pulled around by the first. Every day they were taken out for a period of activity in this container and afterward were returned to the dark. This was continued for several weeks while their eyes opened and they learned to see. The question is, What happens when after a few weeks you take these two cats out of this controlled situation and let them out in the world? The animal that was allowed to walk in the striped room could walk around normally in a regular environment, even though it had first begun to see in such a restricted environment. It did not bump into things and did not fall off the edges. It behaved like a normal cat. The other one, although its eyes, nervous system, and legs were absolutely intact, behaved like a blind cat. It bumped into things and fell off edges. The common saying, that cats see with their feet, is not just a joke from the neuroscientists' point of view!

We can conclude from this that, clearly, perception is not merely a matter of having an object outside and getting an image of it inside. The brain is an active configuration that participates in the organism's interaction with its environment. It's as if the brain actually makes the world come through in perception. It responds to all the integrated processes involved in interacting with the world.

LIVINGSTON: I would like to tell you about an experiment that can be done with humans. This is an experiment in which there are three small rooms. They are like a dollhouse. These rooms are accessible from a chair, which can be moved from one position to another to enable a subject to see the three rooms through a peephole. These rooms are set up in relation to the peephole and they appear correct. One is correct. It is an ordinary little room. Another is distorted with the left wall twice as high as the right wall, the roof sloping down, and the floor sloping up. Still, from the peephole it looks correct and ordinary. The third one has a top-down distortion. The walls lean out. All the rooms are decorated with furniture, curtains, windows, and so forth, all correspondingly distorted. All three rooms look normal because they project to the point where the peephole is as if they were rectilinear with one eye. When people who don't know the experiment sit in a chair and look with one eye into rooms A, B, and C, they say that the rooms look the same.

Now the experiment is this: We put subjects in a position where they are viewing the left-right-distorted room. We give them a stick and tell them to touch the butterfly on the left wall. They reach out and don't get close to it. They reach further and further without reaching it, and finally they start to giggle, because things are countering their expectation. They finally reach the butterfly, and then we tell them to touch the fly on the opposite wall. They try and hit the back wall, then they hit the side wall far from the fly, and so on. They miss again and again and laugh, because that's unexpected. After about ten inaccurate attempts, they finally begin to see the room as left-right distorted.

Once they have learned to do this correctly, you ask them to look at room A, which is the ordinary room. They look at room A and see it, too, as left-right distorted. At this point, they are just as inept at touching the fly and the butterfly in this room as they were earlier in the distorted room. They must readjust again to the normal conditions. The point is that you cannot know the room without behavior. Purely on the basis of passive perception, you can be fooled, and this is something that can be generalized.

VARELA: This is interesting from the point of view of epistemology. From this point of view, it's impossible to say that something, this pen, for example, is "out there" with any kind of substantial quality, in spite of the fact that, as we have been discussing, that is the belief in the West. Conventionally, you would say about your perception of room A, "Oh, that was a mistake; that was an error." But in fact what we discover by looking at the brain this way is that it is not an error; rather, it is something that is normally the case. We learn that the world is shaped according to expectations, to history, to the way we are wired, to development, so that the picture of the world is inseparable from that particular brain or, I should say, person. This raises for Westerners, too, the question of what I mean when I say that there is something objectively "out there." What is "objectively"? The usual answer Westerners give is that there is some kind of physical quality at least. But even that becomes suspect, because the physicist says that this physical quality is in itself not very easy to find and specify.

DALAI LAMA: The Yogacharins find in their analysis that external reality is not substantial. When you search beyond the conventional level, you can't find it. However, they conclude there is a subjective kind of reality that is truly existent. They assert substantial existence of the subject of experience, because one can feel it. In neuroscience, when you analyze along the lines you spoke of through the examination of the brain and how it perceives, you find there isn't any substantial entity "out there." When you apply this analysis to the neurons, the subjective side, do you feel the same way?

WALLACE: His Holiness' question is simply: When you're looking out, you find that there's nothing substantial out there. Now, leaving outside a nonphysical cognition, if the subject is actually the brain, do you say that the brain that is doing the perceiving is also as nonsubstantial as anything out there, in which case you have nothing substantial out there and nothing substantial on the subject side? Is that the conclusion for you as a neuroscientist?

VARELA: I will speak only for myself, because at this point you have to realize that we're dealing with an area that lies outside any prevailing consensus. The prevailing view, even in neuroscience, is that there *is* a pen out there, and in spite of the fact that there are little things going on inside my brain, basically there is an image of the pen inside. What I am saying in fact is that this view can be questioned on the basis of science itself. That one can re-understand neuroscience and show that there is no basis for this belief that there is a stable solid substantial reality that we can rely upon, so in fact cognition is not a representation in any way. Now let me see if I can follow your question well.

WALLACE: Let's forget the whole issue of whether there is consciousness apart from matter. We're taking the neuroscientists' viewpoint that it is the brain that sees and the neurons that are doing all the cognizing. Let's assume that this is the context we're speaking in. Forget Buddhist doctrines for the time being. On the objective side, when we use this kind of very perceptive approach that you're dealing with now (although you say most neuroscientists don't penetrate that far), you say the evidence that there are these substantially existent external entities out there really seems to start falling apart. Well, similarly, wouldn't you also have to conclude that the neurons, the stuff inside the subject that are presumably making these perceptions, lack that substantiality in the same way as anything out there? In which case, what are you left with?

VARELA: That's right. There are two steps there. I think that, mostly, the first reaction you get in discussing this with colleagues is, "Oh, if you don't think there's anything out there, then you must believe in some internal reality that is projecting what appears to be the outer world. You must believe in some solid, some kind of innate categories that are real." That is, they would assume that we must hold some kind of a subjectivist or idealist position. This is, in fact, not at all the case, because we can show that you can influence what you perceive as the world, by manipulating it. So you can manipulate your perception from outside, but you can also manipulate it from inside. The only real conclusion is that you cannot find substantiality either inside or outside. So I would say that on purely scientific grounds, you can defend the position that the perception of this world is in fact a codependence, a strict codependence of what we call the world and what we call the brain. These two things meet together and merge, making this reality. So purely on scientific grounds, we do come closer to a more Buddhist, Prasangika, point of view. But it must be said that while some of us would hold this view, it would not be a majority view. On the other hand, I think it is scientifically a perfectly reasonable point of view, and I think Dr. Livingston or I could stand up and argue this point of view with our colleagues without being thrown out of the building! They might think we were a little crazy, but still they wouldn't think we had completely gone off the deep end.

LIVINGSTON: Yes, I agree.

When Is a Perception Valid?

DALAI LAMA: In the neuroscientists' approach, identification of everything that is cognitive, like perception and so forth, is made on the basis of something that is physical matter, like neurons, and so forth. On such a basis, how do we discriminate between a wrong perception and a valid perception? We assume that individual neurons or the whole system, the whole circuitry of the neurons, cognizes. This occurs whether there is a valid perception going on or an invalid perception going on. Since they're all working either way, how do you make any distinction from a neurophysiological point of view?

VARELA: My nervous system will function and identify something, such as food. All the programs say "food," but then if I try to eat it, I may find I cannot. There is feedback from the environment saying "misrepresentation, wrong take, correct your approach." So it is like that: back and forth, trial and error. If you make too many mistakes, you die. So evolution carries on by making many attempts until something is arrived at that is appropriate or adequate. That is how you discriminate between correct and incorrect, by the consequences of that perception. A perception would be established as valid if it allowed a life form to do what it needed to do—to eat, to reproduce, to plan behavior, and so forth. The consequences decide.

DALAI LAMA: There is no way of making the distinction at the time of the actual experience?

VARELA: Neuroscientists can find many ways to cause the nervous system to make an error. Because the system works the way it does, you can trick it into perceiving things that only another action can convince you is not so. This is what is called perceptual or sensory illusion. As an example, close one eye and look at your thumb with your arm outstretched, and then bring it back half the distance toward your eye. Do you see your thumb doubling in size? It becomes a little larger but it doesn't become double the size, does it? Although the image of the thumb on the retina has doubled in size, you don't see it as double. Check it as follows: Put your other thumb close to your eye as a reference point and do the same experiment with the first thumb. You will see that the thumb now looks bigger. Doesn't it? So there you are. Which is the valid perception of the thumb?

DALAI LAMA: In this case I think that a lot of environmental factors have to be taken into account. For example, let's shift now to conceptual cognition. Let's imagine a continuum of conceptual cognition in which a prior moment of awareness of conceptual cognition is in fact a false cognition. It was mistaken, but now you come to a new cognition, a conceptual cognition that is valid. Being valid, it damages or refutes the preceding conceptual cognition that was wrong. Now in that case, from the neurophysiological point of view, how would you describe the refutation of the prior cognition?

VARELA: We could call it "learning," I suppose, that is, the process I described before. You have a hypothesis that something is food and you try it out. You then have a perception that doesn't match your expectations. The nervous system rearranges itself by making synaptic changes so that the next time you see that something, the assocation with food won't be there. This is a perfectly good example of an emergent property: before, the notion of food came up; but the next time, the notion of food will not come up. The system rearranges itself; it learns.

But I didn't feel that we were finished with the less conceptual example of the thumb's size. If you ask yourself, What is the real size of the thumb? which one do you choose? Surely putting one thumb next to the other doesn't affect the size of the first one.

Nevertheless your perception at the moment of having the experience is that it does.

DALAI LAMA: All these terms for measurement are based on human convention. Now, for example, for a cat or dog, would the whole concept of size and things like that be different?

VARELA: Surely these same things would happen for them. In fact, you can trick dogs and other animals into believing that there are things where there are none. For example, you can take a frog's eye and cut the retina and rotate it and sew it back into place after the rotation. Normally the frog sees a fly and snaps it up very precisely. After rotation of the eye, you show the fly and the frog behaves as if the fly were behind it. Never in its life will the frog learn again to catch the fly with its tongue. That is an invalid perception in the sense that the frog won't eat.

DALAI LAMA: In Buddhist terminology you would say that the source of the deception is actually within the eye organ, because you have changed it. In the case of my thumb, the source of deception is within the object.

VARELA: Why is it in the object? You haven't changed the object! What you have done from a scientific point of view, I think, is change the context of perception. The rotated eye creates another context of perception, and it is not possible to say that this is more real than that. If I see my thumb in the context of another nearby object, then I use one evaluation. If the context changes, the evaluation will be different. This is again the problem of trying to say what is the real valid cognition of the size of a thumb. From this point of view, there is no such thing as the true perception of the thumb. It's only in reference to a previous action; it's not valid in itself.

LIVINGSTON: I have two more experiments I would like to present. If you show a picture very briefly, people may not be able to perceive the picture exactly or accurately. These experiments, done at Harvard, were the following. There was a classroom full of students and a big screen and a big projector that could make a very abrupt flash of an image on the screen. The students were to look at the screen. At first maybe they just saw a flash. Then the image was exposed just a little bit longer. As soon as they got some impression of what this image was about, they were to write it down in their notebooks. Then these notebooks were collected. It was found that even after considerable exposure of the image, the students would maintain an incorrect interpretation of it and would continue to do so even to the point where the exposure was so long that somebody coming in from outside could easily perceive that it was mistaken. The students started perceiving something and they got locked, anchored, into a certain perception. They stayed with that, clung to that, until it was absurd. They had a very long exposure of the image, and they still saw it in the original inaccurate way.

I'll give you an example: They had some very simple pictures, such as a bicycle leaning up against a fire hydrant somewhere on the campus, with some steps of a building in the background—something that these students should have seen at one time or another. When the picture was exposed to some students, they said: "I see a ship. It's a full rig ship, it has a wave under it, and it's coming full blast toward me." They wrote this down in their notebooks and kept seeing that ship and the waves and so on until they had seen the image exposed to four times the length of time it would take a new person to see it's a bicycle against a hydrant in front of some steps! I'm trying to illustrate the problem that once you form an image about somebody or some room or some thing or some event, you may be unable to let it go.

A second experiment that is relevant, I think, is the following: It was found early on in the experiment described above that if an image was disagreeable to the person who was being tested, it would take a long time, with a lot of exposure being built up, before the person finally saw what it was. Now, it could be said that this result was due to the quality of the picture, or the way it was being presented, or some other variable. So they set up an experiment with four images at once. The experimentalists showed the subjects sets of four pictures in sample tests, so that they became familiar with looking at four figures with a brief exposure. Then the experimentalists took the picture that was disagreeable to somebody and put it once in one corner and another time in another corner. They randomly sorted those disagreeable pictures among the others. In this way they were able to find out what a person was sensitive to, didn't like, was fearful of, or what a person found immoral or had a censorship impediment about. For example, you could have four pictures of animals in a zoo. You'd have monkeys in one quarter, elephants in another and dogs in a third. Then you would have dogs fornicating in the fourth quarter. The pictures were equivalent for light and dark and so on, so irrelevant factors like those were ruled out. Now, the subjects would go on trying to identify what is in the pictures until they get them all correct. When the unpleasant picture was put in along with the other animal pictures, people would guess the three other pictures correctly very quickly and would then have to get ten times more exposure to see the picture that they were censoring.

The reason I bring this up is that it suggests very powerfully, I think, that before we see anything, we already have exercised a certain censorship in respect to that image. Before we perceive, the image has already gone through some filters that say, we like this, or we don't like it, or we must avoid it, and so on. The point is that the visual cortex or some other part of the brain is already exercising before you get to a conceptual confirmation.

WALLACE: Maybe on some subconscious or semiconscious level there is already identification, suggesting that the subconscious is a bit faster than the conscious mind?

LIVINGSTON: That's the conclusion that Western scientists came to. I must say something a little conservative about this, because what is known is that the subjects do not give testimony that they perceive the image correctly. They tell us, and we experience ourselves, that we do not see the picture clearly. But that doesn't tell you exactly what's going on. It may be that the brain is protecting the individual from being exposed as a person who would talk about something as bad as dogs fornicating, and that protection is sufficiently strong to maybe wipe out or blur or otherwise modify the image. It doesn't tell us exactly where these processes take place or exactly what is taking place.

WALLACE: Concerning how you translate "subconscious" in Tibetan, I must mention that Tibetans do not speak in terms of subconscious and conscious, but in terms of the grossness and subtlety of mind. The subconscious is a subtle level of mind, and what we consider identification or ascertainment is a grosser level. So when I translated the experiment to His Holiness, he responded, "Doesn't this imply that the more subtle mind is faster?"

VARELA: This is confusing for me. Previous discussions had led me to think that the occurrence or nonoccurrence of mental ascertainment had nothing to do with levels of subtlety.

WALLACE: I think we are working with the temporary hypothesis that during the waking state there are two levels of mental ascertainment, the gross one that you can talk about, but possibly also a preceding one that is more subtle and is already conditioning how long it takes for the grosser, expressible mental ascertainment to occur. Both ascertainments have to be there for you to know whether you like something or not. If you're seeing fornicating dogs and you don't like to see that, both kinds of ascertainment have to be there. Whether or not both kinds of ascertainment belong to the gross level of consciousness still or have been shifted down to subtle consciousness is a point of discussion. His Holiness was open to the possibility that there is some degree of subtlety.

He now raises a further point. Imagine a single event, on the one hand, that is actually experienced while in the waking state, and then on the other hand, an identical event experienced in the dream state. To each of these events we have an emotional response. When you wake up from the dream, if it was a bad experience, you kind of feel lousy even though you've awakened. So the question is, Given these two states of mind, waking consciousness and dream consciousness, and given a similar event to which you're responding, is there a different strength to the emotional response? The reason for the question is that, from the Buddhist point of view, the dream consciousness is a more subtle one, more akin to a subconscious level of mind. That it is more subtle than waking consciousness suggests that it would be more powerful.

ROSCH: When the original experiment of this type was done with words, it was found that people took much longer to say that they had seen "dirty" words than regular words. So the criticism was that they saw them just as fast, but they didn't want to say them because they were taught not to. So whether it was on the level of perception or expression was never resolved completely. This is a very controversial area of research in psychology, and the controversy comes from the fact that in the psychoanalytic tradition that Freud and Jung began, there is a very intelligent unconscious. This is a major point, and it's so major that it has become a cultural belief among educated Americans that they have a thing called the unconscious. They feel that this unconscious is implicated if they ever notice some kind of impermanence or discontinuity in their consciousness in daily life, or when they notice some change in themselves from one situation to another or from childhood to adulthood. All of the things that Buddhists point to as evidence of impermanence—all these discontinuities—can be denied or discounted by referring back to a presumably continuous unconscious. Such a personified, functioning unconscious is also a great challenge to scientific method, since by definition it cannot be observed directly. So there has been a huge amount of research to try to see whether people actually perceive things and think and defend themselves perceptually on the unconscious level, without conscious awareness.

How Does Buddhism Validate Perception?

VARELA: I would really like to hear His Holiness' comments on how, from a Buddhist standpoint, one can establish what a valid perception of my thumb is?

DALAI LAMA: One criterion for proving a valid cognition is by its consequences. You have three criteria for existence in the Prasangika system: first, being in accordance with convention; second, not being damaged or refuted by a valid or conventional cognition. Then there's a third one, which is similar to the second one but invokes another experience, the Yogacharins' viewpoint. According to this third criterion, what certifies the existence of an object is a valid cognition, therefore it is the subjective mind that certifies whether or not something exists. If the validation of the cognition in turn depends on the object, then the subjective experience wouldn't have much authority. Therefore, according to the Yogachara school, the validation of this cognition depends on some other factor called apperception, or one could also call it self-cognizing awareness. So this self-cognizing consciousness is a factor of the subjective mind that validates cognition.

Now the Prasangikas' view is that the Yogacharins have to go through such a complicated process because they have this basic theory of something inherently existent, the *alaya,* consciousness. Because of this they have to search for some kind of objective essence, some final authority that really confirms cognition. And since you can't get it from the object side (which, from their point of view, doesn't exist), you must get it from the subject side. But it can't be the initial perception, because it has to be something that confirms this initial perception. Therefore, they had to posit this self-cognizing awareness. Because the Prasangikas negate the inherent existence of both the objective and subjective, they say that just as the validation of the object depends on the subjective condition, in the same manner the subjective condition depends for its validation on the object. This corresponds closely to how we validate cognition in our everyday life. If you perceive something in a certain way, then you relate with the object to check that perception. When you find the object to be in accordance with your perception, then you know that your cognition is valid. So, for the Prasangikas there is no such thing as inherently valid cognition. Even a direct experience of shunyata, emptiness, is not intrinsically valid.

HAYWARD: Then how is the cognition of shunyata validated?

DALAI LAMA: When you have the experience of emptiness, the Prasangika view is that the actual existence of emptiness is not perceived by that consciousness, only the total absence of inherent existence. Emptiness is approached by the negation of inherent existence. The wisdom that directly realizes shunyata does not realize the *existence* of shunyata. We make a distinction between shunyata and the existence of shunyata. It's only in a subsequent recollection that you say, "Oh, I'm now aware of shunyata." At this point, the existence of shunyata is once again a conventional reality. Shunyata itself, simply shunyata, is ultimate reality. An awareness that perceives the existence of shunyata is already a recollection and not the direct perception. Shunyata itself is a concealed entity in the threefold classification we mentioned before. The three categories were: evident, slightly concealed, and extremely concealed. Shunyata is slightly concealed. The existence of shunyata is evident in that it is a conventional designation that doesn't require inference. The reasoning processes through which you reach the conclusion that things lack inherent existence also prove that the experience you have of it is valid. The very reasoning process that proves the emptiness of phenomena also proves the validity of that cognition, because it tallies with reality.

Another way to verify it is to look at what the consequences are of a direct cognition or direct perception of shunyata, and this is also a strongly validating factor. That is, what effect does it have on the mind in terms of how your kleshas, your mental distortions, are doing? A direct perception of shunyata would drastically reduce the level of mental distortion and also give rise to tremendous powers that are opened up by the sheer force of that realization. If you have a fraudulent realization, that is, you think this is direct realization but it's actually fraudulent or far more superficial than you think, it will not have that impact on the mind, neither in purifying the mind nor in enhancing its power.

Another point in the Prasangika view is the intimate relationship between phenomena existing as dependently related events and their having an empty nature or lacking intrinsic existence.* And so another effect of the direct realization of shunyata is that, following that experience, even seeing a slight interaction of causality or conditioning of one entity by another, we get a very, very penetrating ascertainment or certainty. The force

---

*A fundamental doctrine of Buddhism is dependent arising (Skt., *pratityasamutpada*), according to which phenomena arise in interdependence on each other, that is, as part of a web of causation through which phenomena mutually condition each other. In virtue of this interdependence, no phenomenon can be said to have an inherent existence of its own.

of your meditative experience very strongly enhances your insight into everyday phenomena. When the Prasangikas explain emptiness, they include emptiness with dependent arising. They're not isolated from each other. Actually the meaning of emptiness is something like the absence of independent existence. The absence of independent existence is actually the basis of all the things that can move. This great certainty, that even the slightest cause can bring about a great impact on the effects, is a result of this experience. And this certainty also validates the authenticity of your realization of emptiness.

Evolution
of Life

FRANCISCO J. VARELA
AND LUIGI LUISI

How Were the Main Ideas of Evolution Formed?

The question of how things originated is very important for Westerners. How did this body or this brain come to be the way it is? Where is the beginning? We have heard one kind of beginning, the development of an individual from birth to adulthood. But then there is the question, What is the origin of the wisdom of the sperm to swim up and find the ovum? Or how does it come about that my brain knows to have eyes in this very nice position that is just right for giving me the sense of three dimensions? The question of how things get to be the way they are is a way of phrasing the primary concern of biological evolution. This is what I would like to discuss this morning. But before we move into that we need some perspective on the history of evolution and how the main ideas have been formed.

Evolution is concerned with how things get to be the way they are, functioning in the way they do. Looking for the origin is a very old concern in the West; certainly since the time of the Greeks it has been a prominent one. We will not cover the entire history of that idea, but will begin with the point that evolution became a science, in our sense, with the publication of Charles Darwin's book *The Origin of Species* in 1859. We have a very specific birthdate for the beginning of *modern* evolutionary theory.

Unfortunately, Darwin's work has been widely misconstrued in popular accounts, and people talk in a very loose sense about what he said. It's really important to go back and try to see with some precision exactly where he began. Darwin lived in a time when the study of the diversity of the animal kingdom was popular. People were fascinated as much as we are that fish can swim and don't drown, that horses have strong legs, that birds are actually able to grip branches and don't fall off. All of this seems absolutely wonderful, and people of Darwin's time were also astounded by the diversity of life and the way it all seems to work together. Darwin, like many other people at that time, went around the world making very detailed notes about the diversity of animal life.

During this time he convinced himself of something that his contemporaries were not clear about. This was not yet a theory, just an observation. He said: "Maybe the way to understand this diversity of life is to think that a current member of a species changes a little bit from its predecessors, and by slight changes in every generation, species get to be different." For example, he observed many passerine birds in South America, and he realized that when the groups of birds had adjacent territories, they tended to be similar. That meant, he thought, that such groups must have had a common ancestor in times not long past. When animal groups are widely divergent, it means that their common ancestor was way back in time.

Modification by Descent

In brief, he formulated a new notion: that animal evolution might work through *modification by descent*. This was a great innovation in the description of observation. Though merely a descriptive device, it was very important. I want to stay with it for a moment.

If you take Darwin's book and you look for a figure in it, you won't find pictures of birds or turtles or dinosaurs or whatever. There is only one figure, only one, and it's something like a lineage tree. For example, we can think of a lineage tree for the Buddhadharma.* The main origin is Shakyamuni in the fifth century before Christ. As we move up in time we have the origin of the Theravadan school in Burma, Vietnam, or Ceylon. Then we have

---

*The Buddhist teaching and enlightenment experience is thought to be transmitted directly down through the generations from teacher to disciple, beginning with Shakyamuni Buddha.

the Mahayana in India, which seems to have been stopped by the invasion of Islam; and then the origin of Tibetan Buddhism, with its Old Translation school and New Translation school. As a result of small modifications, step by step, one sees in the present, the twentieth century, all of this diversity of teaching, but all with the same common ancestor.

The idea of modification by descent does two things. On the one hand, it explains diversity, and on the other hand, it introduces this notion of something beginning with a common ancestor. This point is absolutely crucial to Darwin but must be separated from a further idea that made Darwin the real scientific hero of the West. The difficult question is what *mechanism* can account for this succession of little steps of transformation, one after the other. It's obvious, for example, that Buddhist history starting from Shakyamuni could have taken many different shapes. How did it happen that it took the shape it has today? This is the question Darwin pondered for many years. The story goes that one day he was riding in his carriage reading a book, and, the roads in England being not as good as they are today, the carriage hit a bump, causing his book to fly up into the air. At that moment he said: "Of course, natural selection!" [laughter] We'll see now what he meant by that. (We love to have these stories of the moment of great inspiration. As you know, it is said that Newton conceived of gravitation when an apple fell on his head!)

The important point here is that natural selection is not the same as modification by descent; it is one good mechanism for accounting for modification by descent. I want to emphasize that it is *one* good mechanism, because this is the way Darwin saw it. He didn't say that it's the only one or the sufficient one. This Darwin himself stated.

Now, what is natural selection? Darwin explained it much as we understand it today. The idea is the following: Suppose you have a population of individuals. Think of dogs or birds. There is variation among individuals. Some of this variation could be passed from parents to offspring. This point has led to a notion that is central in evolutionary theory—the notion of *heritable* variation, that characteristics can be inherited, causing diversity. It is not enough to say that individuals vary. The key point that

Darwin saw at the time was that some of this variation can be passed on, can be replicated in the descendants. This heritable variation is then also subject to environmental factors.

A good example of environmental factors at work is that all of a sudden on the planet the temperature changed a lot. It became very cold and there was a glacial period. At that time some individuals were able to withstand the cold a little better, say, because they were fatter or had thicker fur. If those factors for withstanding cold are heritable, in the next generation the descendants of individuals with cold-resistant characteristics will be represented in greater numbers in the new population, because more individuals with those characteristics will have survived to reproduce and pass them on to their offspring. Hence, environmental pressure naturally selects certain individuals, creating modification by descent. We now have the mechanism, how it works. Environmental factors *select* among the various characteristics. The phrase *natural selection* has all sorts of associations in people's minds, but from the point of view of an evolutionary biologist, it has a very precise meaning. The meaning is: What is selected is the inheritable variation, and it is selected not by an agent but by environmental conditions. This was the inspiration Darwin had in the carriage.

Darwin as a young man spent a lot of time on farms. Many farmers would do breeding experiments with domestic animals, horses and dogs. Dogs are a very good example. If we take two dogs and mate them, it is easy to observe how that gives rise to various characteristics. Now, a person may like a particular puppy and so selects this one and mates it again. This is all very easy to understand when there is a human agent doing the selection. Darwin realized that one does not need a human agent to do that selection! Darwin combined something obvious, namely that the environment imposes limits, with his knowledge about heritable variation; both conditions amount to a mechanism for modification by descent. So instead of modification by descent being just a mere description, it now became an actual theoretical explanation, because a description of the mechanism by which it worked was now included.

Figure 16 is an example of an actual lineage tree. It shows that,

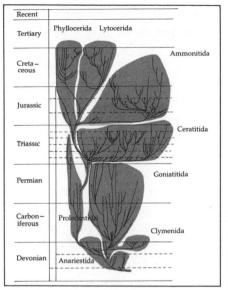

Recent
Tertiary
Cretaceous
Jurassic
Triassic
Permian
Carboniferous
Devonian

Phyllocerida Lytocerida
Ammonitida
Ceratitida
Goniatitida
Prolecantitida
Clymenida
Anariestida

FIGURE 16. Expansion and extinction in lineages of a group of trilobites, animals that existed between 300 and 500 million years ago.

in fact, when one examines the fossil record left by animals, particularly animals like marine molluscs with shells that leave a very clear fossil record, one does find precisely the kinds of things that Darwin talks about. Although he didn't have such rich evidence, it has now been completely confirmed that if you trace the shapes of these shells over great periods of time, you see that changes in the shape of the fossils follow patterns that resemble lineage trees. Biologists give these clusters of slightly similar shells family names. At various points one can see, for example, that how what used to be a very small lineage compared with other very dominant ones later became the sole survivors when something happened that completely wiped out all the other families. That family was naturally selected.

So modification by descent is explained by natural selection, which is bound up with the idea that there will continuously be significant environmental changes that will cause some characteristics of a species—or a whole species—to be preferred over others. And this becomes a testable proposition; one can go back and see if this was the case. I have to be quite straightforward here and say that although most biologists deeply believe that natural selection is the effective mechanism of evolution, it is not that clear that in every case it leads to explanations, or even less, to predictions. For the time being I'm just painting the picture as Darwin saw it.

Adaptation

We will come to the current criticisms of natural selection in a bit, but before that I have to introduce another idea that came along with natural selection. This was the notion that natural selection always produces an optimal or a good *adaptation* to the environment. An adaptation was measured by the degree to which the organism was actually successful in leaving descendants. This is a subtle but important point. When we talk about adaptation we normally mean that fish can swim and horses can walk. This is not what is meant in evolutionary theory. In evolutionary theory a well-adapted plant or animal is one that can leave many descendants or whose descendants can be sure to survive, either one. If a species doesn't leave descendants, then there's no way that it's going to be seen later on. So either the animal has many descendants, which gives them a good chance to continue the lineage, or there are a few descendants that are so well protected that one is sure to survive. Humans work with that second strategy; insects use the first strategy. Either way, one ensures the continuity of descendants, and that is the measure of adaptiveness.

Up to now, we have the story through the 1910s or the 1920s. At that time people began to ask the question, What is the mechanism behind hereditary variation? How can something be transmitted from one generation to the next? People were beginning to look for the mechanisms of heredity. Finally it was discovered that during the process of generating a new life, in the fertilization of an egg by a sperm, distinguishing elements inside the nucleus of a cell—chromosomes—are present. There's a fixed number of them in each cell, and they make copies of themselves right before the next new cell is formed. This is a mechanism through which father and mother can pass on to a descendant something that embodies genetic variation.

DALAI LAMA: How does DNA (which is considered to be the main carrier of the genetic code) relate to the chromosomes?

FRANCISCO J VARELA: The chromosome is something that you see in the microscope as a fairly large, coiled worm. If you move another step in magnification and analyze deeper, you find that the chromosome is like a network of two components, some proteins and the nucleic acids, including DNA (desoxyribonucleic acid). The DNA is very highly packed thread inside the chromosome. If I were to take the DNA out of a cell of any animal, and just lay it out straight, it would cover many, many kilometers. This thread is compacted so tightly inside that it fits into a tiny chromosome.

The New Synthesis

DNA wasn't discovered as the central genetic material until 1950, but already in 1920 people knew that the chromosomes were essential for genetic transmission. Later on, our knowledge became refined to the level of the DNA, and later on even to the level of finer molecular bits. In any case, here on the one hand is Darwin's theory of natural selection, and on the other, the studies on hereditary mechanisms. In 1930 or 1940 biologists felt that both these together were enough for a coherent theory of evolution. This was called the new synthesis (of genetics and evolutionary biology); sometimes it was also referred to as neo-Darwinism. It was announced with great pride. I myself was raised in that mood of triumph in biology, and people were busy actually finding many interesting results.

With the new synthesis, people doing studies became confident that in fact the whole of life could be explained on the basis of a common tree of life. We know, for example, that a fish and a horse are more closely related to each other than to various other species. They're closer to each other in the lineage than to, say, the amoeba, and certainly the amoeba is closer to the plant than to the fish. One can draw a tree that is like a stream of water running down a mountain, giving rise to all of the varieties that we have observed, and little by little, one can reconstruct the path up to the top of the mountain, which is of course the very origin of life.

DALAI LAMA: Perhaps this is not a profound question, but since biologists seem to be tracing the origin of life, and according to science there is a beginning somewhere where everything is empty like space, how would you explain the origin or emergence of life, or whatever you may call it, from that? Once this planet is already existent and there is already an environment, the origin of life becomes explainable. But if there isn't any environment. . . . Before this planet or this galaxy formed, life must already exist.

VARELA: The argument of the scientists goes in exactly the opposite direction. We have a lineage, life, and an environment. Starting with that, we go back and back and back and back, and then we can observe through the geological record that there is a point at which there is only environment, there is just planet. We can then observe that there is a moment, which is something like five billion years ago, when there was no life whatsoever. There was only planet. So the scientist says, At this point life must have started!

B. ALAN WALLACE [interpreter]: His Holiness was referring to the time before this planet actually existed.

VARELA: Then, for the scientists, there is obviously no life. Life can only originate when there are some conditions, and so the argument is that there must have been some conditions. These must derive from something before, when there was a galaxy or sun or a supernova, or whatever the astronomers say. I'm very glad that you're asking that question, because it is the logical question to ask and this is precisely why we wanted to ask our friend Dr. Luisi, a specialist on molecules, to give us an account of this. Before life, there is only the environment, which means some molecular state. After a moment, there is life. How can scientists look at this problem of the origin of life? One key issue is a better understanding of molecules. I'll now ask Luigi to give us a brief explanation of this.

Molecular Evolution

LUIGI LUISI: The questions I will discuss are: What are molecules, and how are they linked to life and to the other issues we have been talking about? Let me start by recalling something you all know: that there are atoms and there are molecules. Atoms are the basic components of all matter. There are over one hundred different kinds of atoms, for example, oxygen, hydrogen, nitrogen, carbon, zinc, sodium, and so on. All these atoms combine according to precise rules into stable aggregates, which are called molecules. A molecule is the constituting element of a chemical substance: a pure substance is identified by one type of molecule. For example, the molecule of water is constituted by two atoms of hydrogen and one atom of oxygen. A molecule of hydrogen is constituted by two atoms of hydrogen, and so on.

There is already one very important point that we can make: Although water is constituted only by hydrogen and oxygen, its properties cannot be derived and understood on the basis of the properties of isolated hydrogen and oxygen. When different atoms come together to build a molecule, there is an emergence of new properties that are characteristic of the molecule and not of the constituting atoms. We will come back to this point of emergence a little later, when we speak about the "molecules of life."

The concept of the molecule and the identification of a particular molecule with a particular substance is central to quite a large range of the modern sciences. Chemistry, biochemistry, molecular biology, but also clinical medicine and agriculture, are completely based on this molecular concept: namely, that the properties of a substance are intrinsically determined by its chemical structure, that is, by the constituting molecule. Also in our everyday life, we are surrounded by chemicals that have been synthesized more or less directly according to this concept: cosmetics, perfumes, textiles, plastics, dyes. Progress in all these fields today is closely bound with the concept of the molecule.

Now I would like to consider a couple of points relevant to our meeting. One is about the dynamic properties of molecules, properties connected with movement or change. Let me elaborate on this through the example of a glass of water. Many people are not aware of the fact that the volume actually occupied by water molecules in this glass of water is very small, perhaps one percent or less of the total volume. The rest can be considered as empty space. The same is true for all other liquids, and even more so for gases; but it is also true, although to a lesser degree, for solids.

DALAI LAMA: The water molecules are not touching each other?

LUISI: They are interacting with each other, but over a certain distance, so that there is a lot of space between them.

DALAI LAMA: But in this empty space are there particles of air? Is it just purely empty space?

LUISI: In pure water, it is empty space. You can say, however, that there is a field of energy.

WALLACE: This is a very interesting point, because there is a lot of discussion on this in Buddhist philosophy—about whether there is empty space between particles and how they interact.

LUISI: Because of this large empty space, the molecules of water enjoy a large movement. This constitutes the dynamic properties I mentioned. The molecules continuously change location and orientation. Seen in this way, the glass of water has a dual character: it is something static, always the same, as we like to consider it in everyday life; but if you consider the movement of the molecules, a glass of water is never the same. One can attempt a parallel, or if you like, a metaphor: all this looks like the concept of the mere self we have talked about in other sessions of our meeting, namely, something that has a continuity although it has no intrinsic substantiality. The same is true for a human being: our body appears always the same from day to day, but actually our cells continuously die and are replaced by new ones, so that every morning each of us is actually a new being!

Generally in the chemical and physical sciences, we often encounter a situation in which physical reality can be depicted in these two apparently contradictory ways: in terms of a dynamic or a static view. You can study the properties of an object, like the density and weight of water; or you can add sugar to water and measure the heat arising from its dissolution. These are all equilibrium properties—properties that describe a balance that can be regarded as relatively static. But you can also look at the details of the molecular structure and measure the velocity of the tumbling molecules and their mutual interaction. In this way your view is no longer static, but dynamic. The static and the dynamic views are complementary. It is not that one view is wrong and the other is right. The view taken depends simply on the observer's standpoint.

Molecules are not living. The expression "molecules of life" simply means molecules that constitute the structures of living organisms. What are these molecules of life? Many textbooks divide molecules into two large families, the inorganic molecules and the organic molecules. The inorganic are, for example, the molecules forming salts such as the carbonates, silicates, sodium chloride—the mineral salts. The organic molecules are those constituted essentially by carbon atoms. They may be synthetic or natural. The molecules constituting the structures of life are organic molecules; and they contain, in addition to carbon, three other elements: nitrogen, hydrogen, and oxygen. Others (phosphor, certain metal atoms) are, in terms of percentage, negligible. And yet elements such as carbon or nitrogen, which are essential for life structures, are not at all important on a universal scale. If atomic chemists measured the atomic composition of our universe, practically all they would find is hydrogen. The rest is present in such small amounts that they would be unable to measure it (if it were diluted homogenously throughout the universe).

But on our earth, organic molecules are essential. The most important molecules are proteins and nucleic acids. Both of them are macromolecules—namely, very long molecules, constituted by thousands of atoms linked together in a linear chain. Nucleic acid, in the form of DNA, is involved in inheritance. Proteins display many functions. For example, silk and wool are proteins; our skin, our muscles, our hair, are constituted essentially by proteins. Hemoglobin is a protein that carries oxygen in the blood; insulin, a hormone, is a protein. Antibodies are also proteins. Enzymes, too, are proteins; they are the molecules responsible for all chemical transformations in our body and all living structures: the synthesis of vitamins, digestion of food, burning of sugar, and so on.

How is it possible that one single family of compounds (proteins) displays such a variety of properties? I would like to explain this because it is central to the question of evolution. Proteins are constituted by amino acids, which are the blocks that are linked together to form the long chain of the macromolecules.

In nature there are twenty different amino acids, that is, twenty different chemical structures. It is like having an alphabet of twenty different letters; with these you can build an almost infinite number of words.

To make only one calculation, suppose you want to know in how many ways you can build a word using sixty characters (i.e., in how many ways you can build a protein with sixty amino-acid residues; this would be a very small protein actually). Imagine a chain of sixty consecutive boxes, each box filled with any one of the twenty alphabet letters (amino acids). The theoretical number of possibilities will be 10^{70}, which is larger than the number of atoms in all the universe!

One important general feature of proteins is their folding pattern. Each protein acquires a well-defined, stable shape in space, which we call native conformation, or native folding. A protein is active only when it is folded right. The form, the three-dimensional form in space, is essential for the biological activity. Proteins display their biological function because they are able to recognize a partner molecule, and for this recognition the three-dimensional shape is the most important structural parameter.

Often, for this recognition mechanism, one part of a protein has a concave shape, a cavity, and the partner molecule (e.g., a substrate in the case of enzymes) fits perfectly into the cavity. Actually, this complementarity of forms is central to all molecular mechanisms of life, and for that matter, to life in general. It is like the bottleneck and the cork, the hand and the glove, the key and the keyhole, the masculine and the feminine genital apparatus. In molecular biology, there is a lot of inquiry about this kind of complementarity of form. A protein works only when this particular type of fitting with a partner molecule takes place. This interaction is the trigger of many biological processes.

How is the structure of proteins linked to the structure of nucleic acids, the second important class of life molecules? The link is through a gene. A gene specifies the structure of a protein. For each one of the proteins, there is a gene, namely, a linear DNA structure. Thus, when your body needs to make hemoglobin, the corresponding gene is activated, then copied—actually, the copy is made out of another nucleic acid, RNA (ribonucleic acid), and not of DNA—and this linear sequence of RNA induces the synthesis of the needed linear sequence of amino acids, the specific protein, hemoglobin in our example.

This chain of events forms the central dogma of molecular biology, according to which there is a linear flow of information going from DNA to the protein. The structure of the DNA piece, the gene, determines the structure of the protein, and indirectly also its folding. So, there is a linear causality chain going from a gene to the tridimensional folding of a protein, and hence to its biological activity.

DALAI LAMA: This is true for all animals as well as bacteria?

LUISI: This is a so-called universality of the biochemical world. We mean by this expression the fact that our cells, as well as those of plants and microorganisms, all obey the same biological mechanism. Not only that, but they all have the same structures of life molecules: DNA, RNA, and proteins. And the interactions of these life molecules obey the same mechanisms throughout the whole living world. This is a strong argument in favor of the general theory of molecular evolution, according to which all living structures originate from a common, ancestral cell.

I want to point out that the causality chain that describes the events of life ceases to be linear when you realize that amino acids are the elementary units for building proteins, but amino acids are produced by proteins. DNA is necessary for producing proteins, but you need proteins (in the form of enzymes) to build DNA. So the causality chain is not linear but circular, and actually more than circular—it is a complex three-dimensional net of events, all dependent one on the other. But no beginning, no starting point of this causality net can be pointed out. How did it all start? This is the question Francisco will be dealing with, so I will turn the floor over to him again.

The Origin of Life

VARELA: It was important to have this interlude about molecules, because when the question of the origin of life comes up, biologists are faced with a novel situation. We have to go back to molecules and understand how these "molecules of life"—DNA, proteins, and so on—become cells. And so the question of the origin of life has come to be a matter of both chemistry and biology.

We know that life didn't exist, say, 5 billion years ago. We know that life has existed for 3.6 billion years. So what was the world like when life appeared? One thing we know is that at that time the sea existed. There were many electrical discharges because the atmosphere was composed differently than it is now. There was a lot of sun radiation that existed at that time that doesn't exist now. This was simulated in the laboratory, and when the chemists sampled water from this simulated environment, to every scientist's delight, they found amino acids—which are the main components of proteins—and the beginnings of nucleic acids. I will make a very long story short and say that there is some evidence coming from simulation of this primitive earth scenario for the spontaneous emergence of proteins and nucleic acids owing to the cooperative conditions present.

How then can there be more and more complex molecules? The study of this question is extremely technical today and has produced no clear conclusions. But the current idea is that there is no insurmountable mystery preventing explanation of how these molecules arise. Once you have proteins and nucleic acids, they can link up together in this unique pattern that is the cell. From the Western point of view, it is important to say that in going up the stream of time, once you get to the cell, *that* is the beginning of life. But that beginning of life can in turn be explained by emergent molecular properties, and there is a substantial amount of experimental evidence for that view.

The field of study of the origin of life is full of debates and controversies. But I think it's fair to say that no biologist or chemist doubts that, one way or the other, emerging links can be found to explain what you find in this remarkable picture [see figure 17]. These are the oldest fossils ever encountered. They were found somewhere in Africa. These old stones can be dated to 3.6 million years ago. They contain cell-like profiles, which can be compared with this, for example, which is a living bacte-

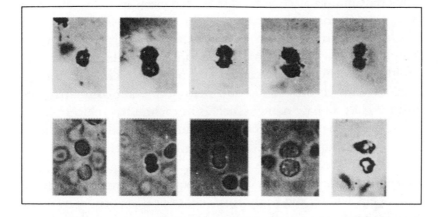

FIGURE 17. *Top:* Photograph of fossils presumed to be bacteria found in deposits more than 3 billion years old. *Bottom:* Photographs of living bacteria whose form is comparable to that of the fossils.

rium. You can see why the scientist would say that these were among the first cells that ever arose on this primitive earth. An interesting point is that they actually look very much like the ones we see today. The lineage, in this case, has stayed absolutely unbroken, and the evolutionary tree we saw is a direct stream. As offshoots, you find all the rest of life.

So this is how science understands the origin of life. Cells didn't exist before, and then they actually came into being through the kind of chemical and atmospheric processes we just described. Here is an area that is highly interdisciplinary. One needs a chemist to go into the details of the chemistry. One needs a biologist to study the cellular part, and one also needs the people who study the history of the planet, the geophysicists, to go into the details of what the environment was like at the time cells are supposed to have arisen. As it turns out, there is not one initial point for the origin of life but, more likely, many initial points. There are many kinds of bacteria. Some of them look like little worms; some of them look like little rods with tails that wiggle around. Many kinds of bacteria seem to have originated independently, looking much as they do today. The origin of life wasn't one event in one place but a distributed event in many different places and forms, and we can see traces of those forms even today.

One interesting point here, from the point of view of understanding life as other than a competitive struggle, is that what biologists normally call a cell is a complex structure containing a nucleus with chromosomes and many other subcompartments inside. They all have names (such as mitochondria, chloroplasts, etc.). I can't go into the interior structure of the cell in detail here, but it's as though inside there is a little city with many things happening. A bacterium is also a cell, but it's a simpler cell, because these compartments inside do not exist. We speak of a true cell, or eukaryote, and a primitive cell, or prokaryote.* The point here is that it is currently accepted that the simple cells actually give rise to the complex cells that compose our organism by a process of coming together, of cooperation, so that some cells begin to live inside of others. Thus the cells that compose our bodies are in fact what we can call symbiotic unities. Each of the compartments inside the modern cell was originally the cell's ancestor. It's one of these simple bacteria that have learned how to live with others and help each other in maintaining and supporting their continuity. So it is quite interesting to see that for most of the history of life on earth, three-quarters of the time that life has been on the planet, life has been only bacterial life, single-celled life. Only in the last quarter of the time have these more complex cells emerged. Only then were many of these cells able to come together to constitute animals and plants. It is important to note that nowadays evolution doesn't just mean plants and animals going through classical natural selection, but it also means life traced back to its very roots in the microworld. We're used to the macroworld of plants and animals, but in terms of both time and sheer volume, the microworld is heavily predominant.

Altruism

So around 1950–1960, people in evolutionary biology felt that they really had a very clear picture, joining together natural selec-

---

*A prokaryotic cell lacks the membrane-enclosed nucleus and membrane-enclosed organelles found in true, or eukaryotic, cells. Organelles are bodies with specialized functions suspended in the cytoplasm of eukaryotic cells.

tion and genetics. This new synthesis seemed to be the answer to all of their questions, and there seemed to be no clouds on the horizon other than details. However, soon large clouds started to appear, and I think that it is very fair to say that in the 1980s evolutionary theory was in enormous turmoil and disarray. There are many open questions, and people debate very passionately. There is certainly no sense that evolutionary biology is a unified science as it used to be twenty years ago. I would like to convey to you then some of the objections that were raised against neo-Darwinism that seem quite fundamental.

One of the most simple objections I know you will find interesting, because it is tied in with an issue of compassion. It's a very simple question. In natural selection, since it is based on heritable variation, there can be selection only at the individual level, that is, only one individual can increase its chance of leaving more descendants. This is very clear. Now, when biologists look at nature, they find the clear fact that animals not only take care of their own young, but they take care of each other beyond that. This is what biologists call altruism, that is, working for the benefit of the group. For example, at the South Pole you find almost nothing but ice, but there are also penguins. Penguins are very interesting birds, because in order for them to get enough food, they have to go out and fish all day long. So this is a problem. How are the parents, both the father and mother, going to care for the eggs if they have to go out and catch fish all day? Penguins have solved this problem by creating kindergartens. A few birds stay behind and take care of the eggs and the young of the whole group, while the parents go out and fish. Then when everybody comes back, they all take care of the children.

This observation is not unique. So, around 1960 this exploded into a controversy in biology. People rightly asked how this altruistic behavior could be accounted for. It appears to totally contradict natural selection! For example, in a pack of wolves, if there is an attack from another group of animals, one or two of them will stay behind and be killed to let the other ones escape. From the point of view of natural selection, this is not understandable, and the logic is very simple. If I have a tendency to be good to others and I let myself be killed, how is that tendency going to be transmitted to the next generation? It doesn't make any sense.

So, interestingly enough, the issue of love and kindness beyond just individual descendants—since there is no reason from the point of view of natural selection why it should evolve—created an enormous debate in evolutionary biology. It showed that natural selection could not entirely account for evolution.

The way scientists have tried to resolve this difficulty is by seeing natural selection as acting not only at the level of the individual but also at the level of the group. The classical notion was "the survival of the fittest," meaning the individual. Now we have not just individual fitness, but inclusive fitness. It means that if I am good to my neighbor, in the long run this will be good for me as well. If we try to formulate a logic for this, we come up with the probability that the kinds of genes that I have will be transmitted, perhaps not by me, but maybe by somebody else in my group. There is kind of a pattern of taking in the hereditary material individually and distributing the responsibility for it to the entire population, so that now selection can happen at the level of the entire group. Is that understandable?

DALAI LAMA: First of all, I raise the instance of a dog sacrificing itself for its master. Here you have a dissimilarity of species and no possibility of a hereditary benefit unless you think on a very large scale. Is it accepted that such altruism or self-sacrifice occurs across species?

VARELA: Well, as has often been the case in this conference, Your Holiness, you seem to anticipate the scientists' questions. That is precisely the kind of evidence that people started gathering for this debate. There are plenty of cases of cross-specific altruism. For example, there are cases of children who have been raised by wolves. There are even a few documented cases of dolphins in the sea who have saved shipwrecked sailors. They carry them up onto the beach. It's not that they just grab onto them like a fish might bite. It's deliberate. So this is an open problem and one that I find absolutely fascinating, because in fact that potential for undirected compassion and openness seems to get always wider. It seems to be expandable even in animals beyond what biologists can explain in the classical way.

So this is one criticism of neo-Darwinism. It can be summarized by saying that although natural selection happens only at the individual level, today it is clear that evolution happens at many levels. At the group level, the species level, the individual level, the cellular level, and even, we would say, at the genetic level.

DALAI LAMA: I'm wondering what similarities there are here with Buddhist theory. In the animal kingdom, animals like us are endowed with cognition. They are also subject to the mental distortions of attachment and anger, as well as having the potential for compassion and altruism. Now, I am wondering how a Buddhist might explain the fact that altruism may be primarily devoted to any species.

ROBERT B. LIVINGSTON: Altruism is even found in some plants, you know. Insects and plants have many interdependent behaviors, the plants favoring the insects' survival and the insects favoring the plants' survival. This occurs in every phylum, in every part of the great tree of evolution. It's not that there isn't conflict; it's that there is mutual cooperation. The interdependence that exists has the appearance of doing work or inventing or learning and adapting—which are complicated biological processes—on behalf of mutual survival, not simply individual survival.

VARELA: Life altogether does not seem to be possible at all without a degree of openness in responding to others. It is interesting to note that even the species-specific cooperative response may already be generalized enough to account for cross-specific altruism. For example, when the penguin's response in taking care of the young of other penguins might even go beyond its own species. Dolphins seem to engage in cross-specific altruism all the time, and so do chimpanzees and even wolves. This quality of openness in animals seems to be extendable to the kind of altruism that is without a predetermined object. Although sometimes the object is predetermined, there seems to be a continuum from animals all the way to the full potential for undirected compassion possible in humans.

Species Are Not Getting Better at Living on the Planet

Another big, big criticism of neo-Darwinism that has come up is this: Since natural selection is supposed to be going on continually, species should get better and better adapted to their environments. Species should be getting better and better at living on this planet. This is a testable observation. It implies among other things that the more recent species, since they are the product of more adaptation, should be able to create more new species, since each one of them should be fitter and fitter for producing surviving offspring. Is this the case? One can go back and study, for example, how many new species there are of certain marine animals that leave enough fossil remains that one can trace their history all the way back to the origin. Does one find that from their origin until today that they spin off the same number of new species, or is it only more recently that more develop? The clear answer is that the number of new species is constant over time. Thus, in this respect there is no sense of getting better all the time. Evolution is just carrying on at the same pace. The idea of progressive adaptation finds no confirmation from these kinds of observation.

This has become a big problem, because people don't have a clear idea of what they mean by fitness in the evolutionary context. In the 1950s and 1960s, the idea of fitness was very clear: it could be measured by the number of descendants. Today it's far from simple, because all of the measures of fitness that have been tried simply don't work. They simply don't tally with observation. Just the idea of fitness has become the subject of great debate. But if one doesn't know how to measure fitness, the whole point of view with natural selection at the center of it falls apart. That has been a second major focus of debate and criticism.

Selection Pressure Is Not the Main Factor in Adaptation

A third criticism of neo-Darwinism—and this will be last—is something like this: From the point of view of natural selection, characteristics change in response to the environment. This is like the behavioristic model—responses happen when there are stimuli. Here the environmental change is the stimulus, and the change in the species through natural selection is the response. It's a very behavioristic point of view. It is as if the inside of the population of animals is a black box as the mind was a black box between stimulus and response in behavioristic psychology.* In fact what happens is not at all like that. As we know, something that is a stimulus for the brain doesn't have a single predetermined effect, because inside the brain there are enormous numbers of things that relate to the stimulus and transform it and interpret it in many different ways. Exactly the same has turned out to be the case in evolutionary biology. For a change to occur, there must be two factors in play. One is that selection will be on the basis of genes. However, genes are not collections of little balls in a box, where you can know whether you are passing on a particular gene to an offspring. Genes are like points in a network or in a matrix, because they are all interdependent with each other; so if I want to increase the presence of one gene in a population, I also have to work with all the others that are tied to it. There is also a problem with getting one gene in one organism to change. The process of development of an organism is very, very complex, so one gene cannot be changed without altering an enormous quantity of things in the resulting adult. One cannot select isolated traits or characteristics.

Suppose that the environment becomes colder. It would be selectively advantageous to have hair grow on the body. However, it is not so simple as just putting in one gene for hair. To have hair on the body you have to in fact restructure the entire body, because to have hair the skin has to be changed. To change the skin, you need to change all of the biochemistry inside the body. To change the biochemistry inside of the body, you need to change the physiology. So just to have a little hair grow means restructuring the entire organism. This cannot be done every time from point zero. It is as though organisms impose their own point of view on what changes are possible, so that at every moment not everything is possible. There are only a few little changes possible, and they are very restricted. It is much like perception, where one has expectations and cannot perceive things that are not within them.

The view that the environment delivered "pressures" that would force selection is now usually referred to as the view of

---

*See earlier section, "Cognitive Psychology," on pages 84–106.

adaptationism, because the idea was that all responses were to challenges in the environment and the species just adapted to them. But this does not tally with observation at all. One needs to take into account the internal factors at the genetic level and input at the embryological level that comes from the organism itself. These are called the *intrinsic factors* in evolution. So, the theory must take into account not only the external factors of environment and natural selection, but the internal factors imposed by genetic interdependence and embryological interdependence. These last two are very important. In fact today outstanding evolutionary biologists affirm that a large proportion of the key factors in evolution—and therefore the most useful factors in explaining the diversity of life—are internal factors rather than external selection pressures. Yes, it is true that if the planet gets very cold, animals have to change, but how they go about it is the result of internal factors much more than of external factors. It's as if external factors impose very broad constraints that do not, cannot possibly, determine what will happen. I find this very interesting, because it is an exact parallel to what we learned in talking about perception. Yes, we need light and we need some stimulation to the retina. Those are the constraints. But what we see depends on internal factors; and the two together, internal and external factors, give rise to some kind of stable perception. The case here seems to be much the same. The environment creates some constraints; then we have internal factors, and together these two give rise to species and evolution. The internal element is all the more significant in that what we call the environment is to an important degree the result of life itself. Life produces environment, which becomes a constraining factor, which then, again together with life, produces results. These two things, life and environment, really define each other interdependently. One cannot say the environment was just there and animals were sort of parachuted onto the earth. That was the view implicit in the adaptationism of neo-Darwinism. The environment was just there and provided the selection pressures, and the different animals are just dropped into the environment and are further selected through evolution. This was a kind of behaviorists' view of evolution.

In conclusion, it is fair to say that today there is no coherent theory of evolution. Some aspects of Darwin's view are intact, but the idea of natural selection as determined by external environmental pressures has softened greatly. The environment is now regarded as the source of only broad constraints. There are many other mechanisms operating that are only fractionally understood.

Evolution, Karma, and Compassion

A Conversation

Criticism of the Popular Idea of the Struggle for Survival

FRANCISCO J. VARELA: People have made much of the notion, attributed to Darwin, that life is a competitive struggle. It's a struggle for survival because resources are limited. Therefore, individuals and species have to fight with each other, because otherwise they won't survive. Darwin did say something like this, and here derived much inspiration from an economist, Malthus, who spoke about limited resources for human populations. But the fact that some resources are limited and the overall conditions of the environment change, providing selective pressures, was just one of his inspirations, by no means the only one.

JEREMY W. HAYWARD: But the way that evolutionary biology is taught in schools and colleges greatly emphasizes the importance of competition and the limitation of resources!

VARELA: That's why I said, and want to reiterate, that what Darwin actually said and the way biologists also nowadays see the doctrine of natural selection is not what journalists, popular accounts, and even schoolteachers have made of it.

ROBERT B. LIVINGSTON: Yes. In the West there has been a distortion of three teachings: Darwin's, Freud's, and Marx's. In each of these three, the distortion has been in favor of competition and conflict. The original people, Darwin, Freud, and Marx, did not emphasize that aspect as much as modern philosophers and teachers do. As a consequence, for example, with Darwin, the emphasis on conflict allows the mercantile business philosophy to say survival of the fittest means you can do anything to the other guy. It's your cunning and your survival against his.

But actually Darwin, Freud, and Marx were equally concerned with cooperation, and I think it is important for His Holiness to recognize that this is a distortion in the West that I think real biology, real psychology, and real economics do not countenance.

VARELA: I agree. This, I think, is quite important. But there is a difference here between, on the one hand, studying cooperation as a topic that has not been fashionable until just recently, and on the other hand, the idea that natural selection can only be explained on the basis of struggle. There's a difference there. When people in the West talk about struggle for survival, it means I kill another because there is only food for one of us. It's not that I struggle to live. It's that I kill others so that I can survive. This is the popular idea.

DALAI LAMA: If we consider one bigger tree and one smaller one, it is almost as if the bigger tree is killing the smaller one in order to survive. This is also related to changes in the environment.

VARELA: Let me see if I understand the point. Consider one of the classical examples of natural selection (which in fact turned out to be false, but let's leave that for the time being). There are little moths that have a white color identical to that of the tree that is their habitat. This coloring prevented the birds that feed on them from seeing them. This was the natural condition. Then industrialization came to Victorian England and produced a lot of smog that made dark stains on the trees. Now these white moths stood out and the birds could eat them. Biologists observed that more and more of these moths started to be a little darker, so that they looked like the dirty trees. They said, "Fantastic, here is natural selection at work." This was not a case of one moth killing another to survive. They all changed in accordance with environment. Wouldn't you say that this is different?

DALAI LAMA: There is a difference. It's not like struggling at the expense of others.

VARELA: Exactly, although Your Holiness is also right that between these two things, there are some gray areas where the adaptation is partly one and partly the other. It's not so clear that it's always either killing one another or just changing with the environment. It's a mixture of both.

LIVINGSTON: If you have exposure to cold as in the time of the glaciers, then the physiological adaptation may be better in one individual than in another, and nature will select for the improvement of temperature control, shivering, and other actions, and also in favor of cooperation in doing things like building a shelter or a fire or making clothing. The kind of Darwinian evolution that Francisco talked about included these kinds of physiological adaptations and intellectual adaptations for humans.

VARELA: I'm glad we clarified this distortion of Darwin's ideas because although there might be some differences in emphasis among the scientists themselves, my feeling is that the real biologists don't take the struggle for survival very literally. The picture is more complex. The important thing is that it was the idea of natural selection that became science, not "nature red in tooth and claw."

HAYWARD: You said that there is, today, no coherent theory of evolution, but there are many mechanisms operating that are only very fractionally understood. Is this the view accepted by a majority of mainstream biologists?

VARELA: Widely respected biologists like Steve Gould and Richard Lewontin, and others, have made some of these points. There are, of course, degrees of criticism of the classical view that nobody will deny. As I was growing up and as a student, I never heard one criticism of the neo-Darwinian view! It was solid doctrine, and it seemed that it explained everything.

HAYWARD: I was reviewing a college biology textbook recently, an introductory course, and none of this was mentioned. This was a 1983 or 1984 edition.

VARELA: Your Holiness, this is part of the sociology of science, that textbooks are way behind. When a textbook says something, you have to think "twenty years ago."

Karma and Evolution

VARELA: In the Buddhist tradition, karma is a term used for causal relationships and the consequences of human action. It seems that there is also a Buddhist idea of causality in the world of, for example, seeds and plants and water—in the world of nature. Now, the Western notion of evolution seems to suggest a link between human life, or animal life for that matter—sentient life—and this causality in nature. Do you see any equivalence between the Western notion of evolutionary transformation and the notion of karma? What do you see as the similarities and differences?

DALAI LAMA: I find this a very complex issue, because in Buddhist texts the theory of karma is very much related with actions that are directly related to living beings, actions that bring feelings of pain and pleasure. Thus, in this context the external environment is also spoken about in those terms. When you really get into the details [of nature], the actual physical substance and the environment, then I feel that matters are again open [not bound to the karmic pattern]. The fact that consciousness or cognition arises in the nature of clarity indicates that, from the Buddhists' point of view, knowing isn't related to any karmic theory at all. It's just nature. And in the same way the fact that external objects, like particles, have their own nature is also not related to the karmic theory. These questions are not discussed in that context as karma.

If you take a piece of paper, for example, the piece of paper arises from the continuum of the substance that preceded it, that preceding substance being a substantial cause. Now, if we're just looking at the paper and how it arises from substantial causes, I really have my doubts whether this is in any way related to the idea of karma. But on the other hand, the fact that there's now a pad of paper before me and it's there for me to use—as soon as it is contextually related to me—it is a matter of karma. It is there for something. Whose karma? My karma, the person to whom it belongs and who utilizes it. Likewise, if it's eventually eaten by some insect, then the presence of that paper will be related to that insect's karma. Now, concerning the external environment, how trees and plants and so forth arise: On the one hand, the environment naturally relates to sentient beings, because the type of trees that there are, the type of fruit that they bear, whether bitter or sweet, and how all these things relate to sentient beings, is a matter of the karma of sentient beings. It's related to the sentient beings themselves, on the one hand. On the other hand, if you say, "Let's take the mountains and leave out organisms altogether," and we understand the question purely in terms of causal sequences, I once again have my doubts about whether this is really a matter of karma or even related to the whole theory of karma, because it is spoken of out of the context of sentient beings.

Similarly, concerning the whole evolution of the cosmos, if we go back to the Kalachakra system and space particles,* then in a general way we can say, Yes, the evolution of the universe is related to the karma of sentient beings. They're responsible in a general way. But as soon as you get to particulars—if you take one space particle and follow its evolution for however many billion years and all the interactions it enters into with the rest of the environment—then once again, as soon as you're not speaking in the context of sentient beings' experiencing this, I feel very doubtful whether it is really a matter of karma.

The whole topic is very difficult, but let's take something on this planet, for example, changes in weather patterns. There can be one area that's receiving drought while another area is receiving flood. On the one hand, this is understood in the scientific manner as simply causes and conditions coming together "out there." But insofar as this is affecting sentient beings, then the karma of the sentient beings is acting as a cooperative cause in this occurrence. So there are substantial causes and cooperative causes, and with the juxtaposition of these two, these events will arise.

Now let's take a specific community. Imagine a community in which there is intense and pervasive hatred or anger. I feel that such a state of negative emotion might have an impact on the environment, for example, might contribute to bringing about great heat or drought. If there is a community in which great attachment or craving is very strong and pervasive, this could perhaps lead to a lot of moisture, flooding. I'm just pondering these issues, not making definite assertions. But it is true,

---

*See pages 77–83.

whether you're dealing with an individual or a larger community, that the activity, the behavior, the mind-state of the individuals of that community will, on a daily, monthly, and yearly basis, influence their environment.

VARELA: But what about the future? Your answer is interesting and I'd like to come back to that, but it doesn't seem to address the kinds of causalities that evolutionary biologists look at. The question of weather and the larger picture of the environment, I agree, seems a lot more difficult and certainly not a question that scientists could deal with today. But I would also be interested in the area where there would seem to be an overlap, which is the area concerned with the direct consequences of sentient beings' actions for sentient beings. For example, from the Buddhist point of view, if I take rebirth as a human being, then the fact that I have this body is a form of karma—I am inhabiting this body because there is a history—which is also what evolution is about. So it seems there's a way in which the actions of sentient beings that impact on themselves and other sentient beings is certainly a matter of evolution, and we have seen how scientists deal with this. But it is also part of karma directly. This is the area of my question: How can the Buddhist analysis and the scientific analysis be connected here?

DALAI LAMA: If the evolution of, let's say, the human species, is entirely a matter of the environment and the modification of genes, chromosomes, and so forth, then there really isn't a place for karma at all. It simply wouldn't fit because all the effects would presumably be entirely accounted for by their physical constituents. However, cells evolve to become more and more complex, and then later evolve into human beings. Just as Dr. Livingston described,* there are many options, some seventy trillion, that one human could become [based on the assortment of the parental genes]. Yet just one option is taken, and if the question is asked, Why? then karma is directly related to this question.

VARELA: Right! Which is again why the question about

---

*See pages 169–170.

karma arises, since the evolutionary theory attempts to answer why. You see, Your Holiness, it's a very simple-minded question. When an animal, or a human being for that matter, looks for another animal to mate with and there is desire, attraction, there is also a sense of care for the young, and there is good karma of love and kindness, and the couple may perform altruistic acts for the group. These are all factors that from an evolutionary stand-point affect what will happen in the future, because they affect probabilities concerning the descendants—all the mechanisms of sex, heredity, and so on. These are also all karmic matters in the Buddhist sense, because they have to do with actions, meritorious and nonmeritorious actions. So it seems that whether I take care of my children or not can be seen from both points of view, from an evolutionary point of view and from a karmic point of view. The question is, Would it be possible in your mind that these two are related to each other, much like the brain and the consciousness, with one being the cooperative cause of the other?

DALAI LAMA: First of all, the hair on my head, does it occur as a result of karma? Definitely. In previous lives I established the karma for rebirth as a human being, and this has yielded my present human body. So this hair, being part of the body, is definitely there as a result of karma, but now imagine shaving the head. You have some hair in your hand and you toss it up in the air. Part of the hair goes to the east, is taken by little gusts of wind to the east, and part of the hair blows to the west. Is that event a result of karma? Very questionable.

Actually I doubt that the fact that human beings have hair, in the same manner that different trees have different leaves, is a direct result of karma. Since generally my body is a result of my own karma, from that point of view my hair is also a result of karma, but it is questionable to attribute to karma the fact that human beings have hair and other species don't.

It's very difficult to make a demarcation between the impact of the environment, that is, of the natural facts, and that of karmic action. It's a very fine line.

HAYWARD: Maybe we could take an example that's more particular to Buddhist doctrine—the example of aggression.

Now, we won't worry about hairs on a person's head but about this person who has a lot of anger. The biologist would say that this anger is a characteristic that came from the genes of the mother and father, and in turn from their parents, and so on, back and back. The Buddhist explanation is karma. Do these two explanations coincide or not?

DALAI LAMA: I find that these two presentations are really not incompatible. There's no question that if a person is hot-tempered by nature this would relate to his heredity, parents and so forth, and a person's intelligence is also related to heredity. This is not new knowledge for the Tibetans. But I do not find this incompatible with karma, because the question arises as to why that sentient being entered into the womb of that particular mother? There's where the karma would slip in.

HAYWARD: So there are two separate causal streams, the stream of the material body and the stream of consciousness?

VARELA: It seems, then, you would say that in fact the evolutionary explanation is part of the cooperative cause?

DALAI LAMA: This is so; I agree to these points. What is the substantial cause whence the individual's intelligence arises? It is the intelligence of the whole continuum of consciousness, which goes back to that individual's previous life. What are the cooperative conditions that give rise to this particular intelligence in this lifetime? They are the brain, the genes, the whole biological system. I feel that the specific aspects of karmic actions and their results are quite beyond ordinary understanding. They are very concealed phenomena, the third category, the very, very subtle.

Is There a Direction to Evolution?

DALAI LAMA: This morning you said that 3.6 billion years ago there were various bacteria that had the potential to generate symbiotic relationships [and thus form more complex cells], but for three-fourths of this period they did not. Was it simply environmental conditions that caused this shift three-fourths of the way through, when they did start doing these wonderful things?

VARELA: Basically, we don't know. One classical answer

would be, It must have been some environmental pressure. But we don't know.

DALAI LAMA: It's not a question of these bacteria increasing their potential for symbiotic relationships?

If I could rephrase the question: Something happened three-fourths of the way through. Leading up to that point, was it a change in the internal mechanism of the bacteria that made it so that now they had a greater potential for entering into a symbiotic relationship? That is, was the chief cause internal or was it external, in the sense of being environmental?

VARELA: Your Holiness is absolutely right in insisting on this question. It is a question that all biologists are asking, and the answer is that we don't know. Probably, in the classical sense, it is a combination of both—some new potential, as you say, and some environmental change leading to this possibility. But it's worth remarking that nevertheless this new potential didn't exclude the earlier possibilities because the earlier forms have continued to exist.

DALAI LAMA: We had at some point, perhaps, a very different environment, brought about through electrical discharge, solar radiation, and so forth. How long did the universe exist before that started to happen?

VARELA: Yes, I see your question. The planet is quite old already. If you and I were to go back five billion years and look around, we would see a panorama not totally unlike what we would see today but with some major differences. There were no trees, no plants, no animals. The oceans dominated the surface of the earth, and there was a great deal of volcanic activity. The atmosphere was totally different. There was no oxygen, for example; oxygen is a product of life.

THUBTEN JINPA [interpreter]: Life creates a kind of new environment?

VARELA: Exactly. And this is a very, very beautiful scientific puzzle, that life affects the environment just as much as the environment affects life. There is no question today, it seems, that our environment is, in a fundamental way, the expression of the history of life. Oxygen is the most dramatic example of that. At the beginning of life, oxygen was a poison. If any animal came in contact with oxygen, it would die. But gradually organisms began to learn ways to avoid being poisoned by oxygen, and eventually it became our source of breath! So there is this kind of dance between the environment and life. Some organisms would find ways to protect themselves, but then others might get poisoned. To this day there are bacteria that cannot live in the presence of oxygen, so they live in environments that are totally protected. They're called anaerobic, which simply means they require a nonoxygenated environment. We can see many things like this in the fossil record of early life, which we have really begun to appreciate in detail only recently. So the history of life, as you can see, has many, many detailed steps. And these are not only on a large scale, like the multiple origins of species, but also on a small scale, like the transformation from primitive cells to complex cells, and so on.

JINPA: Speaking from evolutionary theory, can we presume that human genes could also go through another cycle, that at a certain time we could become nonhumans or some other kind of human beings?

VARELA: There is no doubt from an evolutionary standpoint that this will happen! As we have transformed so much in the development from primates to humans, there is no doubt in an evolutionist's mind that we will continue to transform and that this transformation will eventually lead to something that is completely another thing.

NEWCOMB GREENLEAF: Or the branch of humans might die out.

VARELA: Sure, this is another alternative. Suppose there is a nuclear war. Nuclear war will wipe out all plants and animals. However, it will not touch the smaller creatures. In fact, there is evidence that at many points in history, most of life in the form of plants and animals was completely eradicated. Bacteria didn't even notice it, because they're much more resistant. So as Newcomb suggests, the evolutionary branch of humans might disappear and life might continue along another branch. We don't know. But there is no doubt that humans will continue to transform, and in fact there are even observations on the rate of transformation of humans and other animals.

GREENLEAF: Another common feeling about evolution is that somehow the human species is the point of the whole thing, that evolution is directed toward us, that we are the finest product of evolution.

VARELA: That is again part of the neo-Darwinian paradigm. The idea there is that evolution is progressively getting better, and since we are the latest we must be the best. But if you want to know how well adapted a species is, look how long it lasts. By this measure of fitness, the fittest are the bacteria. They have survived all throughout evolution. We could imagine that at one point, while the dinosaurs were around on the earth, there was a big celestial body that hit the earth so hard that it was the equivalent of exploding an atomic bomb in every major country of the planet simultaneously. So much heat was generated that all the seas evaporated. That meant a dramatic impact on life; at that point life was virtually abolished. Who stayed? Our little friends the bacteria. They were untouched. We might wipe ourselves off the planet with atomic bombs, and this probably wouldn't end life on the planet. In fact, from that point of view you can reverse the evolutionary tree and put the bacteria on top. They're the best. So, you see, this whole thing about who is at the pinnacle has become quite silly. The obvious answer is, It depends on what you're looking for. One measure of adaptation, for example, is how widespread the species is on earth, and by that measure, cockroaches and sparrows do a lot better than we do!

LIVINGSTON: And among big brains, the dolphin has a brain that is larger than ours, and it evolved about sixteen to twenty million years ago as compared with ours, which evolved only five million years ago.

DALAI LAMA: Do the biologists describe some kind of ultimate point in evolution?

VARELA: No, that approach doesn't seem to be regarded as valid. That question wouldn't arise, because we know that evolution will continue to happen. Whether it will get somewhere, reach some omega point, would be classified as a purely theological question.

Can Compassion Be Learned?

DALAI LAMA: Now, I have what is possibly a silly question, but it is very important for me. Politicians, for example, are often speaking in terms of black and white; this is good and this is bad. The idea of relative is not there. Actually, things are very much relative. So this absolutist quality of mind—this is good, this is bad—tends to be prevalent among politicians, whereas scientists are presented with issues that have made the mind become more subtle, so that it is not dealing with absolutes. I wonder whether it has been discovered that scientists have slightly less strong mental distortions? Perhaps not scientists in general but those dealing with the types of issues we have been talking about. Has any research been done on that?

VARELA: Certainly no research. All we have I think, all of us, are some anecdotes. It's hard to say. I have thought about this often, and I can only report to you my personal experience. We should hear other people here, but my experience is that among scientists the prevalence of fixations and the power of attachment are as widespread and strong as in any other group of people.

HAYWARD: We were actually talking about this at lunch a couple of days ago. We thought that even among Nobel Prize winners and other great scientists that we know, many are supremely arrogant. They believe in the world as they see it. Even creative scientists who are very playful with their rational mind in thinking about a world outside, still very often don't apply this playfulness to their own lives.

VARELA: My feeling—and I don't have data on this—is that the percentage of creative scientists with freer minds is just about the same as the percentage of creative businesspeople and creative homemakers and parents. I don't know. I wouldn't be surprised.

DALAI LAMA: I have another question concerning the possibility of learning. There are two types of cognition: mistaken and nonmistaken. The mistaken one misconceives things in the ordinary way—I am not talking about any involvement of religion. Is there any difference between the two, the mistaken and the nonmistaken, that would make it possible to significantly increase correct ascertainment and to diminish the incorrect one in human beings?

VARELA: Just purely as a professional, I would say that one can make people a little better. People can be educated to some extent to be able to be less wrong, but there's a limit. Human beings inevitably get to a point where they will make mistakes or will forget, misperceive, and so on.

DALAI LAMA: It is not a question of whether human beings can be rid of misperceptions or misconceptions. The question is between two particular instances of cognition: a misconception and a valid cognition. One can be proven by reasoning and the other cannot be proven; one has a valid objective support and the other one does not. Could the instances of valid cognition be increased and the other decreased?

VARELA: I think it is the same answer. Human beings can get a little better, and that is I guess what we would call educating somebody, making them more responsible, more able. We know that without education, if one doesn't provide the means for human beings to learn, they will be more often wrong. But this educational process is limited.

DALAI LAMA: I have understood that in raising a child there are two factors. One is that the child must get sufficient nutriment, and this is a purely material matter. The other factor is tender loving care, the affection of the parents; and you said if a child receives both, then it lives up to its full potential. However, if the child has full nutrition but the parents are indifferent and let the child feel lonely and insecure, you say its development does not come up to its full potential. How is this explained from a material point of view; how does it work?

LIVINGSTON: Yes, well, there are many aspects of tender loving care, and one aspect is touch. Touch turns out to be an essential element in the development of the infant. The child is also very interested in motion and very interested in the sounds of the human voice. Incidentally, the newborn infant knows the mother's voice and distinguishes the mother's voice when it's first born. This is known. Now, if a child is not sufficiently touched, if the infant is not touched in graceful ways, in many ways, over the whole body, if it is neglected in this way, then the child becomes fretful and cries a lot and doesn't sleep well and doesn't eat well. It's not hungry, so it begins not to thrive, and it will show a decline in growth. It should be growing fast and now it slows its growth.

DALAI LAMA: Do you think that it is only because of this touch? I want to know if it is really this act of touching that is crucial, a purely physical event of touching, or because touching in such a case is actually an external expression of what you feel toward the infant and thus maybe it is the emotion of love and tenderness that is instrumental here rather than the actual physical expression?

ELEANOR ROSCH: There is a very classic experiment in psychology with newborn baby monkeys. Some monkeys were put in a cage with a wired device in the shape of a mother monkey that they could get milk from, but it was hard. They put other monkeys in a cage with a soft cloth in the shape of the mother that they could get milk from also, so the only difference was touch. The ones with the soft mother grew up much healthier than the ones with the wire mother.

What would happen is that the little baby monkeys with the cloth mother would cling to the cloth the way a baby monkey clings to its real mother, and there are pictures of these little monkeys clinging to this cloth thing. The little babies with the cloth mother were almost like normal monkeys but not quite. There were things that were a bit wrong with them when they grew up, so the real mother was better. The babies with the wire mother would just sort of lie there apathetically, and they didn't grow and develop. When they grew to adulthood, they stayed that way. They wouldn't relate to other monkeys. They wouldn't mate. They were very sick.

LIVINGSTON: And they were inadequate as parents. I think this stresses, in at least the human situation and probably the higher apes, monkeys included, that there is intergenerational signaling. The mother signals to the baby, the baby signals to the mother, and these signals must be built in correctly on both sides. Some babies don't seem to get from the mother the kind of signals they need, and when these babies, who are like the babies that were not touched enough, come into the hospital, the nurses seem to understand what they are lacking and start giving the babies much more care that arouses response and interest in them. These babies will then start to be hungry and communicative. It's a kind of reciprocal relation. The more the baby evokes proper behavior from the mother, the more the mother gives proper behavior, the more the relationship becomes constructive for health and development. It's a nice story.

In the West we have an expression, "practice makes perfect." This is not really valid from a neurophysiological point of view. It's only when the consequences of that practice are made known to the individual, that practice makes perfect. It's this feedback of the consequences that becomes instrumental in making the perception better, or making the act better. I think that this has its social as well as its physical consequences.

VARELA: But on the other hand, we know that experiential evidence doesn't seem to come through to human beings very easily. One has to put in extra effort. For example, there is plenty of evidence that people can live in peace with each other, but people often don't. There is that paradox of not learning from evidence.

LIVINGSTON: But in a sense one has to train for that in the same way that one trains to be a musician. You have to have a discipline of training.

ROSCH: From the psychological point of view, if you take even behaviorism (which seems so far from being reasonable), since the increase of love and compassion is actually more satisfying to a person than hatred and anger—that is, in behavioristic terms, it is more reinforcing—then what you have to do is get the person to actually experience that or just to be a little bit more compassionate, and then the reinforcement will come and they will do more and more of it. It's a matter of that first stage of getting them there.

VARELA: I wish it would work that way!

DALAI LAMA: The process of examination that the scientists use is actually like searching for the essence of the designated object. In Buddhist practice, there's much discussion of the different levels of selflessness, and it has to do with this analysis of seeking out the nature of the designated object. The point of this in the Buddhist context is to apply this insight as an antidote for the mental distortions, for the kleshas such as anger, and so on. So, in the Buddhist context, especially in moments of very strong passion—very strong desire, hatred, or aversion—the object of the passion tends to appear to the mind as if it's very, very substantial, existing by virtue of its own inherent nature. If one then brings in the wisdom that comes from investigating that designated object, one finds that under analysis the designated object is not to be found. That insight then acts on the passion of the mental distortion and decreases it.

This is the case in the Buddhist context. In science as you have described it, a similar process seems to be occurring in terms of seeking out the nature of the designated object. Has there been any attempt to apply this to the arising of mental distortions and to actually heal the mind? On the one hand, there seems to be a similarity of process on the Buddhist and the scientific side, although the motivation or the context for these two processes is very different. The motivation from the Buddhist side, which I described above, is quite clear, and the motivation from the scientific side is also quite clear—simply trying to see truth. The question I am posing here is, If one simply follows the scientific process, if one were to adopt that very process totally from science, just as scientists do it, and were to apply it to the arising of mental distortions, do you think it would be effective? Is this an experiment that could be done?

VARELA: An experiment in the sense of seeing what would happen, yes, absolutely! In fact I think the experiment could take something of the following form: Suppose you expose somebody to the idea that maybe our emotions are not solid, that there is the possibility of investigating our mind a little deeper, then an ordinary Westerner would say, "That's impossible; the world is solid, I'm solid," and hold to usual Western dogmas. Typically in the Western mind there would be this split, when analyzing self, of continuing to hold onto the view of an objective world. So if we do the scientific analysis that you have just described, in fact it might create an opening for a more Buddhist analysis with the motivation of self-examination. The two things could meet in a more harmonious way.

Typically, practitioners of meditation in the West have for years kept their scientific mind in one compartment and their practitioner's mind in another. It is very difficult for them to allow them to meet. We have tried to take them through this analysis, and it seems to help quite a bit. Now, this is just a very timid beginning, but I think Your Holiness' point is very well taken and I have great hopes—which is one of my motivations for being here—that there can be a point of contact.

HAYWARD: One time we were having a class in Buddhist doctrine with people who had been practicing and studying for some years. We were reading the *Bodhicharyavatara* and discussing the practice of exchanging oneself for other.* It was in this discussion that I first realized the heavy weight of classical scientific beliefs—about perception and the self, for example—that people in the West absorb as they grow up, and how often Buddhist philosophy and practice is quite a superficial layer on top of this. So one way to counteract this is through further scientific understanding, as we have been discussing here.

DALAI LAMA: In the field of religious practices—what I usually call universal religion, in which it does not matter whether you believe in the next life or not—I'm fully convinced that as a human being the best source of happiness, the best source of tranquility, is compassion and love, while mental anger and hatred usually brings trouble, mental unrest. So I'm always repeating this. Now I want to ask you, as a neuroscientist, is there any

---

Bodhicharyavatara (Skt., "Entering the Path of Enlightenment") is a classic Mahayana Buddhist text by the great Indian teacher and representative of the Madhyamika school, Shantideva (fl. 7th–8th century C.E.). The practice of exchanging self for other involves mentally taking on oneself the suffering of others and radiating goodness toward them.

difference between distorted conceptions like desire or hatred (which are mistaken consciousnesses) and virtuous states of mind like compassion, love, or valid cognitions? From your professional viewpoint, is there a possibility to lessen the anger-and-hatred side and slightly increase the positive mind?

VARELA: A typical biologist would say if one doesn't have any form of defense and territory and self-maintenance and some aggression to go with them, then one couldn't survive. On the other hand, if I don't relate to others, if I don't have any kind of love and compassion for my children, then life is not possible either. So the two things are always there, some form of defense and some form of love. The question of whether one can increase compassion as in the Mahayana path has never arisen in biology, as far as I can see. It's never even been imagined.

DALAI LAMA: We are not involved with whether there is a next life or not, or with nirvana. So there is no question of the involvement of the Bodhisattva. We are just talking about a normal human being, not particularly highly developed beings.

VARELA: The answer, I think, would be yes. We know that the capacity of human beings to learn is enormous, therefore that also can be learned. I see no intrinsic reason why that would not be possible. Certainly that could be possible.

LIVINGSTON: I agree.

DALAI LAMA: Certainly one major obstacle is simply ignorance itself. Ignorance not so much in the specific Buddhist sense of ignorance grasping to ignorance itself, but simply ordinary ignorance, not knowing; not knowing the consequences that will ensue from one's actions. So here I always believe that education is very important, the way we educate the next generation. Because I always feel, not necessarily from the viewpoint of religion, but as a reality from the scientific viewpoint, that cooperation toward genuine unity is precious. This is not a question of morals or religion, but simply a question of survival, a question of further development in a positive way. I was very struck in your presentation, Dr. Livingston, by the impact of how we treat our children during the first few years. This is care in a basic sense, not religious, but simply responding to children's need on a biological level for lovingkindness, for care, for contact. I'm very, very impressed by this. This is essential, I think. It lasts all through life. So we need love, we need human feeling, not regarding others as an enemy, as destroyers, but rather as helpers. Whether there is a positive outcome depends on our will, our effort. We can see this from our own experience. There may be a person who in early life is very evil and then later transforms into a very different person, a very wholesome person. This is seen experientially.

I feel there are many positive factors. There are many fields that offer new knowledge. For example, the importance and efficacy of the attitude of lovingkindness toward other human beings has now been established from the scientific viewpoint. Things like this are very, very positive factors. In previous times, these things weren't there. In regard to the importance of love and kindness for survival, some people may feel: "Oh nonsense! I can manage very well without any sense of universal responsibility." But today it is manifest that in reality this is not the case. That is quite clear, isn't it?

LIVINGSTON: I think the new way of scientific thinking that is emerging—it may yet be a long way from reaching the textbooks, but when it does it will be a very positive contribution— is that genetic potentiality all over the world is precious to everyone. We are so interdependent. The potentiality of a child anywhere in the world making a contribution to all of humankind is very great. If we neglect that child out of a billion children, it is our fault and is a tragedy for everyone. I think the basis for our failure is ignorance and false ideas. Scarcity dominates many countries, many societies. In the world as a whole, we do not have scarcity that requires people to starve. We do not have scarcity that requires people to be homeless.

DALAI LAMA: That's right, that's right! This business of "us and them," "this is we, this is they," "they're facing starvation, we're not" is a division we humans created. But in the economic field, nobody speaks like this. If you find some good marketplace, you rush there! So it could be the same in terms of bringing happiness.

Closing Remarks

FRANCISCO J. VARELA: Your Holiness, I feel that during this week we have had enormously interesting conversations. We have been very happy here. I think I speak for everybody when I say that, overall, our greatest happiness has been to be of some service to you, so that you can continue to manifest the spirit of love and kindness that you represent to everyone. I think that this is our greatest satisfaction. We will be happy to have done even a little that might help to further your message, which we all profoundly share!

DALAI LAMA: Thank you very much. I very much appreciate it. It's a responsibility for all of us. Since I have nothing to lose, therefore I've been most vocal in this field! Since we already lost our own country and many things, there's not much to feel that selfish over! It is easier to speak about these things when you have no country—nothing! [laughter]

From our point of view, actually, we are like tourists visiting this globe. It is as though we come from some different planet! So you see, as a tourist, the important thing while you are visiting a foreign country is to be a good person, at least not a troublemaker. If a tourist visits a place and creates a problem there, that is nonsense. [laughter] It is much more reasonable to go there, enjoy yourself, and have a good rest. Likewise one's own life should be a meaningful life, with a positive purpose. I'm not talking about nirvana, or the next life, but about this life on earth. If you are a happy person, it creates a happy atmosphere.

During the last few days, one of the ultimate sources of satisfaction for all of us has been the atmosphere of sincerity. There has been real human feeling here, and this brings some kind of benefit. If the atmosphere were different, too formal or too reserved, then we would not get this kind of satisfaction! So this is the real source of happiness. Thank you very much!

We've discussed a number of complex issues during this week, and it's been very, very good, considering the limited time. These are not subjects that we can discuss exhaustively, nor can we come to any definite conclusions. These are issues that need to be researched from generation to generation. I'm quite sure that this event is a small contribution toward starting some new approaches, realizing other dimensions to reality.

About the Participants

NEWCOMB GREENLEAF holds a Ph.D. in mathematics from Princeton University. After spending many years as a research mathematician, Dr. Greenleaf has been active in developing innovative teaching methods that integrate mathematics and computer science. He is currently a professor in the Computer Science Department at Columbia University.

JEREMY W. HAYWARD holds a Ph.D. in Physics from Cambridge University and spent several years at Massachusetts Institute of Technology doing research in molecular biology. In 1974, he helped to establish the Naropa Institute, an accredited college based on Buddhist philosophy, of which he is now a trustee. He has published two books, *Perceiving Ordinary Magic*, which discusses the dialogue between science and spirituality, and *Shifting Worlds, Changing Minds*, which deals with the meeting of cognitive science and Buddhism.

THUBTEN JINPA (interpreter) was born in Tibet in 1959. He received his monastic training at Zongkar Choede Monastery and Gaden Monastic University in India, leading to his degree as Lharam Geshe in 1989, equivalent, in the Tibetan monastic tradition, to a doctorate in Divinity. Since 1986, he has been the principal translator for His Holiness the Dalai Lama on philosophy and religion. In 1989, Jinpa joined Kings College to study Western philosophy, and received his honors in 1992.

ROBERT B. LIVINGSTON, M.D., has been involved in neuroscience research for over three decades. He has taught and published extensively in many areas, particularly sensory physiology and human developmental neuroanatomy. He is the author of many scholarly articles and of the book *Sensory Processing, Perception and Behavior* (Raven Press, 1978). In 1990, he retired as Professor Emeritus from the Department of Neuroscience at the University of California in San Diego. Dr. Livingston is also the current president of the Association of Physicians against Nuclear War.

LUIGI LUISI holds a Ph.D. from the University of Rome. He is internationally known for his research on macromolecular chemistry and bioplymeres, and is a frequent contributor to professional journals. He is also the author of prize-winning children's stories. Currently, he is a professor at the Federal Institute in Zurich.

ELEANOR ROSCH, Ph.D., is well known in the world of cognitive science for her pioneering studies on color categorical perception, and is the author of numerous scholarly articles. In her current teaching and writing she has been active in introducing a dialogue between psychology and the Buddhist tradition. Dr. Rosch is a professor in the Department of Psychology at the University of California at Berkeley.

FRANCISCO J. VARELA holds a Ph.D. in biology from Harvard University. He has published numerous articles in the fields of sensory physiology, biological modeling, and immunology, and is the author of several books. His most recent book (co-authored by E. Thompson and E. Rosch) is *The Embodied Mind: Cognitive Science and Human Experience* (MIT Press, 1991). He is currently Fondation de France Professor of Cognitive Science and Epistemology at the Ecole Polytechnique in Paris.

B. ALLEN WALLACE (interpreter) received his B.A. at Amherst College in Physics and Philosophy and is currently a Ph.D. candidate in the Department of Religious Studies at Stanford University. He has studied the Tibetan Buddhist tradition intensively for over twenty years. He is the author of *Choosing Reality: A Contemplative View of Physics and the Mind* (Shambhala Publications, 1989) and of articles on the epistemology of science and religion.

Sources of Illustrations

Figure 2. Redrawn from R. Buchsbaum, *Animals without Backbones* (Chicago: University of Chicago Press, 1948).

Figure 3. Redrawn from R. Buchsbaum, *Animals without Backbones* (Chicago: University of Chicago Press, 1948).

Figure 4. Redrawn from T. H. Bullock, *Introduction to Nervous Systems* (San Francisco: W. H. Freeman and Co., 1977).

Figure 5. Modified from E. V. Evarts, *The Neurosciences: A Second Study Program* (Cambridge, Mass.: MIT Press, 1975).

Figure 14. Modified from D. Purves and J. Lichtman, *Principles of Neural Development* (Sunderland, Mass.: Sinauer Associates, 1985).

Figure 15. Modified from D. Purves and J. Lichtman, *Principles of Neural Development* (Sunderland, Mass.: Sinauer Associates, 1985).

Index

References to illustrative figures are in italics. The abbreviation AI in parentheses refers to artificial intelligence.